New Labour's Policies for Schools

Raising the Standard?

Edited by Jim Docking

Written by the National Education Policy Course Team
University of Surrey Roehampton

David Fulton Publishers Ltd
Ormond House, 26–27 Boswell Street, London WC1N 3JD

First published in Great Britain by David Fulton Publishers 2000

British Library Cataloguing in Publication Data

A catalogue record for this book is available from the British Library

ISBN 1–85346–611–5

Typeset by FSH Ltd, London
Printed in Great Britain by The Cromwell Press Ltd, Trowbridge, Wilts.

Contents

Preface

This book is about the policies for schools in England pursued by the New Labour Government during its first 2½ years of office (May 1997 to October 1999). Effectively, it is a sequel to our 1996 publication *National School Policy: Major Issues in Education Policy for Schools in England and Wales, 1979 onwards*, which covered most of the 18 years during which the Conservatives were in power. Its purpose is the same: to provide the main facts about current national initiatives for schools, and to offer a framework for reviewing these critically and informatively.

We believe this book will appeal not only to undergraduates and post-graduates on relevant courses (our core audience) but also to a wider readership – politicians, LEA officers, school governors, parents, teachers and lecturers – indeed, all who care about the direction of so much government activity in the field of education.

Jim Docking
Roehampton, London
November 1999

Contributors

Jim Docking was formerly Head of Education at Whitelands College and Chairman of the School of Education, Roehampton Institute London, where he is now a senior research officer in the Centre for Educational Management. He edited *National School Policy*, to which this book is a sequel, is author of books on managing classroom behaviour and parents and schooling, and has co-authored or co-edited books on special educational needs, alienation in the junior school and disaffection at Key Stage 4.

Peter Jackson writes on philosophy and literature, chairs the Froebel Council Research Trust and was formerly Head of the BA and MA Education Programmes at the Roehampton Institute.

Ron Letch started his career as a teacher in Essex. He then moved into teacher training as a senior lecturer in Education at Whitelands College. He went on to become a senior inspector for Surrey County and then a chief inspector in the London Borough of Hounslow, where he was finally Deputy Director of Education. Currently he is a research associate at the Centre for Educational Management, Roehampton Institute London.

Jane Lovey taught in mainstream schools in England and Africa for 12 years before spending 15 years with pupils who were either excluded from school or had excluded themselves. She then taught at the Roehampton Institute London before joining the research staff at Cambridge University School of Education.

Pat Mahony is Professor of Education at Roehampton Institute London. She has worked for many years in teacher education and has published widely on the significance and impact of government policy in this area, with particular reference to issues of social justice. With Ian Hextall, she has recently completed two ESRC funded research projects that form the basis for their forthcoming book *The Reconstruction of Teaching*. Pat is British Editor of *Women's Studies International Forum*.

Roger Marples is Senior Lecturer in Education at Roehampton Institute London, with responsibility for the BA in Education Studies, having previously taught in primary, special and secondary schools. He has published in British and American journals on topics relating to philosophy and education, and has recently edited *The Aims of Education* (Routledge, 1999).

Derek Shaw was formerly a lecturer in education at Roehampton Institute London where he was Inservice and MA tutor in the education of children with special needs. He also taught courses concerned with able children and thinking skills.

Graham Welch is Professor of Education and Director of Educational Research at the Roehampton Institute London, having been Dean of the Faculty of Education from 1991 to 1997. He has acted as a consultant on education development for the UAE, South African and UK government agencies as well as the British Council in the Ukraine and Argentina. He is also Director of the Institute's Centre for Advanced Studies in Music Education (ASME) which is one of the UK's leading centres for research in aspects of musical development and education.

Note: Since this book was completed, Roehampton Institute London has become the University of Surrey Roehampton.

Introduction

Jim Docking

In June 1999, Tony Blair became the first Prime Minister to address a teacher union conference, symbolising his personal crusade to raise standards in schools. 'Never before', he told the National Union of Head Teachers, 'have we possessed at the same time a national quest for change, a government committed to state education and a programme of educational reform with huge support'. Any failure to capitalise on this opportunity, he added, would 'betray our generation and those that follow'. Whether or not one accepts the claim for 'huge support', and whatever views people take about this 'opportunity not to be missed', there is no doubt that recent developments in education have been far-reaching, challenging and profound, affecting every local authority, headteacher, school governor, teacher, pupil and parent.

This book covers the first 2½ years of New Labour's programme of school and local education authority reforms that affect England. There is no single education policy for the UK, though some aspects are similar. As Raffe *et al.* (1999) point out, Scotland has had its distinct educational system since before the union in 1707. The Scottish Office, established in 1885, was given responsibility for school education, while the new Parliament, set up in 1999, enables the country to enjoy greater political autonomy. In Northern Ireland, the Stormont Parliament was responsible for education, and when this was suspended in 1972, education continued to be administered by the province's own Department of Education as, of course, it is now under the new Northern Ireland Government. Differences between English and Welsh education have been much less marked. Even so, the Welsh Office has had responsibility for education since 1970, and the new National Assembly for Wales will open the door for more distinctiveness. Comparisons between the education policies within the UK would make a fascinating study, of course – but for another book!

Although each contributor provides a personal perspective on a key aspect of national school policy, the main sub-headings are common to all chapters (with some exceptions in Chapter 1):

- **Previous policy** – a summary of developments under the Conservatives
- **Present policy** – an outline of New Labour's approach
- **Issues for debate** – discussion of 2–4 controversial issues
- **Further Reading**
- **References**.

The chapters are grouped in two parts. Part I, comprising two chapters written by the editor, sets the scene. The first chapter examines the background to the standards debate and the Government's rationale for increasing investment in education and pursuing an interventionist programme to raise standards. The assumption in the White Paper (DfEE, 1997) that educational standards and economic performance are tightly coupled is questioned, and the Government's claim that English pupils are underachieving in comparison with their peers in many other countries is regarded as an over-simplification of the data. Two issues are then discussed: should we imitate the teaching methods of countries that seem to have the highest rates of student achievement? and are standards in this country improving or slipping?

Chapter 2 presents an overview of successive governments' policies to raise standards, comparing those of New Labour and the Conservatives. The extent to which present approaches to the problem represent a continuity or discontinuity with those of the previous administration is discussed, as is whether focusing directly on schools and teachers is likely to be as effective in raising standards as focusing on decreasing levels of child poverty. Other related issues that are raised are the impact of market forces in a programme of curriculum and structural intervention and the degree to which high standards depend on a high degree of central planning.

The ten chapters that make up Part II examine aspects of national school policy in greater detail. In Chapter 3, Derek Shaw explains the means by which standards are monitored and schools challenged through target setting, inspection and assessment. He discusses problems of benchmarking, which depends on the availability of reliable data about school performance and the suitability of the criteria by which schools are grouped for comparative purposes. He also considers the difficulties in producing 'value-added' data and meaningful performance tables, and sketches out the debate about the role of the Office for Standards in Education and its beleaguered chief inspector for schools.

In the next chapter, Jim Docking reviews the national programmes to raise standards in literacy, numeracy and information and communication technology plus the supporting strategies to provide study support, extra tuition and regular homework for primary and secondary pupils. He suggests that asking whether the literacy and numeracy strategies will improve standards raises wider issues than questions about the likelihood of the national targets being met, and that assumptions about the value of homework may not be as evidence-based as the Government implies in its guidelines. In Chapter 5, he traces the story behind the revised National Curriculum and the innovative statement on the purposes of the school curriculum, and examines the controversy over citizenship and the debate about whether the National Curriculum, based as it is largely on traditional subjects, is appropriate for the twenty-first century.

In discussing developments in early years education, Peter Jackson (Chapter 6) explores the issues surrounding the Sure Start initiative, class size, the inspection of nursery education and childcare, the different settings for pre-school education and the new foundation curriculum. He then considers whether such radical reform of early years provision is necessary, whether the new early years partnerships will prove effective and whether the pre-school programme is likely to raise standards.

Special educational needs is the subject of Chapter 7. After describing the main policies as outlined in the Government's Green Paper and subsequent Action Plan, Ron Letch discusses the highly controversial drive to place more children with SEN in mainstream schools, and, more specifically, the problems this raises with respect to children presenting emotional and behavioural difficulties and the role of special school staff in supporting their mainstream colleagues.

Next, Roger Marples examines the complexities of provision for the 14–19 age group and the policy to make better provision for lifelong learning, which New Labour sees as not just about enhancing employment prospects but achieving personal autonomy and fulfilment. While finding much to admire in aspects of these policies, he expresses concern about the present triple-track system (academic, vocational and occupationally specific) and the stranglehold of A-levels, concluding that, although ministers are moving in the right direction, they are doing so 'with an occluded vision of where they ultimately wish to go'.

In their examination of policies for reforming the teaching profession (Chapter 9), Graham Welch and Pat Mahony note how both the volume and the prescriptive nature of the legislation is circumscribing teachers' autonomy. After outlining the new requirements for teacher training and Qualified Teacher Status, the induction period, salary progression, advanced skills teachers and headteachers, together with arrangements for a General Teaching Council, the authors note the significance of the Government's promise to ensure that decisions about changes in the profession are supported by research findings. They then discuss whether teaching can be properly regarded as a profession, the appropriateness of the standards against which teachers are now to be judged, and prospects for the General Teaching Council.

Chapter 10 by Ron Letch focuses on the changing role of local education authorities and the plethora of demands to which LEAs have recently been asked to respond. These include: drawing up Education Development Plans, School Asset Management Plans and Behaviour Support Plans; implementing the policies of 'best value' and 'fair funding'; facing the challenge of Education Action Zones; setting up school admission forums and developing constructive relationships with schools; being subject to inspections from OFSTED and the Audit Commission; and playing a significant part in promoting policies for social inclusion. Four questions are then considered: Is there really a future for LEAs? Is partnership between LEAs and schools rhetoric or reality? Can LEAs help to raise standards while schools function as largely autonomous institutions? And finally, does the LEA have a unique role as advocate?

Chapter 11 is about New Labour's policies concerning choice, diversity and the development of partnerships. After outlining the main features of Education Action Zones and the 'Excellence in Cities' strategies to give new life to schools in poor and depressed areas, Peter Jackson looks at strategies to regularise school admission policies and to develop partnerships between home and school, business and schools, and independent and maintained schools. He then raises various questions concerning action zones, re-empowering LEAs, and handing over the management of schools and the services of 'failing' LEAs to private firms.

In the last chapter, Jane Lovey examines New Labour's policies to arrest pupil disengagement and reduce the incidence of truancy and exclusion from schools. She explains how these issues relate to: the establishment of the high profile Social Exclusion Unit; the legislation governing procedures for excluding pupils from school; the role of local authorities in combating truancy, reducing rates of exclusion and providing for the education of excluded pupils; and the setting up of 'nurture groups' in infant schools. She then goes on to discuss the place of mentoring as a strategy to re-engage disaffected secondary students, the role of pastoral support programmes, and the connection between problems of disengagement and the demands of the National Curriculum.

Of course, many policies have application in more than one area. Those concerned with social inclusion, the development of partnerships, targeting and assessment and Excellence in Cities are obvious examples. There is therefore a degree of overlap between some chapters. We have tried to keep this to a minimum, but decided not to eliminate it entirely. Had we done so, the reader would have been irritated by constant cross-referencing, and the contributors would have been restricted in developing distinctive lines of argument. However, since some policies are discussed in more than one chapter, expedient use of the index would be advisable.

Two years before assuming power, the Labour Party (1995) acknowledged that 'education is now at the top of the political agenda'. Whether or not the policies of the party now in power are seen to represent an extension of the Conservatives' or a fresh approach, the pace of change continues unabated and with a missionary zeal. This frustrates some teachers, but the Government is clearly determined to make schools change in the face of what the Prime Minister calls 'the forces of conservativism' in the profession. It is too early to say if the strategies are working, but what is to count as 'success' must be more than meeting national performance targets which are about improvements in average levels of attainment. Among the questions to ask will be:

- Are the strategies likely to sustain long-term improvement in children's achievements at school? Assurances about this will depend on engaging the goodwill of the teaching profession as well as tackling the more deep-rooted problems of child poverty.
- Are the strategies effective for all groups of students – both boys and girls, both lower-attainers and able children, both those in working class and middle class families, residents of both depressed and affluent areas, and all ethnic groups?

- Are the strategies effective not only in improving standards in the 'basics' but in furthering personal development and interests, inculcating a love for learning and encouraging a determination to go on learning?

Time will tell.

References

Department for Education and Employment (1997) *Excellence in Schools.* London: Stationery Office.

Labour Party (1995) *Excellence for Everyone.* London: Labour Party.

Raffe, D. *et al.* (1999) 'Comparing England, Scotland, Wales and Northern Ireland: the case for "home internationals" in comparative research', *Comparative Education*, 35(1), 9–25.

Part I

SETTING THE SCENE

Chapter 1

What is the Problem?

Jim Docking

Nobody who has followed developments in New Labour's policies for schools can doubt its commitment to change the shape of the education system, the curriculum and classroom practices. When the party won the General Election in May 1997, it did so largely on the back of its policy of 'education, education and education'. Two months later, this slogan was used as a heading at the start of the White Paper *Excellence in Schools*, in which raising standard in schools was described as 'the Government's top priority' (DfEE, 1997, p.9). Subsequently, David Blunkett, the Education Secretary, staked his reputation on 11-year-olds reaching the national literacy and numeracy targets by 2002. Whatever one's criticisms might be about the nature of the policies, the energy behind them is unmistakable.

Why all the fuss? The argument goes like this:

1. In order for Britain to survive as a prosperous nation, we must be able to compete in world markets.
2. Success in this enterprise depends upon having a highly numerate and literate workforce.
3. However, standards in our schools are not rising fast enough, and in this respect England compares unfavourably with many other countries, especially those in the Pacific Rim.
4. The Government must therefore raise expectations among teachers by setting challenging targets for students' achievement.
5. In order that these targets might be realised within a few years, the Government needs to shake up school pedagogy through initiatives that ensure everyday classroom practice is in line with the best methods available and that ineffective strategies are discarded.

This line of argument, in which education is regarded less for its intrinsic value and more as an instrument for shaping the economy, was spelt out in Chapter 1 of *Excellence in Schools*. Education was described there as 'the key to creating a society which is dynamic and productive'. 'In the 21st century', we were told, 'knowledge and skills will be the key to success. … Britain's economic prosperity and social cohesion both depend on achieving that goal.' Although the 'wider goals' of education, in terms of ensuring that 'children and young people learn respect for others and themselves' were also acknowledged, the central message of the White Paper was that reforms in education were essential if this country was to catch up with its industrial competitors. Unlike Britain, which had traditionally relied on private schools to produce the country's elite, these other countries 'recognised that a strategy for national prosperity depended on well-developed primary and secondary education for all students, combined with effective systems of vocational training and extensive higher education'. It was necessary to raise the education standards of all children in this country since 'we face new challenges at home and from international competitors, such as the Pacific Rim countries'. And to push this matter home for anyone in doubt of its importance, the place of England in the international league tables was portrayed graphically in an appendix. Interestingly, the recent statement of values in the revised National Curriculum makes some shift of emphasis, placing 'the well-being and development of the individual' at the top of the list and 'a productive economy' lower down (QCA, 1999c).

In his speech to the Labour Party Conference in 1998, David Blunkett, the Education Secretary, reinforced the Government's view that educational standards and the economy were closely linked:

> We recognise the very real challenge facing manufacturing industry in this country and the way in which we need to support and work with them for skilling and re-skilling for what Tony Blair has described as the best economic policy we have – 'education'. (quoted in Ball, 1999)

Yet this kind of governmental message about the importance of making education more relevant for the workplace and raising standards in the 3-Rs was nothing new. The Labour Prime Minister James Callaghan had said as much in his much-publicised address to Ruskin College in October 1976. In her account of this speech, its background and legacy, Kathryn Riley (1998) relates how Callaghan spoke about fitting children to do à job of work as a key goal of the education system. He said that parents were uneasy about informal methods of teaching, and he deplored the low standards of numeracy among school-leavers. He wanted prescribed national standards, a common core curriculum, and closer relations between industry and schools. According to Riley, the significance of the Ruskin speech was that

> it raised questions about curriculum control and suggested that teachers were not the only legitimate group to have an interest in the curriculum. … Ruskin undoubtedly signalled a political change in that national Government indicated that it wished to set policy objectives for education and to apply criteria to the public sector. (p.70)

When Labour lost the election in 1979, the Conservative administration took up this challenge. The various Education Acts between 1979 to 1997 were designed to improve standards to match those of other countries and meet the needs of the world of work. This was made quite clear in the White Paper *Better Schools* (DES/Welsh Office, 1985, para. 9), which pre-empted New Labour in addressing the needs of the new millennium:

> But the Government believes that, not least in the light of what is being achieved in other countries, the standards now generally attained by our students are neither as good as they can be, nor as good as they need to be if young people are to be equipped for the world of the twenty-first century. By the time they leave school, students need to have acquired, far more than at present, the qualities and skills required of work in a technological age. Education at school should promote enterprise and adaptability in order to increase young people's chances of finding employment or creating it for themselves and others.

A later White Paper *Choice and Diversity* (DfE/Welsh Office, 1992) went further in insisting that Britain 'can match and outstrip' the standards of other leading nations (para. 15.2).

In effect, therefore, New Labour's policies for schools are based on assumptions about standards in schools and the relationship between education and the economy developed over the previous three decades. But are the underlying assumptions well-founded? It is to this question that we now turn.

TIMSS and international performance

Does the performance of English students really compare badly with those in other countries?

As we have seen, New Labour's White Paper (DfEE, 1997) drew explicit attention to England's place in the international league tables. These have covered attainment in reading, mathematics and science. The main evidence for reading comes from a study comparing the achievements of 1,817 nine-year-olds in England and Wales with those in 27 other countries (Brooks *et al.*, 1996). The tests were wide-ranging, covering both narrative and factual extracts as well as the ability to interpret documentary material such as charts and tables. Overall, the English and Welsh youngsters came out as average, alongside countries that included Belgium and Spain, being out-performed by France, Finland, New Zealand and some other countries. Of particular concern, however, was that the tail of underperformance was longer than that elsewhere.

The main evidence cited in the White Paper, however, was the Third International Mathematics and Science Study (TIMSS), carried out between 1995 and 1997. England was one of 26 countries involved in a study of more than 175,000 nine-year-olds in 4,000 schools, and it was also one of over 40 countries involved in a study of nearly 300,000 13-year-olds in about 6,000 schools. (Scotland also participated, but not Wales.) Students in the samples were given booklets of written tests in mathematics and science and also practical tasks.

According to the White Paper, 'international comparisons support the view that our students are not achieving their potential. For example, our nine- and 13-year-olds were well down the rankings in the maths tests in the Third International Maths and Science Survey' (p.10). However, as an inspection of Tables 1.1 and 1.2 shows, this is a partial and misleading summary of the TIMSS findings. In the written tests, English students of both age groups performed better relative to other countries in science, while in the problem-solving performance tests (involving both maths and science) English students were *among the top performers*. True, English students did come out badly in mathematics overall, but, as we shall see, not in all aspects of this subject.

Taking the written tests first, among the nine-year-olds, those in only three of the 26 participating countries – USA, Japan and Korea – obtained significantly higher overall mean scores in science than their English counterparts (6,142 in 134 schools). Indeed, English students scored above the international average in all four content areas (earth science, life science, physical science, and science and the environment), and 13 per cent were among the top 10 per cent across all countries. In contrast, the overall mean scores of English students in mathematics were significantly below the international average and lower than the scores of students in about half the countries, among which the best performers were Singapore, Korea, Japan and Hong Kong – all in the Pacific Rim. However, together with their counterparts in Australia and Hong Kong, English students were among the highest scorers in geometry, outshining students in Singapore, and they were above the international average in data representation and analysis (Harris *et al.*, 1997).

The same pattern of results was found with respect to the English 13-year-olds (3,700 in 127 schools) (Keys *et al.*, 1996). They too scored well above the international average in the science tests, with students in only four other countries – Czech Republic, Japan, Korea and Singapore – performing significantly better overall. Indeed, around one in six were in the top 10 per cent internationally, and the results showed an improvement since a similar study in the early 1990s. However, in mathematics the English students performed significantly less well than their counterparts in 24 other countries and slightly below the international average. Countries in the Pacific Rim, most of Western European and some of Eastern Europe were ahead. Also, their performance in this subject internationally had deteriorated somewhat since previous studies. None the less, as with the younger students, it was not all bad news in this subject: the 13-year-olds scored above the international average in data representation, analysis and probability; it was in fractions and number sense, geometry, algebra, measurement and proportionality where they fell below average.

But this is not the end of the story, for TIMSS also administered a set of 12 hands-on tasks to assess the 'performance skills' of 15,000 13-year-olds in 1,500

Table 1.1 TIMSS: Comparisons between England and other countries in the written tests

9-year-olds		13-year-olds	
Mathematics tests	Science tests	Mathematics tests	Science tests
Australia, Austria, Canada, Czech Republic, Japan, Hong Kong, Hungary, Ireland, Israel, Korea, Netherlands, Singapore, Slovenia, United States	Japan, Korea, United States	Australia, Austria, Belgium (Flemish), Belgium (French), Bulgaria, Canada, Czech Republic, Netherlands, Hong Kong, Hungary, Ireland, Japan, Korea, France, Russian Federation, Singapore, Slovak Republic, Slovenia, Sweden, Switzerland	Czech Republic, Japan, Korea, Singapore
Cyprus, ENGLAND, Latvia, New Zealand, Norway, Scotland	Austria, Australia, Canada, Czech Republic, ENGLAND, Ireland, Netherlands, Scotland, Singapore, Slovenia	Denmark, ENGLAND, Germany, Israel, Latvia, New Zealand, Norway, Scotland, Thailand, United States	Austria, Australia, Belgium (Flemish), Bulgaria, ENGLAND, Hungary, Ireland, Netherlands, Russian Federation, Slovak Republic, Slovenia
Greece, Iceland, Iran, Kuwait, Portugal, Thailand	Cyprus, Greece, Hong Kong, Hungary, Iceland, Iran, Israel, Kuwait, Latvia, New Zealand, Norway, Portugal, Thailand	Columbia, Cyprus, Greece, Iceland, Iran, Kuwait, Lithuania, Portugal, Romania, South Africa, Spain	Belgium (French), Canada, Columbia, Cyprus, Denmark, France, Germany, Greece, Hong Kong, Iceland, Israel, Iran, Kuwait, Latvia, Lithuania, New Zealand, Norway, Portugal, Romania, Scotland, South Africa, Spain, Switzerland, Sweden, Thailand, United States

Countries in the middle row include those whose overall mean scores were not significantly different from England's. England's scores were significantly lower than those of countries listed in the top row, and significantly higher than those of countries listed in the bottom row.

Data derived from Harris et al., 1997; Keys et al., 1996

schools in 21 countries. (A smaller study of nine-year-olds did not include England.) Each task lasted either 15 or 30 minutes and was designed to tap students' investigative, problem-solving and analytic skills in mathematics and science. For example, students were asked to find out how pulse changed both during and after a specified exercise and to explain their results; and in a task using scale models, they were asked to determine which pieces of furniture would fit round a bend in a corridor, and then to suggest a rule that would save trial and error. During activities such as these, students had to demonstrate a range of skills such as designing the investigation, taking measurements, recording their findings in a systematic way, drawing conclusions and making predictions on the basis of their data.

In contrast with the results for most of the written mathematics tests – but in line with those of the science tests and also the element in the maths tests involving data representation and analysis – the findings for these practical tasks revealed that the performance of English students (450 in 50 schools) was superior to that of their counterparts in most other countries (Harris *et al.*, 1998). Overall, England came second out of the 19 countries (see Table 1.2). In the tasks that involved mainly mathematics, they ranked seventh equal and performed better than the same students did in the written tests, with only Singapore doing significantly better; in the science tasks, their performance was about the same as in the science written tests and challenged Singapore's for top place.

In short, the TIMSS findings do not demonstrate that English students, across the board, did badly compared with other countries. Although they compared unfavourably in certain important areas of mathematics such as number, they performed well in relation to other countries in data-handling and statistics and very favourably in science and problem-solving tasks that involved both maths and science. But there is also reason to question the representativeness of the English sample in the maths tests. Warning against using international data selectively to suit your preferred policies, Margaret Brown (1998) has pointed out variations in sampling practices that infringed the rules laid down by the researchers, especially with regard to low achievers. For instance, whereas nine European countries excluded at least a fifth of their lowest-attaining 13-year-olds and a further ten excluded between 10 and 20 per cent, England excluded just 1 per cent. These variations would almost certainly have affected the rank order of European countries.

Why was England one of the few countries to do better in the science written tests than in mathematics? One reason for the subject discrepancies in the results for English students might simply be that, compared with the maths tests, the science tests and performance tasks reflected more closely the demands of the National Curriculum at that time. Margaret Brown (1998) argues that the written tests in maths contained some sorts of items (adding complex fractions, for instance) that were not emphasised in the National Curriculum for that age. This could mean that the tests underestimated children's ability in some maths areas. Other factors could be differences in the time spent in school, in the curriculum areas tested, in whole-class teaching in maths and on homework, plus the fact

Table 1.2 TIMSS: Comparisons between England and other countries in the performance tasks (mean scores among 13-year-olds)

Mathematics tasks (International mean: 59%)		Science tasks (International mean: 58%)		Overall (International mean: 59%)	
Singapore	70%	Singapore	72%	Singapore	71%
Romania	66%	ENGLAND	71%	ENGLAND	67%
Australia	66%	Switzerland	65%	Switzerland	65%
Switzerland	66%	Scotland	64%	Australia	65%
Norway	65%	Australia	63%	Sweden	64%
Sweden	65%	Sweden	63%	Scotland	62%
Slovenia	64%	Czech Republic	60%	Norway	62%
ENGLAND	64%	Canada	59%	Romania	62%
Netherlands	62%	Slovenia	58%	Czech Republic	61%
New Zealand	62%	Netherlands	58%	Slovenia	61%
Canada	62%	New Zealand	58%	Canada	60%
Czech Republic	62%	Norway	58%	New Zealand	60%
Scotland	61%	Romania	57%	Netherlands	60%
United States	54%	Spain	56%	United States	55%
Iran, Islamic Republic	54%	United States	55%	Spain	54%
Spain	52%	Iran, Islamic Republic	50%	Iran, Islamic Republic	52%
Portugal	48%	Cyprus	49%	Portugal	47%
Cyprus	44%	Portugal	42%	Cyprus	46%
Columbia	44%	Columbia	42%	Columbia	39%

The samples of two other countries, Hong Kong and Israel, were too small to be included in the international comparisons.

Data derived from Harris (1998)

that children in Pacific Rim countries are much more likely to receive private tuition than students in many other countries (Keys *et al.*, 1997a and b).

Perhaps the main point to make is that international comparisons of test scores can only be interpreted in the context of the differing national cultures. If schools in this country place greater emphasis on problem-solving than on applying learned procedures (adding up correctly, etc.), it is no wonder that English students scored higher in the former than the latter. The Government has effectively acknowledged this in its National Numeracy Strategy, which aims to introduce more mental arithmetic in the classroom. Of course, the question about whether this switch of emphasis is the *appropriate* one remains open (see Chapter 4).

The TIMSS cohort of students who were tested in 1995 at nine years of age were re-tested at age 13 in the spring of 1999. The results when released in 2000 will show whether the performance of English students has changed over time and relative to other countries. Also, the OECD (Organisation for Economic Co-operation and Development) has recently launched a three-yearly international survey called PISA (Programme for International Student Assessment). Focused on performance in reading, maths and science among 15–16-year-olds, the survey will be carried out in 30 countries, with the first results expected in 2001.

Will raising standards in education improve the country's economic performance?

Peter Robinson (1997) argues that improved educational standards may help certain individuals, but not nations, to succeed economically. Using the TIMSS evidence, he demonstrates that there is no clear correlation between countries that do well educationally and those that are the most economically successful, as measured by GNP per head. Writing before the collapse of the Far Eastern markets in the late 1990s, Robinson acknowledges the apparent link between educational and economic performance in most of the Pacific Rim countries. But as regards Hong Kong students, he notes that their improvement in mathematics since earlier international studies did not precipitate economic growth but followed it. Elsewhere, he could detect no positive relation of any kind. The United States, for example, is one of the world's most successful industrial nations, yet its TIMSS scores for 13-year-olds were similar to England's for mathematics (and significantly below this country's for science). Conversely, students from eastern bloc countries, such as the Czech and Slovak republics and Bulgaria, performed better than their English counterparts, yet their countries are far from being economically prosperous. Robinson's comparisons of the TIMSS results and economic performance across 39 countries lead him to conclude that the correlation between attainment in maths and per capital GNP 'was so weak as to be meaningless'.

What, then, about the prosperity of individuals as opposed to countries? Does improved educational performance lead to better prospects in the labour market? On this point, Robinson acknowledges that those with really low levels of literacy and numeracy are at a clear disadvantage when competing for jobs. Citing a longitudinal study of people born in 1958, he notes that of the 9 per cent of men with poor attainment in literacy and numeracy, only 69 per cent were in full-time employment when they were 37 years old compared with 89 per cent in the sample as a whole. This is in line with findings from the Youth Cohort study (1999b) which reveal that employment at age 18 was highly influenced by performance in GCSE. Thus raising the levels of achievement among the bottom 10 to 15 per cent of the attainment range would certainly be likely to help the individuals concerned economically. But this is not to say that raising average levels of school attainment will have obvious economic effects more generally.

This, says Robinson, is partly because the numeracy skills that employers say they require are much more rudimentary than those assessed in the National Curriculum (he was writing before the National Numeracy Strategy), so that better performance in National Curriculum tests will not necessarily mean an improvement in basic computational skills. Moreover, referring to the Government's Skills Needs Surveys of the mid-1990s, he maintains that employers are less concerned about employees' skills in English and math-ematics than in information technology, personal motivation, the ability to communicate effectively with other people, and skills in management. In any case, as Coffield (1998) has emphasised, much depends on the employment opportunities in the area where you live. Factories like Siemens and Fujitsu do not close down because the workforce lacks skills: plans for education and training, without associated economic strategies, will therefore not bring economic prosperity for individuals.

Of course, if, as the Government believes, we are moving towards a 'knowledge economy', then recent correlations may not be relevant. Although the theory is untested, it could well be that, as knowledge becomes of increasing importance in most areas of work, our economic standing will depend more and more upon it. The question then is whether the kind of national curriculum we have is appropriate for the needs of the twenty-first century, a matter taken up in Chapter 5.

Issues for debate

1. Given that the Pacific Rim countries did so much better than England in most of the TIMSS mathematics tests, should we imitate their teaching methods?

As we have seen, the best performing countries in the TIMSS studies were all in the Pacific Rim. This factor played into the hands of the then Conservative administration, which wanted a legitimate reason to introduce both mental arithmetic and calculator-free papers into national mathematics tests. According to Margaret Brown (1998), in spite of an agreed embargo, Education ministers on 3 July 1996 ordered the comparatively low ranking of English 13-year-olds in the TIMSS study to be leaked to *The Times*, which conveniently responded with a front-page headline 'English students plummet in world maths league'.

Official encouragement to adopt the classroom practices of eastern countries has continued under New Labour with support from the Office for Standards in Education. In recent years, teachers have been urged to adopt more whole-class interactive teaching, to engage in regular testing and to focus more sharply on the core subjects. The implicit message in the national strategies has been that teachers should stop treating any interference in teaching methods as an encroachment on their professionalism and be more like their colleagues in the Pacific Rim countries by regarding themselves more as applied technologists.

It is dangerous, however, to assume that effective classroom practices in one country will be equally successful in another. As Robin Alexander (1997) has pointed out, imitating the teaching methods in, say, Taiwan and Japan will not necessarily yield the same results as in the original country whose cultures are very different from our own. History, says Alexander, teaches us that:

> simple 'off-the-peg' borrowing of educational practices, of the kind that is currently being commended for primary schools, may not work, because it treats such practices as value-neutral and fails to explore the way they relate to the wider culture of which classroom life is a part. (p.97)

A comparison between French and English cultural and educational traditions illustrates this point. In the QUEST study of 400 9- to 11-year-olds in French and English schools, Broadfoot *et al.* (1998) found marked differences in attitudes to schooling and students' own learning as well as differences in learning outcomes. Moreover, these differences remained apparent regardless of socio-economic factors and the geographical location of the school. But the researchers concluded that these differences could not be explained in terms of different teaching styles without reference to general cultural expectations. If this is true, they say, the effects of any particular teaching strategy – and therefore its value – cannot be predicted without an understanding of a nation's larger cultural context.

For instance, they found that, compared with their French counterparts, English teachers tended to make a greater effort to interest students and to avoid giving negative feedback. In spite of this, both boys and girls in France seemed to be more positive about school than English students and to have clearer notions of their own educational goals. They did not place so much significance on the personality of the teachers because they already shared their values about educational success and the purpose of education. According to the researchers, the French make a clearer distinction than the English between work and play, focus more on academic learning in their schools, and place more value on students learning established procedures than on problem-solving.

For example, an English maths lesson (this was before the National Numeracy Strategy) would typically involve tasks for children to complete on their own, though with permission to talk to help each other, while the teacher moved around giving encouragement and support. In contrast, a French maths lesson would often begin with an explanation to the whole class of a procedure such as multiplying decimals, which would be followed by much classroom questioning based on a manual. No wonder, then, that the French children generally performed better in tests requiring the application of known procedures and the English were more successful in open-ended tasks where the procedures to follow were less obvious. Not surprisingly, both English and French students obtained higher scores on their own national tests. All this, say the researchers, questions the usefulness of international league tables such as those we discussed earlier.

We must also be wary of interpreting other countries' practices in terms of a crude 'back to basics' approach. A key example here is repetition by the whole class. This is a feature of many classrooms in Pacific Rim countries, but it is not the same as 'rote learning' as formerly practised in English classrooms. Crucially, the repetition comes only after an intense period of classroom interaction. Teachers do not see themselves as 'delivering' the curriculum but as posers of carefully sequenced questions to stimulate learning, as this extract from a recent observational study in South Korea makes clear:

> Instructional and practice sequences were dominated by the teachers' question/answer patterns which first directed students' attention to the known, to the critical parts of the problem, to the procedures needed to solve

the problem, and often to the rationale for using the procedure. ... Teachers then use leading questions to guide students through the procedures using more and more complex and abstract examples. Students are required to give the answers, often in choral response. When individuals answer, the rest of the students are required to evaluate, in choral response, whether the answer is right or wrong. This repeated pattern... seems to keep most of students consistently on task. (Grow-Maienza *et al.*, 1997, p.8)

The irony is, however, that just as New Labour seems to be embarking on policies and practices akin to those in the Pacific Rim, so are some Far Eastern countries taking up some aspects of English methods. They are appreciating that high control over school learning may discourage children learning to work independently and creatively. They are also aware that teaching children in one large group for most of the time may not be the best way to prepare them for the small collaborate group situations that are a feature of modern industry (Pennington, 1999; Reynolds, 1997).

In Singapore, for example, a Government-appointed review team (which included members of high tech companies) recently expressed concern over highly structured lessons and teachers' emphasis on drilling to produce high exam scores. Since 1999, the national syllabus has been reduced to allow more time for schools to develop creativity, team project work and a greater focus on the holistic development of children. A Centre for Teaching Thinking was opened in June 1998 to provide 100 hours of training for all teachers in helping children to use their minds more creatively (Spice, 1998). Japan too is revising its education system. Mary James (1997) has related how the exercise is being conducted in the spirit of *ikiruchikara* (literally 'zest for living'), which, implies self-reliance, co-operation with others, sensitivity to others' feelings, learning to identify problems for yourself and make independent judgements, and the health and physical strength to lead a vigorous life. The new national curriculum, introduced in April 2000, reduces the proportion of time devoted to whole-class teaching, which has traditionally dominated lessons, and enables teachers to introduce more child-centred learning, individual instruction, creative activities and collaborative group work (Fitzpatrick, 1999).

It would therefore be foolish for us to discard those features of our own teaching culture that many Pacific Rim countries are trying to blend with their traditional practices. As Mary James (1997) explains:

If we put all our effort into building an education system designed to produce high scores on standardised tests on the assumption that this will enhance our economic prosperity (confusing correlation with causality) we are likely to run into the same problems from which Japan is now so earnestly trying to escape.

Similarly, as Ball (1999) suggests, any narrowing of the curriculum through drilling students to pass the national tests at the expense of investigative, cross-curricular and open-ended work that encourages group collaboration and initiative will not, paradoxically, respond to employers' concerns about deficiencies in people's skills for engaging successfully in international competition. David Reynolds, who pioneered New Labour's numeracy strategy, is an advocate of Far Eastern teaching methods, particularly those used in Taiwan. But even he has insisted that what we need to do in this country is to keep what we do well while also learning from, but not slavishly embracing, the practices effectively adopted in other countries (Reynolds, 1997).

The question, then, is not so much whether we should use methods that have been successful in other cultures but how we can harness this experience in the most effective way, given our different traditions and expectations of schooling.

For discussion
'The answer is a blend, not a slavish cult worship of what others do' (Reynolds, 1997, p.21). What would be the implications of this advice for national policy and school practice?

2. Are standards of English pupils improving or declining?

There has been a steady improvement in the grades awarded at GCSE and A-level, though rates of progress have slowed down in recent years. For example, the proportion of 15-year-olds achieving five or more passes at Grades A* to C in GCSE or the GNVQ equivalent increased from 32 per cent in 1990/91 to 43 per cent in 1993/94, but improved to just 48 per cent (still under half) in 1998/99 (see Figure 1.1). At the same time, according to a Government-commissioned report by Sir Claus Moser (1999), there is a 'horrendous' lack of basic skills among young people. For instance, roughly a fifth of adults have such severe problems in literacy and numeracy that they cannot do their job properly – 'a sad reflection on past decades of schooling and policy priorities over the years' (p.2).

When it comes to the national test results (see Figure 1.2), the percentages of 11-year-olds reaching Level 4 or above in English show a year-by-year improve-ment, with particular gains for boys in 1999. In mathematics, the percentages are lower than in English but show improvement up to 1997 and from 1998 to 1999. (The dip in 1998 was probably due to the introduction of a mental arithmetic test that year.) The highest percentages are in science, which is consistent with international findings.

Key Stage 2 results, however, reflect only trends since the mid-1990s. What about comparisons between today and earlier periods? The evidence is mixed. Surveys of reading attainment based on standardised tests have been carried out among eight-year-olds by the National Foundation for Educational Research since the late 1980s. These show that the average score fell by 2.4 standardised score points between 1987 and 1991 – equivalent to about six months of reading age – but then rose between 1991 and 1995, returning to the 1987 level (Brooks

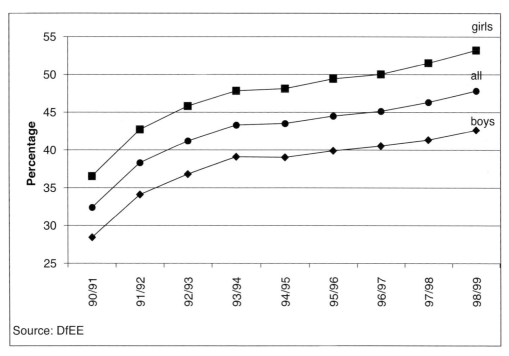

Figure 1.1 Percentage of 15-year-olds obtaining 5+ A*–C grades or GNVQ equivalent (England)

et al., 1997). On the other hand, Galton *et al.* (1998), using adapted versions of the Richmond Tests of Basic Skills, found that average marks in a sample of over 400 children fell between 1976 and 1996 from 56 to 45 per cent in maths, 43 to 36 per cent in language skills, and (most dramatically) 63 to 48 per cent in reading and vocabulary. Galton places the responsibility not on teachers but the National Curriculum, which reduced the amount of time teachers could spend on literacy and numeracy. However, as Galton recognises, comparisons over time are difficult because of changes in the kind of question that has meaning to children from one generation to the next.

Another factor in the standards debate is whether performance at school is different according to locality, ethnicity and social class. Thus the proportion of students obtaining five good GCSE passes in 1998 increased by at least 2 per cent in some LEAs but fell back by the same percentage in others (Audit Commission, 1999). The Youth Cohort Study (1999a) shows that, although there has been continuing improvement for all ethnic groups, performance at GCSE of Pakistani, Bangladeshi and, most of all, Black school students is still below that of their white contemporaries, while the performance of Indian and other Asian students is better than that of any other ethnic group. As regards social class, the same study suggests a big improvement in the number of children of manual workers with five GCSEs at Grade C or better; even so, by the age of 18, students with two or more A-level passes are three times more likely to have

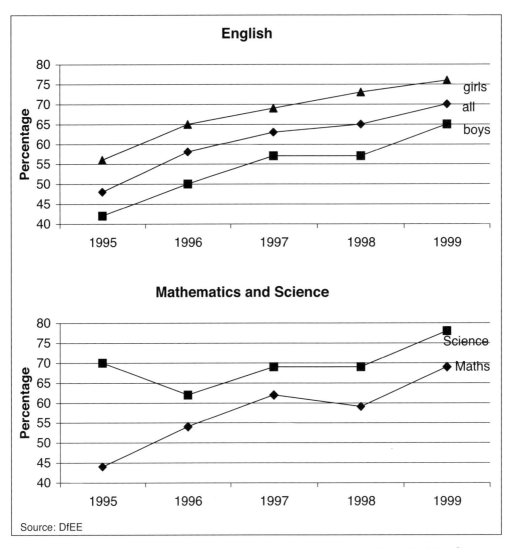

Figure 1.2 Percentage of 11-year-olds achieving Level 4 or above in Key Stage 2 national tests (England)

parents in managerial or professional occupations than in unskilled manual backgrounds (Youth Cohort Study, 1999b).

Then there is the much publicised 'gender gap', which is evident in national tests for English by the time children are seven years old and persists to GCSE, though levels of achievement have been rising for both boys and girls (see Figures 1.1 and 1.2). At A-level, differences are less noticeable. However, the issue is more complicated than is often portrayed in the media. For instance, a gender gap is not so evident in mathematics and science or at all levels of attainment. Gender differences are also tied up with social class and race: according to Arnot *et al.* (1998), Asian and African-Caribbean boys from the professional and intermediate classes go against the trend in outperforming girls.

Whether the gender, ethnic and class gaps are growing or decreasing is a matter of some dispute, depending on what criterion is used to determine the nature of the gaps. Thus, a team at Cardiff University led by Stephen Gorard (Gorard *et al.*, 1999) criticises the convention whereby the simple difference between percentages is used as a measure of the gap in achievement. Instead, they argue in favour of an alternative method that calculates the change over time adjusting for differences in entry rates. Their reanalyses of data for Welsh pupils demonstrate contrasting pictures from the commonly accepted ones, with gaps between groups becoming smaller, not greater, over time. (More recent figures have shown that in the 1999 English national tests, boys at 11 years appeared to be catching up with girls in reading, though not writing, on the simple percentage gap basis.)

It is difficult to account for the gender gap, but Sukhnandan's recent review of the literature (1999) identifies two broad kinds of explanation. The first is school-related factors. These are partly associated with curriculum changes that have encouraged a wider range of learning experiences and modes of assessment. Girls (it is said) are more attentive and willing to learn than boys, qualities that stand them in good stead in open-ended, process-based project work; boys on the whole do better in traditional classroom situations that focus on memorisation of facts and abstract rules that have to be acquired quickly. Boys also tend to have a more negative attitude to school, and teachers interact more negatively with them. However, the issue may also be bound up with what tests measure. In English, where the 'gap' is particularly evident, boys apparently demonstrate greater technical skill and a better vocabulary than girls, but they fall down at GCSE because they write more shortly while focusing more on action and less on explanation (QCA, 1999d).

Secondly, and arguably of more significance, are factors that lie outside the school, particularly the different socialisation experiences that predispose boys and girls towards different sorts of interests and ways of learning, which in turn have an effect on school achievement. This factor is compounded by the change in girls' attitudes towards career-planning, family and work, and also by the loss in recent years of employment opportunities in the manufacturing industry and manual jobs that traditionally recruited boys. Of these two sorts of explanation, one based on school factors the other on social and economic changes generally, Arnot *et al.* (1999) argue that

> girls' academic achievement nationally cannot be accounted for by educational actions, whether small-scale changes in individual school subjects, new forms of assessment, including coursework, or examination modes... What is clear is that successive generations of girls have been challenged by economic and social change and by feminism. (p.150)

It is often alleged by business leaders and university lecturers that the apparent rise in standards generally can be put down to less rigour in marking examination papers. Is this true? There certainly have been well-publicised inquiries into marking procedures following discoveries of errors in gradings awarded to GCSE students. In one case, as many as 114 mistakes were found in the grades that had been awarded by the Northern Examination and Assessment Board to students in just one school (*Guardian*, 6 February 1999). Recent evidence has also demonstrated marked differences in grading standards among the awarding bodies, at least in some subjects at A-level (QCA, 1999a). There is also much controversy over the reliability of the key stage national tests and the appropriateness of using those for 11-year-olds to monitor progress (e.g. Robinson, 1997). But an independent panel vindicated the Government and the Qualifications and Curriculum Authority over allegations of political interference and 'fiddling' to take account of the difficulty of the tests for 11-year-olds in 1999. However, the real controversy is whether standards have fallen on a national scale over time. A major problem here, of course, is that syllabuses and question style have changed, and course work now supplements written examinations, which in turn are now more about candidates' ability to apply skills rather than memorise facts. For instance, history A-level papers before the 1980s simply offered a choice of essay questions, but more recently have contained document-based questions asking candidates to evaluate sources. These factors make comparisons over time a highly complex exercise.

The former School Curriculum and Assessment Authority set up a rolling programme of reviews by panels of specialists to ensure that examination demands and standards of grading were being maintained, and this has been continued by SCAA's successor, the Qualifications and Curriculum Authority (QCA). Although the investigators were hamstrung by syllabus changes and even loss of scripts, they concluded that, overall, examination standards at GCSE in English, chemistry and mathematics had not changed significantly (SCAA, 1996). A later study reached the same broad conclusion with respect to French, religious education, physical education and geography (QCA, 1999b). At A-level, analysis also suggests that standards have generally been maintained in mathematics, physics, history, government and politics, and German (Bell *et al.*, 1998; QCA, 1999b). Evidence from the Office of Standards in Education confirms these findings. In a two-year study by inspectors of 2,000 exam scripts and several hundred coursework assignments in 70 schools in 1996, standards in the modular A- and AS-level courses were found to be as high as in traditional end-of-course examinations (OFSTED, 1997).

But the debate continues. Adopting a different approach to the problem, Coe (1999) compared changes in GCSE and A-level grades in a range of subjects since 1988 while holding constant the effects of general ability, as measured by certain tests. He found that grades achieved by students of the same general ability had tended to increase by at least one grade for A-level and nearly half a grade for GCSE over the ten-year period. He notes that this could be due to grade standards slipping, but suggests a number of other possibilities. These include more effective teaching, better exam tactics, the introduction of course work and modular exams which help candidates to demonstrate their ability more easily, and demographic changes that have seen rising numbers of middle-class adolescents (who traditionally do better in exams). Because of all these factors, Coe concludes that it is not possible to say definitively whether or not grade standards have slipped.

For discussion

'Given the uses to which GCSE and A-level results are put, what matters is that the candidates are accurately ranked each year. The debate about grade slipping is therefore an irrelevant, as well as an inherently inconclusive, issue.' Do you agree?

Further reading

On the relationship between education and the economy, see Robinson, P. (1997).
Look out for the new TIMSS report, to be published by the National Foundation for Educational Research, and the first PISA survey results (OECD).
On gender differences, see Arnot *et al.* (1998) and Arnot *et al.* (1999).

References

Alexander, R. (1997) 'International comparisons and the quality of primary teaching', in C. Cullingford (ed.) *The Politics of Primary Education*. Buckingham: Open University Press.

Arnot, M. *et al.* (1998) *Recent Research on Gender and Educational Performance*. London: Stationery Office.

Arnot, M. *et al.* (1999) *Closing the Gender Gap: Postwar Education and Social Change*. Cambridge: Polity Press.

Audit Commission (1999) *Local Performance Indicators 1997/98· Education Services*. London: Audit Commission.

Ball, S. J. (1999) 'Labour, learning and the economy: a "policy sociology" perspective', *Cambridge Journal of Education*, 29(2), 195–206.

Bell, J. *et al.* (1998) 'Investigating A level mathematics standards over time', *British Journal of Curriculum and Assessment*, 8(2), 7–12.

Broadfoot, P. M. *et al.* (1998) *The Quality of Primary Education: Children's Experience of Schooling in England and France*. End of Award Report to the Economic and Social Research Council.

Brooks, G. *et al.* (1996) *Reading Performance at Nine*. Slough: NFER.

Brooks, G. *et al.* (1997) *Trends in Reading at Eight*. Slough: NFER.

Brown, M. (1998). 'The tyranny of the international horse race' in Slee, R. *et al. School Effectiveness for Whom?* London: Falmer Press.

Coe, R. (1999) 'Changes in examination grades over time: Is the same worth less?'. Paper presented at the British Educational Research Association Annual Conference, University of Sussex.

Coffield, F. (1998) 'Easy come, too easy go', *TES*, 18 September, 15.

Department for Education/Welsh Office (1992) *Choice and Diversity*. London: Stationery Office.

Department for Education and Employment (1997) *Excellence in Schools*. London: Stationery Office.

Department of Education and Science/Welsh Office (1985) *Better Schools*. London: Stationery Office.

Fitzpatrick, M. (1999) 'Dawn of a new creativity', *TES*, 18 June, 24.

Galton, M. *et al.* (1998) *Inside the Primary Classroom: Twenty Years On*. London: Routledge.

Gorard, S. *et al.* (1999) 'Revisiting the apparent underachievement of boys: reflections on the implications for educational research'. Paper presented to the British Educational Research Association Annual Conference.

Grow-Maienza, J. *et al.* (1997) 'Mathematics Instruction in Korean Primary Schools'. Paper presented to the American Educational Research Association Conference.

Harris, S. *et al.* (1997) *Third International Mathematics and Science Study, Second National Report, Part 1: Achievement in Mathematics and Science at Age 9 in England.* Slough: NFER.

Harris, S. *et al.* (1998). *Third International Mathematics and Science Study, Third National Report: Performance Assessment.* Slough: NFER.

James, M. (1997) 'Aims should come first, methods second', *TES*, 5 September, 23.

Keys, W. *et al.* (1996) *Third International Mathematics and Science Study, First National Report, Part 1: Achievement in Mathematics and Science at Age 13 in England.* Slough: NFER.

Keys, W. *et al.* (1997a) *Third International Mathematics and Science Study, First National Report, Part 2: Patterns of Mathematics and Science Teaching in Lower Secondary Schools in England and Ten Other Countries.* Slough: NFER.

Keys, W. *et al.* (1997b) *Third International Mathematics and Science Study, Second National Report, Part 2: Patterns of Mathematics and Science Teaching in Upper Primary Schools in England and Eight Other Countries.* Slough: NFER.

Moser, C. (1999) *A Fresh Start: Basic Skills for Adults.* London: DfEE.

Office for Standards in Education (1997) *GCE AS/A Level Examinations 1996.* London: Stationery Office.

Ouston, J. (1998) 'Educational reform in Japan: some reflections from England', *Management in Education*, 12(5), 15–19.

Pennington, P. (1999) 'Shake-up aims to stem corruption', *TES*, 7 May, 6.

Qualifications and Curriculum Authority (1999a) *GCSE A-Level Standards: A Review.* London: QCA.

Qualifications and Curriculum Authority (1999b) *Five-yearly Review of A-level Standards and 16-plus Examinations.* London: QCA.

Qualifications and Curriculum Authority (1999c) *The Revised National Curriculum. Primary and Secondary Handbooks.* London: QCA.

Qualifications and Curriculum Authority (1999d) *Improving Writing at Key Stages 3 and 4.* London: QCA.

Reynolds, D. (1997) 'East-West trade-off', *TES*, 27 June, 21.

Riley, K.A. (1998) *Whose School Is It Anyway?* London: Falmer Press.

Robinson, P. (1997) *Literacy, Numeracy and Economic Performance.* London: London School of Economics and Political Science.

School Curriculum and Assessment Authority (1996) *Standards in Public Examinations, 1975–1995.* London: SCAA.

Spice, M. (1998). 'Thinking points to way to a second boom', *TES*, 26 June, 27.

Sukhnandan, L. (1999). *An Investigation into Gender Differences in Achievement: Phase 1.* Slough: NFER.

Youth Cohort Study (1999a) *The Activities and Experiences of 16 year olds: England and Wales 1998.* London: DfEE.

Youth Cohort Study (1999b) *The Activities and Experiences of 18 year olds: England and Wales 1998.* London: DfEE.

Chapter 2

What is the Solution? An Overview of National Policies for Schools, 1979–99

Jim Docking

Previous policy

The Conservative Administration from 1979 to 1997 was responsible for an unparalleled spate of educational law-making and regulatory activity. No area of the education service was left untouched during a series of more than 20 Education Acts. The Government summarised its policies for schools in terms of 'five great themes' – quality, diversity, parental choice, greater autonomy for schools and greater accountability (DfE, 1992).

Quality was addressed primarily through the National Curriculum, which attempted to provide all 5- to 16-year-olds with an 'entitlement' to broad and balanced studies, and through a policy of 'differentiation' that tried to match teaching, learning and assessment to the needs of the individual pupil. This was reinforced through national tests and teacher assessments at the end of infant, primary, middle and secondary schooling. But from the start the National Curriculum was beleaguered with charges of centralism and bureaucracy, eventually necessitating slimmed-down prescriptions following a review by Sir Ron Dearing. Even so, there remained some basic problems, such as the rationale for a curriculum based around prescribed subjects (especially controversial in the early years of schooling) and the treatment of curriculum areas not easily subsumed under subject headings. Quality was also tackled through four-yearly inspections by the Office for Standards in Education (OFSTED) and measures to deal with 'failing schools'. Arrangements for teacher appraisal was another important measure, and satisfied teachers as long as it was focused on individual professional development.

The shift in curriculum control from local authorities and schools to the centre was paralleled by developments in initial teacher training. From the mid-1980s, courses leading to the award of Qualified Teacher Status had to satisfy various criteria. The Teacher Training Agency, with membership determined by the Secretary of State, was set up under the 1994 Education Act to regulate teacher supply and recruitment, raise the quality of courses, accredit providers of initial teacher training and act as their funding agency.

The pursuit of quality was also behind the introduction of the concept of special educational needs, which replaced previous categories of handicap with the idea of a continuum of need that covered children in mainstream as well as special schools. Arrangements were set up to identify and assess children with special educational needs and to provide 'statements' of need for those who required special resources, importantly involving parents in the process. The Government was also committed to educating children with special needs in mainstream schools wherever possible, and it introduced a Code of Practice to clarify the responsibilities of schools and set time limits to speed up the statementing process.

For older adolescents, the GCSE (General Certificate of Secondary Education) replaced separate qualifications for higher and lower attainers, while Records of Achievement were introduced to provide wider scope for accreditation in personal and vocational as well as academic pursuits. In spite of arguments for a more radical approach, the Government insisted that A-levels must be retained as the 'gold standard', but it attempted to broaden the curriculum by introducing AS-levels and vocational pathways for pupils at 16-plus. Quality in the early years was never successfully addressed, either in terms of its ideology or its management through a voucher system – but at least something was done to reverse the absence of any sustained initiative by previous administrations by making it possible for every four-year-old to secure a pre-school place.

The main route to *diversity* was accomplished through the introduction of grant-maintained schools that were free from local control. In the secondary sector, almost a quarter (668) of secondary schools went GM, though their popularity varied considerably from one authority to another. But in the primary sector only three per cent (511) were attracted. The Government also introduced City Technology Colleges that were also independent from local control. Additionally, it allowed locally maintained schools to specialise in a curriculum area, and (much more controversially) permitted comprehensive schools to select 15 per cent of the intake on the basis of general ability. Of these policies, the establishment of a separate tier of GM schools was the most contentious. On the one hand, it catered for schools that felt their LEA had not supplied the kind of support they wanted and allowed them to enjoy a large measure of independence in the way they ran their affairs and employed outside services. On the other hand, the policy of funding GM schools more generously than locally maintained schools attracted strong charges of unfairness – though the threat of schools opting out forced LEAs to delegate more money to their own schools and make their services more consumer-orientated. Local authorities also found it difficult to plan school places and to operate a co-ordinated admissions policy.

The objective to provide *greater parent choice* was pursued through quasi-market policies. Parents were given the right to state a preference for the school they wanted their child to attend and could take advantage of appeals systems through tribunals for admissions and special educational needs. The policy of 'open enrolment' placed a duty on schools to admit pupils up to their physical capacity;

and by linking school funding to pupil numbers, schools had an incentive to offer the kind of curriculum and provision that parents sought. The pursuit of choice was also furthered by giving parents the power to choose whether their child's school should become grant-maintained, while the Assisted Places Scheme enabled selected able children from poor backgrounds to receive their education in independent schools. For the early years, vouchers allowed parents to choose from a range of pre-school provision that included the private sector.

In practice, the policy to empower parents through market forces was only partially realised. There were not enough good schools or opportunities for expansion to meet the demand, and some secondaries became progressively 'sink schools' as they were forced to admit pupils that other schools would not accept. The policy created a strategy for the middle classes while disadvantaging working-class families, and in many cases allowed schools to choose their pupils rather than parents to choose the schools. In April 1999, Peter Lilley, deputy leader of the Conservative Opposition, publicly acknowledged that his party's market policies were 'intrinsically unsuited' to education and health, and promised that a future Tory administration would continue to fund these services mainly from the public purse.

The objective to achieve *greater school autonomy* included a range of measures to reduce control by local authorities. As well as those already mentioned, the power of LEAs to dominate school governing bodies was abolished by two measures. One reduced the numbers of LEA representatives and increased the proportion of parents, teachers and co-opted members; the other gave governing bodies significant powers at the expense of the LEA to manage school affairs and determine their spending programme as funding was increasingly delegated to schools. These were probably the most popular of the Conservatives' policies for schools.

Greater accountability was achieved through a variety of measures that were geared to satisfy the public's demand for value in public spending. Performance indicators and output measures were instituted in all Government departments, the performance of individual schools was monitored through the cycle of OFSTED inspections, performance tables were published, and a Parents' Charter was posted to every household. However, performance indicators and inspection were not seen by everyone to be politically neutral devices as controversy ensued about the choice of indicators, whether 'league' tables should include 'value added' data to indicate a school's progress as well as absolute levels of attainment, and what criteria should govern school inspections.

New Labour's policies

The rationale behind New Labour's policies, in terms of raising standards and preparing a future generation with skills that would enable Britain to compete with its industrial competitors, was explained in the previous chapter. Here we look at the general principles and give a summary of the key policies.

General principles

The White Paper *Excellence in Schools* (DfEE, 1997a) set out six 'policy principles':

1. *'Education will be at the heart of government.'* Education was to occupy 'centre stage' and be the 'number one priority', attracting an increased proportion of Government funding.
2. *'Policies will be designed to benefit the many, not just the few.'* The Assisted Places Scheme, whereby able children could win subsidised places in independent schools, would be abolished to free resources for reducing class size for five- to seven-year-olds, and early failure would be reduced through policies to boost nursery education and the three 'Rs' in primary schools.
3. *'Standards matter more than structures.'* Standards would be emphasised by creating 'a climate in which schools are constantly challenged to compare themselves to other similar schools and adopt proven ways of raising their performance'.
4. *'Intervention will be in reverse proportion to success.'* The Government would not interfere in schools that were successful, except to challenge them to improve further, but the DfEE or LEAs would arrange 'targeted interventions...appropriate to the scale of the problem' to protect the pupils – preferably at an early stage.
5. *'There will be zero tolerance for underperformance.'* Schools that were not up to scratch would have to improve, make a fresh start, or close – a principle that would apply also to LEAs.
6. *'Government will work in partnership with those committed to raising standards.'* The partners were to include parents, teachers, governors, local authorities, churches, business, private schools, volunteers and voluntary organisations.

Specific policies

Virtually all the policies set out in the White Paper have now been addressed or a start made. Figure 2.1 lists the Government's main targets for schools, and Figure 2.2 sketches out the chronology of events during the first 28 months.

Within a few weeks of taking office, the Government reinforced its decision to 'put standards at the heart of the education agenda' by setting up the Standards Task Force and the Standards and Effectiveness Unit. Chaired by the Secretary of State and having 24 members (the Chief Inspector for Schools, headteachers, academics and representatives from business and commerce), the Task Force meets four times a year to advise the Government on education policy. It has been particularly influential in policy related to 'Oscar' rewards for teachers, greater involvement of parents and the community in schools, the Standards Website, and the identification of Beacon Schools to spread examples

GOVERNMENT TARGETS FOR SCHOOLS

Targets are to be met by 2002 unless otherwise stated.
Figures in parentheses represent the position in Labour's first year.

Early years
- 66% of 3-year-olds to have nursery places, especially in the most deprived areas. (34%)
- By September 2000: no children aged 5 to 7 years in classes of more than 30 pupils. (477,000)

11-year-olds
- 80% to reach the expected standard for their age in literacy (Level 4 in the National Curriculum Key Stage 2 tests). (63%)
- 75% to reach the expected standard for their age in numeracy. (Level 4 in the National Curriculum Key Stage 2 tests). (62%)

16-year-olds
- 95% to achieve at least one GCSE at Grade G, or equivalent. (92%)
- 50% to obtain 5 GCSEs at Grade C or better. (45%)
- 50% of looked-after children to achieve at least one graded GCSE by 2001, 75% by 2003.

19-year-olds
- 85% to reach at least NVQ Level 2 or equivalent. (72%)

Truancy and exclusion from school
- Unauthorised absence not to exceed 0.5% half days missed a year. (0.7%)
- No more than 8,400 children a year permanently excluded from school. (12,500)
- LEAs to provide full-time education for pupils within 15 days of their exclusion.

Secondary schools
- 800 new specialist secondary schools by 2003.
- 2,000 Beacon Schools by 2002 (75)

ICT
- All schools to be networked by 2002.
- Teachers to feel confident about teaching ICT.
- School leavers to have good understanding of ICT with measures in place for assessing their competence in it.

Figure 2.1

CHRONOLOGY OF KEY EVENTS

1997

May   New Labour won the General Election

Vouchers for pre-school education abolished

Standards and Effectiveness Unit set up to oversee national programmes for school improvement

Targets for performance by 11-year-olds in literacy and numeracy announced

June   Education (Schools) Act abolished assisted places scheme

Standards Task Force set up to advise Government on education policy

Minimal nutritional standards for school meals announced

July   White Paper Excellence in Schools

First Early Excellence Centres set up

New OFSTED grading system to identify incompetent teachers

First school under Fresh Start Policy set up in Newcastle

New Deal for Schools introduced to provide £1.085 million for improving school buildings

August   GCSE targets set

First literacy summer schools for 11-year-olds

September   Hackney LEA taken over by central government

New Start programmes to motivate and re-engage 14- to 17-year-olds who have 'dropped out' of education or training

October   Green Paper Excellence for All Children: Meeting Special Educational Needs

Qualifications and Curriculum Authority (QCA) established, merging work of former School Curriculum and Assessment Authority (SCAA) and the National Council for Vocational Qualifications (NCVQ)

December   Social Exclusion Unit launched under the aegis of the Cabinet Office

1998

January   First honours for school heads to improve image of teaching profession

First Muslim schools get grants

First OFSTED inspections of LEAs

February   Green Paper The Learning Age: A Renaissance for a New Britain outlines Government policy for lifelong learning

April   Extending Opportunity: A National Framework for Study report on support for pupil learning outside normal lessons

Government publishes guidelines on homework

May   Social Exclusion Unit report Truancy and Social Exclusion calls for truancy and exclusion to be reduced by one-third by 2002

Mental arithmetic tests at Key Stages 2 and 3 introduced

July   Sure Start cross-departmental programme launched to promote the development of pre-school children

Teaching and Higher Education Act

School Standards and Framework Act

September   National Curriculum regulations relaxed in primary schools

Crick Report Education for Citizenship and the Teaching of Democracy in Schools

National Literacy Strategy implemented and National Year of Reading launched

All teacher trainees follow national curricula for ICT and, for primary teaching, maths and English

Standards Site launched on the Internet

First Education Action Zones set up

First Beacon Schools identified to spread good practice to other schools

New Deal for Communities to deal with the problems of run-down estates, including failure in schools.

Figure 2.2

| | Schools can give Key Stage 4 pupils more time for work-related learning by exempting them from two of the following subjects: a science, design & technology or a foreign language |
| | |

Schools can give Key Stage 4 pupils more time for work-related learning by exempting them from two of the following subjects: a science, design & technology or a foreign language

Schools required to provide careers education for pupils in Years 9–11

Schools can prepare pre-16 pupils with special needs for Entry level qualifications to credit achievements below GCSE Grade G/GNVQ foundation level and NVQ Level 1

New Key Skills qualification in communication, application of number and IT introduced for 16–19 age group

October　Package of measures designed to address recruitment crises in secondary subjects such as maths and science

November　Government action programme Meeting Special Education Needs

December　Green Paper Teachers: Meeting the Challenge of Change sets out proposals for career structures, professional development, annual appraisal and pay

New grade of Advanced Skills Teachers introduced.

Funds to provide nursery places for 3-year-olds announced

1999

January　Improved funding for local authority music services

Code of Practice on LEA–school relations published

February　First booster classes for Year 6 children with problems in literacy and numeracy

Secretary of State must approve sale of school playing fields

March　Action Plan Excellence in Cities launched to re-vitalise urban schools

April　LEA Education Development Plans implemented to raise achievement and tackle social exclusion in a 3-year programme

Code of Practice on Admissions to ensure local policies meet certain criteria

Fair Funding introduced to improve levels of funds delegated to schools

May　PSHE report Preparing Young People for Adult Life

Robinson Report All Our Futures on creative and cultural education

June　First speech by a serving PM to a teacher union conference (the NAHT)

National College for School Leadership announced for 2000

Guidelines to boost education of children looked after by local authorities

House of Commons Select Committee Report The Work of OFSTED

July　White Paper Learning to Succeed: A New Framework for Post-16 Learning

August　OFSTED given powers to regulate childcare services

September　Grant-maintained schools re-integrated into LEA structures, and all maintained schools re-categorised as community, foundation or voluntary schools

National curricula for teacher trainees extended to primary science and secondary English, maths and science

General Teaching Council established as the statutory professional body for teachers

National Numeracy Strategy implemented

All secondary schools can offer Part One GNVQ, a shortened version of the full GNVQ designed for 14- to 16-year-olds

School governing bodies re-constituted to provide greater representation of parents and the representation of non-teaching staff

Home–School Agreements in all schools

QCA publishes Early Learning Goals establishing a Foundation Stage for ages 3 to 6

2000

January　Maths Year 2000 begins

September　Revised National Curriculum implemented. Citizenship compulsory in secondary schools.

Introduction of new A-level syllabuses and a revised Advanced Subsidiary (AS) qualification (half a full A-level)

Revised GNVQ available at Advanced, Intermediate and Foundation levels of successful practice. The Standards and Effectiveness Unit, headed by Michael Barber, is responsible for many of the national initiatives such as the literacy and numeracy strategies, Education Action Zones, target-setting in schools and approving Education Development Plans drawn up by local authorities.

In a speech to the Confederation of British Industry in July 1999, David Blunkett, the Education Secretary, summed up New Labour's attempts to raise standards in terms of four 'key elements' – laying firm foundations, improving all schools, a drive for inclusion and modernising comprehensive education.

Under *laying firm foundations* he listed the main policies for early years and primary education: the Sure Start programme to provide co-ordinated education and health advice for the parents of very young children; nursery education for all four-year-olds and double the number of places for three-year-olds; reducing the size of classes; and the literacy and numeracy strategies, which include parental involvement.

The second key element, *improving all schools*, applied to secondary and special as well as primary schools. Blunkett described the strategies as a combination of pressure and support. Support included: delegating more resources to schools; supplying benchmarking data to help schools compare themselves with others and set targets for improvement; and giving access to 'best practice' advice (for example, through the Standards Site on the Internet, and the Beacon Schools programme whereby selected schools received extra funding in return for sharing their strategies with neighbourhood schools). Pressure, he said, was supplied through regular inspections, performance targets and published tables of achievement. If either schools or local authorities were not coming up to scratch, he would intervene 'to ensure pupils get the education they deserve' – preferably at an early stage, but if not through tough action as in his recent decision to direct Hackney and Islington to lose some or most of their education services to private contractors.

The drive for *inclusion* encompassed a range of policies to 'benefit the many, not just the few'. Following a Green Paper (DfEE, 1997b), more money was being spent on supporting pupils with special educational needs and improving their access to buildings, while more pupils with SEN statements were being supported in mainstream rather than special schools. Every local authority had targets to reduce truancy and exclusion by one-third by 2002, with increased investment in in-school centres for excluded pupils, electronic registration systems and other initiatives. He acknowledged that some ethnic minority groups were over-represented among excluded pupils, a problem that would be addressed through LEA strategies and annual inspections of high-excluding schools. He also referred to the New Deal for 18- to 24-year-olds to ensure that young people without qualifications are in work or training and receiving the advice they need for further learning.

Admitting that comprehensive schools 'had not delivered what its advocates hoped for', he argued that the purpose of *modernising comprehensive education* was to ensure 'diversity' to meet the needs and aspirations of all children. Where there were grammar schools, it would 'of course' be parents in the locality who would decide their future. For the majority of pupils, he said, we needed 'schools which focus on what works and abandon a dogmatic attachment to mixed ability teaching'. Specialist schools in technology, languages, sports and arts were sharing their expertise and resources with other schools. Their number had already been doubled and would reach nearly a quarter of all secondary schools by 2003. Additionally, the secondary school curriculum had been made more flexible to allow more time for work-place learning, and the revised National Curriculum would make more provision for pupils to develop their special talents as well as introducing citizenship into the curriculum. Alongside these initiatives were programmes to give pupils who needed it extra support through mentoring, to link school learning to life outside school, and summer schools in literacy and numeracy.

Lastly under this heading, Blunkett referred to the Excellence in Cities programme to inject £350 million over three years to develop the aptitudes and arrest the underachievement of secondary pupils in 25 councils. This package of measures (DfEE, 1999a) includes:

- *support for all pupils* – two 'learning mentors' in each comprehensive to advise pupils needing extra help, liaise with feeder primaries, and tackle relationships problems such as bullying and racial abuse; plus curriculum materials to help parents in supporting their children's learning and a low-cost scheme to help poor families and adults lease computers;
- *support for disruptive pupils* – learning units to provide intensive support;
- *support for gifted pupils* – master classes linked to specialist schools, study support, extra teaching, partnerships with independent schools, university summer schools and weekend activities for the most able 5–10 per cent;
- *support for failing schools* – poor schools twinned with successful ones or clustered into small education action zones, maybe involving a single school;
- *a diversity of schools* – a rapid expansion of specialist and Beacon schools;
- *incentives to attract good teachers* – salary bonuses for high performance, subsidised loans to buy computers, and making fast-track promotion for young teachers dependent upon inner-city experience.

David Blunkett also drew attention to three other broad areas of policy and achievement. One was enabling schools to make maximum use of information and communications technology – 'the way to ensuring a confident workforce at the cutting edge of change'. He promised that every school would be networked by 2002, with teachers trained to make ICT of benefit to pupils in the classroom.

A second area was the creation of new partnerships, not only between education and other public services but with private sectors. Some of the examples he mentioned were: collaboration between education and health services (as in the Sure Start programme for children up to three years old and Education Action Zones); special initiatives involving schools working with libraries, museums, universities, football clubs and other partners to improve pupils' motivation and educational opportunities; mentoring schemes; LEAs working together (for instance, in the Excellence in Cities initiative) and with major companies.

Blunkett's final theme was reforms in the teaching profession. Here he mentioned a new national curriculum and set of standards for teacher training, the creation of a General Teaching Council, the national teaching awards on BBC1, more staff development training and reforms in the pay structure. The proposals to make annual appraisal part of the system and give teachers extra money in recognition of certain standards of pupil performance was, he said, 'a serious investment in return for necessary reform'.

Three Education Acts

The legislative basis for most of the measures outlined in the previous section was provided through three Education Acts. The Education (Schools) Act 1997 abolished the Assisted Places Scheme and diverted the funding to reduce the size of infant classes. The Teaching and Higher Education Act 1998 included clauses to set up General Teaching Councils in England and Wales, introduce an induction year for teachers, make it possible for headteachers to be required to have a professional headship qualification, and allow HMI to inspect teacher training establishments.

All the other legislation was contained in the School Standards and Frame-work Act 1998 (see Figure 2.3 for a summary). Although in the Bill's second reading this was described by David Blunkett as 'the most substantial piece of legislation ever brought forward by a Labour Government', it was not in the same league as the epoch-making Education Reform Act of 1988 under the Conservatives. Nor, with its 145 sections, was it as gargantuan as the 1988 and 1993 Acts, which had 238 and 308 sections respectively. All the same, it has had profound consequences for both schools and local education authorities. Raising standards must be the number one priority for schools, while LEAs are given a new statutory duty to promote high standards of education through setting performance targets and by challenging and supporting schools in their efforts to improve pupils' performance.

In the Commons, the measures were criticised by the Conservative Opposition mainly on the grounds that they extended the powers of the Secretary of State to intervene where LEAs or individual schools were performing poorly, abolished grant-maintained schools, were inconsistent in the policy about selection, and created mechanisms for abolishing grammar schools. But the Liberal Democrats wanted the Government to go further by abolishing foundation schools status for ex-GMs, extending class size limits to junior pupils, and allowing LEAs to have more say in appointing headteachers. The Government also encountered trouble in the Lords, where Anglican and Catholic bishops wrung concessions to ensure that the Church's interests in its schools were protected and that its representation on governing bodies was not diluted.

SCHOOL STANDARDS AND FRAMEWORK ACT 1998

Measures to raise standards of school education
- LEAs and school governing bodies have a duty to give priority to the promotion of high standards
- LEAs to have Education Development Plans, approved by the Secretary of State, for raising standards
- LEAs can intervene in the running of a school if pupil performance is unacceptably low; if there is a breakdown in management or discipline; or if there has been insufficient improvement in a school designated as one with serious weaknesses or under special measures
- LEAs can report to the governing body of a school if it has serious concerns about the performance of the headteacher
- The Secretary of State can appoint additional governors to schools in special measures and can nominate one of those governors to act as Chair
- Commitment to reduce class sizes in Key Stage 1 to a maximum of 30

Pupil behaviour
- All schools must have a written school behaviour policy that includes strategies to prevent bullying among pupils
- A procedure for excluding pupils from schools that is common to all types of maintained school
- LEAs responsible for arranging independent appeals on permanent exclusions
- Governing bodies to set targets to reduce level of unauthorised absences
- Corporal punishment abolished in private schools

New framework for maintained schools
- All maintained schools, including GM, to be re-designated as community, voluntary (aided or controlled) or foundation schools
- Governing bodies to set up home–school agreements, drawn up in consultation with parents, that parents are invited (but not compelled) to sign
- Secondary schools may arrange for some of their pupils to receive part of their education in an FE college
- Governing bodies to have more parent governors and a new category of non-teaching staff governor
- The legal framework of governing bodies simplified by abolishing articles of government and shortening instruments of government
- The respective roles and responsibilities of headteachers and governing bodies to be clarified

School admissions
- Code of Practice on Admissions to be issued by the Secretary of State
- No new selection by ability other than banding, and banding arrangements must result in a genuinely comprehensive intake
- Schools with a specialism can admit up to 10% of pupils who can demonstrate an aptitude in that area
- Parental ballots on the retention of grammar schools

Other provisions about school education
- School lunches must meet nutritional standards laid down by Secretary of State and be provided where there is a demand
- Governing bodies and schools no longer required to have written curriculum policies
- Year 10 and 11 pupils can undertake work experience with the consent of the governing body and LEA
- Collective worship can take place off the school's premises
- Former GM schools to adopt the local agreed syllabus for RE

Early years education
- LEAs have a duty to secure the provision of nursery education
- Each LEA must set up an Early Years Development Partnership to prepare early years development plans

Local authorities and school funding
- Secretary of State to issue a Code of Practice on relations between the LEA and its schools
- More funding delegated to schools and a sharper separation of LEA and school functions
- Funding agency for financing GM schools dissolved and all maintained schools in the authority funded on the same basis
- LEA Education Committees to include at least one parent governor
- LEAs must have School Organisation Committees to address the problems of parent choice and school places
- Procedures set out for establishing, altering and closing schools
- Provision for Education Action Zones

Figure 2.3

Issues for debate

1. Do New Labour's policies for schools represent a fresh approach?

It is sometimes said that, for all the rhetoric, the present Government's policies for schools are fundamentally the Conservative's dressed up in New Labour clothes. To a large extent this is true. There have been few outright reversals of policy: abolishing nursery school vouchers, the assisted places scheme, and grant-maintained (GM) schools outside local authority control are the notable exceptions. As we saw earlier, by most accounts nursery vouchers were an administrative disaster. The decision to divert money from the assisted places scheme to reducing the size of infant classes was part of the policy to 'benefit the many, not just the few'. On the GM front, the Government regarded it as unfair that centrally maintained schools should receive more money than their LEA counterparts. It was also concerned that decoupling some schools from the LEA framework reduced co-operation between schools and produced a lack of clarity about accountability in some areas such as admissions arrangements and planning school places (DfEE, 1997a). Now, GM schools have been absorbed back into the LEA network as 'foundation' schools with similar funding arrangements to other schools and with LEA representatives on their governing bodies – though because they retain most of their former powers, including the right to continue an element of selection, a two-tier system and prospects of a pecking order remain (see Note 1 at end of chapter).

Apart from the few policy reversals, virtually all the Conservatives' measures have been left intact. Along with the centralisation policies (the National Curriculum, testing, the Teacher Training Agency, OFSTED and the identification of failing schools), the Thatcherite market policies of competition and choice are still with us – though some changes have been made to the details. Although there are plans to overhaul the qualifications system for 16- to 19-year-olds, A-levels are to remain as the 'gold standard'. Even the national literacy and numeracy strategies are based upon pilot schemes set up under the previous Government. New Labour has also retained the Conservative policy to promote choice and diversity in the secondary sector. It has resisted Radical Left arguments for abolishing the 164 remaining grammar schools (unless local parents want that), arguing in its manifesto that 'Labour will never force the abolition of good schools whether in the private or state sector'.

Although schools that operate partial selection can be, and have been, told by independent adjudicators to reduce the percentage of children admitted on the basis of ability if at least ten parents of primary school children object on the grounds that local children are being squeezed out, the Government has allowed comprehensive schools to continue any pre-existing arrangements for selecting by ability. It has also permitted other schools to make such arrangements provided that their intention is to produce a more balanced intake.

However, there has been a shift from a policy of choice based on school status (grammar and GM schools v. comprehensives) to one based more on curricular diversity (specialist v. general comprehensives). The Labour government has therefore created more funding for specialist comprehensives (which, however, must also attract funds from private sponsors) while also trying to counter Conservative policies that it believed encouraged schools to pursue individual self-interest rather than co-operation.

Some measures have not only been retained but also strengthened or taken a step further. The Government wants more children with SEN to be placed in mainstream schools; LEAs as well as schools are now inspected nationwide; schools are to receive a higher percentage of the local education budget; the requirements for the teacher-training curriculum have been made more rigorous; and, in the face of massive opposition from the profession, teacher appraisal is to be linked with pay. Further, the Conservative policies to centralise the curriculum have been extended to classroom pedagogy and organisation.

The previous Government had made inroads into classroom methodology, for instance in its advocacy of whole-class teaching in primary schools and its legislation in 1986 to ensure that the teaching of controversial issues gave a balanced presentation of opposing views. But New Labour has gone much further in its highly prescriptive and detailed interventions about how to teach and organise classrooms, challenging the professional competence of teachers and their right to make their own professional judgements as never before. Apart from the highly structured literacy and numeracy hours and official guidance on homework, the Government has made the presumption that pupils would be set by ability for at least some subject areas (maths, science and languages), particularly in the secondary schools (DfEE, 1997a; DfEE, 1999a) (see Note 2).

Some say that New Labour has tried to rehabilitate the role of local education authorities, but this is mainly as the chief agent of Government initiatives rather than as unshackled agents. Every LEA must explain, through its Education Development Plan, how it proposes to raise standards in its schools. Where it is not satisfied that a school is performing satisfactorily, the LEA (and, very exceptionally, the Secretary of State) has powers to intervene in the running of the school. The Government certainly has not reversed the Conservative policies that changed LEAs from agents of control to ones that supported largely self-determining schools: on the contrary, it has decreased still further the amount of money LEAs can hold back for central services so that schools can get more. Also, by setting up Education Action Zones, it has robbed some LEAs of their authority over under-achieving schools.

What about Labour's election promise to increase the percentage of the Gross Domestic Product (GDP) on education? A problem here was that during their first two years in office the Government was handicapped by another promise, to keep to the public spending plans of its predecessor. Indeed, spending on education as a percentage of the GDP fell during 1997–98. But in its comprehensive spending review for the three years 1999–2002, Labour trumpeted an extra £19 billion for education in the United Kingdom, raising spending from 4.6 per cent of GDP in 1998–99 to 5 per cent in 2001–02. This does represent higher spending than at the end of the Conservative administration, but it was 5.3 per cent in John Major's first year and higher still in the early 1980s and some earlier years (6.9 per cent in 1974), including previous Labour administrations (OECD figures reported in *Education Journal*, March 1999).

So is anything new? Yes. First of all, New Labour is pursuing social democratic policies in its attempts to reach two parts of the child population that the Conservatives failed to reach effectively. One is children from low-income backgrounds, particularly in inner-cities. This policy has underpinned the social exclusion initiatives, Education Action Zones and policies to revitalise inner city schools through the Excellence in Cities initiative and education maintenance allowances for impoverished 16- to 18-year-olds.

The other aspect is the much more comprehensive programme for the early years. Apart from the measures to reduce class sizes, there are a set of learning goals for children aged three to the end of the reception year. Every local authority now has an Early Years Development and Childcare Plan to show how an education place can be provided for all four-year-olds whose parents want it, and how good quality childcare can be made available and linked to early education. The DfEE also intends, by 2001–02, to extend free education places to two-thirds of three-year-olds, almost double the numbers in January 1997. Also in place in every LEA are Early Years Development Partnerships to plan cross-departmental services with all the early years interests in the area, while Early Excellence Centres are being set up to provide integrated education, childcare and family support.

Secondly, there has been a more rigorous and comprehensive pursuit of partnership policies. Some of this represents continuity with the Conservatives, who had encouraged links between business and education (particularly through sponsorships of some schools and the City Technology Colleges). New Labour has extended this policy by encouraging commercial involvement in Education Action Zones, in privatising services in some 'failing' LEAs, and in arranging for a private company to take over a 'failing' school in Guildford. But the Government's partnership initiatives are not limited to Thatcherite policies, as demonstrated in the programme for the early years, mentioned above, whereby different services are enjoined to work co-operatively.

With help from state funding, partnerships have also been promoted between state and independent schools to share expertise and facilities. Within the maintained sector, partnership has been encouraged through specially chosen Beacon Schools, which receive more funding in return for sharing their effective practices with other schools. Partnership between the Government and teaching profession is being pursued through the General Teaching Council, where, along with union representatives, teachers have a majority. However, only 39 per cent of teachers are directly elected, and the powers of the GTC fall far short of those enjoyed by the General Medical Council. Even so, it will at least speak for the whole profession, not just one section of it. Partnership with parents is a feature of the literacy and numeracy strategies, and every school must now have its own home–school agreement which parents will have been invited – but not compelled – to sign. Additionally, parental representation has been increased on governing bodies and extended to deliberations at LEA level.

We can agree with David Hill (1999) that New Labour's policies in education have more in common with Conservative than Radical Left policies, but also that they reflect a mixture of ideologies. Hill suggests that some policies, such as targeting funding to schools in the poorest areas and using the state as well as the market to raise standards, reflect social democratic principles (e.g. in a commitment to equal opportunities, a degree of positive discrimination, helping to create a more socially just society, and a schooling system to further the economy as well as allow individuals to flourish). Others are neo-conservative (as in its 'basics' approach to the curriculum in schools and teacher training), while others are neo-liberal (as in the policies of privatisation, linking pay to performance, continuing to rely on market forces and restricting public spending on education). It is also the case that, while continuing to rely on the dual strategies of competitive forces and central intervention, the Government has shifted the balance more towards the latter with an explicitly evangelical flavour and sense of mission to its drive to improve levels of achievement in schools.

This was illustrated from the start by the language employed in the 1997 White Paper. Education was to be placed 'at the heart of government', as 'the Government's number one priority', occupying 'centre stage'. Nothing would stand in its way as it pledged to subject schools and LEAs to 'unrelenting pressure', applying 'zero tolerance' of underperformance, and ensuring 'speedy intervention where necessary'. The White Paper asked everyone to share its 'passion' and 'sense of urgency' for higher standards, declaring it was willing to work only with those who agreed with this rallying cry – a policy that was confirmed two years later when the Education Secretary delivered a widely publicised and scathing attack on his critics, accusing them of 'blatant élitism dressed up as well-intentioned liberalism' (Blunkett, 1999).

Whether New Labour's policies, of whatever complexion, are likely to succeed in raising standards is a further question. Certainly there are tensions: more delegation but also increased centralisation; a plethora of initiatives but an exhausted teaching profession to implement them; a more flexible National Curriculum but more prescription in pedagogy; new approaches in poor and depressed areas but a 'bidding culture' in which the more successful schools may find it easier to compete; market forces alongside target-setting and demands for action plans – to name just some. Contributors to Part II of this book examine the policies in detail and ask whether they represent a welcome shift of direction and are likely to achieve their objectives.

For discussion
Are New Labour's policies likely 'to benefit the many, not just the few'? (DfEE, 1997a).

2. Are standards of school performance more likely to improve through changes in schools or in social policy?

A major thrust of New Labour's policies for schools focuses on improving children's attainment in basic skills by improving the quality of teaching. But is this the best kind of policy to achieve the stated objective of raising standards?

Robinson (1997) argues, as many do, that the most powerful policy to raise educational standards is not one that intervenes in teaching methods but one that tackles child poverty. The scale of child poverty and its links with educational attainment has been well established in recent studies (Demack *et al.*, 1999; Gibson and Asthana, 1998; Glennerster, 1998; Gregg *et al.*, 1999; HM Treasury, 1999; Shropshire and Middleton, 1999; Thomson, 1996). These suggest that a third of all children (4.3 million) live at any one time in poor households (defined as those with incomes below half the national average), a three-fold increase since 1979, and up to a quarter live in persistent poverty.

Moreover the situation has worsened in recent years as families with low incomes have not kept up with generally rising standards of living. According to Shropshire and Middleton (1999), there is a sense in which some children 'learn to be poor' since their experiences of deprivation from an early age reduce future aspirations. As early as 22 months, children with parents in professional and managerial occupations are already 14 per cent higher up a cognitive development scale than children whose parents are in partly skilled or unskilled manual occupations; in adolescence, children in these latter bands are 2½ times more likely than those in the former ones to leave school without any qualifications (HM Treasury, 1999).

The cause and effect relationship between education and poverty, however, works in both directions. As Glennerster (1998) has pointed out, not only do the children of poor families do less well in school, but individuals with a poor educational performance record are also more likely to become unemployed or have a low-paid job. The situation becomes a vicious circle. Moreover, the situation is worsening as demand for unskilled workers is decreasing. Glennerster argues that a strategy to raise the standards of the lowest attainers (among adults as well as children) could raise skill levels, reducing the number of low-skilled applicants competing for jobs. This in turn would both raise wage levels for unskilled workers and improve job opportunities for those that had acquired the skills.

The poverty argument is sometimes countered by references to performance tables that show how schools in areas of similar socio-economic circumstances can produce markedly different levels of educational standards. Indeed, some schools in the most deprived areas of the country achieve GCSE results comparable to those in the least disadvantaged localities (Audit Commission, 1999); and, according to OFSTED (1999), children in some schools can be as much as two years ahead of those in others taking pupils from similar backgrounds. This suggests that the gap between the best and worst performing schools and education authorities is not straightforwardly attributable to social conditions. Indeed, the Education Secretary once declared that 'poverty is no excuse for poor standards' (*TES*, 12 March 1998). But that's to over-simplify the situation. Some schools, against the odds, manage to produce good results in spite of the handicap imposed by disadvantage, but this is not to say that teachers can easily bring all children, regardless of background, up to the same standard. As OFSTED (1999) has recently acknowledged, the conditions faced by many urban schools justifies extra resources and smaller classes.

One study suggests that only four per cent of the variability of children's attainment can be attributed to classroom factors such as teaching style (Creemers, 1997). If this is true, it suggests that changing school pedagogy is unlikely to make dramatic differences to national standards. Another study demonstrates that differences between schools in performance at GCSE can be explained to a large extent in terms of socio-economic background factors such as the proportion of unemployment, households with no car, and children not in owner-occupied accommodation (Gibson and Asthana, 1998). Various reports (e.g. NAC, 1997) have demonstrated that for lone parents and families on low income, education has to take second place to the problems generated by poverty, unemployment, alcohol and drug abuse. It is not that these parents are disinterested in their children's education but that they simply have more pressing concerns – and no amount of teacher-bashing is going to put that right. Unfortunately, some Government statements, performance tables and the media may have encouraged the public to believe that schools' examination results are dependent essentially on the efforts of heads and teachers.

The Prime Minister has explicitly acknowledged the link between poverty and failure at school (Blair, 1998), and the Government has begun a programme of redistributive measures to reduce levels of child poverty, such as tax credits to help working poor families, increases in child benefit, the first minimum wage, and grants in pilot areas to encourage teenagers to continue education after the age of 16. The focus is now on prevention as well as relief, with plans to lift 800,000 children out of poverty by the next general election – but that still leaves 3.7 million and Tony Blair says he will need 20 years to abolish child poverty. There's a long way to go.

In December 1997, the Government set up the Social Exclusion Unit to recommend policies that enable the problems of poverty and educational achievement to be tackled together. One example of this strategy is the cross-departmental Sure Start programme to improve support for disadvantaged families and very young children and promote their pre-school development. Pilot Early Excellence Centres are also providing integrated services in education, child care and family support. Another initiative is the New Deal for Communities which, in September 1998, set up 17 'pathfinder' projects and 18 cross-departmental action groups to deal with the problems of run-down estates. In 1999, the Government issued guidance for local authorities on ways of maximising the educational chances of children in their care ('looked after children', as they are called). Education Action Zones also bring together social and educational policies.

In short, this is not an 'either–or' question. Poverty contributes to school failure, and school failure to poverty. Policies to reduce poverty and to raise educational standards therefore need to work hand in hand. The question is not whether to tackle standards through teaching arrangements or anti-poverty strategies, but rather how both such lines of attack can be pursued in the most effective way. But in schools, it is raising standards among the lowest achievers and those from the most deprived families that is likely to contribute most to a reduction in poverty levels, which in turn is likely to raise standards of pupil performance.

For discussion
If some schools in disadvantaged areas can do as well as others in more affluent localities, why can't all?

3. Is New Labour right to believe, as the Conservatives do, that parental choice and competition between schools helps to drive up standards?

As we saw in the previous chapter, standards have risen since 1988, though progress has not been the same for all groups of children or in all areas. But the gains do not mean that the Conservative's introduction of market forces into education were the key factor. Scotland, which has no national curriculum or national inspections, has also seen steady annual improvements in examination results; and GCSE results in England were improving before the introduction of market policies such as performance tables and pupil-led funding. Also, qualifications became increasingly important at a time of high unemployment and the decline in manual occupations.

There have been attempts to tease out the part that increased competition between schools has played in raising levels of performance, but the evidence is conflicting. One study of around 300 schools suggests that in the first half of the 1990s standards increased to above the national average in areas with little or no competition but were below the national average where competition was fiercest (Woods *et al.*, 1999). However, another recent study, based on all 2,657 secondary schools in England and using a different and more complex methodology, suggests the opposite: that the improvement in GCSE standards and school attendance between 1993 and 1997 was greatest where competition was most keenly felt – particularly among schools at the bottom of the ladder (Bradley *et al.*, 1999).

There is also much controversy about whether, as a consequence of market policies, secondary schools have become more or less segregated on the basis of social composition. Some analysts, such as Gibson and Asthana (1999), argue that the operation of educational markets has exacerbated differences between schools: that a vicious spiral has been set up whereby, as successful schools attract more and more socially advantaged pupils, poor families are left increasingly to depend on the least successful schools. In contrast are the findings of Gorard and Fitz (1999), based on data in all 23,000 schools in England and Wales over ten years and employing different definitions of key concepts and different methodologies from those adopted by Gibson and Asthana. Their argument is that

> to our great surprise, socio-economic segregation between schools in England and Wales in terms of student intake has been decreasing since 1989. ...Segregation has declined significantly in every region, in both primary and secondary schools, and as assessed by student poverty, first language, ethnicity and statement of special educational need. (p.2)

But the fact that there is all this inconsistency is important, since it could mean a tension between two planks of New Labour's policies. One the one hand, New Labour has decided to continue the Conservative's policies of choice and competition; on the other hand, it has put in place a package of policies to reduce social exclusion and 'overcome the spiral of disadvantage, in which alienation from, or failure within, the education system is passed from one generation to the next' (DfEE, 1997a, p.3). Clearly, success in the second strategy will be undermined by the first strategy if the market policies are, in fact, leading to a more segregated schools system, and the consequences in terms of both strategies working together to raise academic standards and further a more socially cohesive society would be serious. On the other hand, if schools are not becoming increasingly polarised, as some of the evidence suggests, then the social exclusion policies can work happily in hand with parental choice and competition.

For discussion
What opportunities for school choice are there in your area? What effect do these have on raising prospects for children in the locality?

4. Do high standards depend upon a high degree of central planning?

The centralist, interventionist stance of the Government's schools policies seems to assume that this is the only way forward. This was the subject of a debate, sponsored by the *Guardian* in December 1997, between Michael Barber, head of the Standards and Effectiveness Unit, and Robert Skidelsky, chairman of the Social Market Foundation at the London Institute of Education.

Barber clearly believed Government leadership and pressure to be a necessary condition for creating favourable conditions in all schools for raising standards, given the marked variations between the best and the worst schools. Only in this way could we produce teachers with the requisite skills and a culture of high expectations. He acknowledged that the Government relied on partners – not just teachers but parents and the business community – but Government should be the driving force, linking challenging goals and sufficient investment to its strategies. Barber's optimistic views on the literacy strategy are reported at greater length in Chapter 4.

Skidelsky remarked that it was ironic that this country was going all out for central planning just as it was being abandoned elsewhere. He would prefer more competition between schools, not less, with more incentives for parents to desert poorly performing schools in favour of the more successful. A reliance on central planning, he said, was not a characteristic of successful systems, as witnessed by the effectiveness of the independent sector and the decentralised system in Germany. He likened the Government's faith in centralism to a system whereby people were compelled to buy a product from a single firm, a recipe for low standards. Central planning, he argued, leads to rigidity – you can't easily undo something that turns out to be unsuccessful when it has the force of law behind it. Nor does it increase accountability since statistics can always be given the spin that is wanted. Moreover, as things don't go well, the controllers get anxious and the 'ubiquity of cheating' is stepped up.

For discussion
Who's right?

Further reading

Demaine, J. (ed.) (1999) *Education Policy and Contemporary Politics*. London: Macmillan.

Department for Education and Employment (1997) *Excellence in Schools*. London: DfEE.

Green, A., Wolf, A. and Leney, T. (1999) *Convergence and Divergence in European Education and Training Systems*. University of London Institute of Education. (Chapter 2 contrasts reforms to school policy in England with those elsewhere in the European Community.)

Hill, D. (2000) *New Labour, Education and Ideology*. Brighton: Institute for Education Policy Studies.

Robinson, P. (1997) *Literacy, Numeracy and Economic Performance*. London: London School of Economics and Political Science.

References

Audit Commission (1999) *Local Performance Indicators 1997/98: Education Services*. London: Audit Commission.

Blair, T. (1998) 'Forging and inclusive society', *TES*, 11 September, 21.

Blair, T. (1999) Beveridge Lecture, Toynbee Hall, London.

Blunkett, D. (1999) CBI President's Reception Address, 19 July. DfEE website.

Bradley, S. *et al.* (1999) *School Choice, Competition and the Efficiency of Secondary Schools in England*. Centre for Research in the Economics of Education, Lancaster University.

Creemers, B. (1997) *Effective Schools and Effective Teachers: An International Perspective.* Warwick: University of Warwick.

Demack, S. *et al.* (1999) 'Myths about underachievement: gender, ethics and social class differences in GCSE results 1988–93'. Paper presented at the British Educational Research Association, Belfast, August.

Department for Education (1992) *Choice and Diversity: A New Framework for Schools.* London: DfE.

Department for Education and Employment (1997a) *Excellence in Schools.* London: DfEE.

Department for Education and Employment (1997b) *Excellence for All Children.* London: DfEE.

Department for Education and Employment (1999a) *Excellence in Cities.* London: DfEE.

Department for Education and Employment (1999b) *Learning to Succeed.* London: DfEE.

Gibson, A. and Asthana, S. (1998) 'School performance, school effectiveness and the 1997 White Paper', *Oxford Review of Education*, 24(2), 195–210.

Gibson, A. and Asthana, S. (1999) 'Schools, markets and equity: access to secondary education in England and Wales'. Paper presented to the American Educational Research Association Annual Meeting, Montreal.

Glennerster, H. (1998) 'Does poor training make people poor?', *TES*, 27 February, 21.

Gorard, S. and Fitz, J. (1999) 'The determinants of socio-economic segregation between schools'. Paper presented to the British Educational Research Association Annual Conference, Sussex.

Gregg, P. *et al.* (1999) *Child Development and Family Income.* York: Joseph Rowntree Foundation.

HM Treasury (1999) *Tackling Poverty and Extending Opportunity.* London: HM Treasury.

Hill, D. (1999) 'New Labour and education: new ideology? new politics?'. Paper presented to the British Educational Research Association Annual Conference, Sussex, September.

Ireson, J. *et al.* (1999) 'Ability grouping in English, mathematics and science: effects on pupil attainment', Paper presented to the British Psychological Society Education Section Annual Conference, November.

National Action for Children (1997) *Family Life: The Age of Anxiety.* London: NAC.

Office for Standards in Education (1998) *Setting in Primary Schools.* London: OFSTED

Office for Standards in Education (1999) *Primary Education 1994–98: A Review of Primary Schools in England.* London: OFSTED

Robinson, P. (1997) *Literacy, Numeracy and Economic Performance.* London: London School of Economics and Political Science.

Shropshire, J. and Middleton, S. (1999) *Small Expectations: Learning to be Poor?* York: Joseph Rowntree Foundation.

Sukhandan, L. and Lee, B. (1998) *Streaming, Setting and Grouping by Ability.* Slough: NFER.

Thomson, L. (1996) 'Reading failure and social deprivation', *Educational Psychology in Practice*, 12(3), 166–74.

Woods, P. *et al.* (1999) 'Better education? The impact on school performance of choice and competition between schools'. Paper presented at the American Educational Research Association Annual Meeting, Montreal, April.

Note

1 The 'foundation school' policy has been highly controversial. New Labour insisted from the start that its agenda was one in which 'standards matter more than structures'. In spite of its good intentions here, its policy to bring reluctant opted-out schools back under the LEA umbrella has generated much acrimony at the local level. The scheme was part of a general organisational framework to re-assign all state schools from September 1999 to one of three categories – community, foundation and voluntary (aided or controlled). The first category (about 64% of primary and 69% of secondary schools) consists of former county schools. The second (2% of primary, 17% of secondary) comprises most of the former GM schools, while the latter (34% of primary and 14% of secondary) includes former voluntary (mainly church) schools plus some

former GM schools that wish to emphasise their religious status. Special schools have either community or foundation status. The different categories cater for different arrangements relating to governing bodies, doctrinal instruction, employing staff, owning premises, paying for capital expenditure and admitting pupils. There are also 15 independent City Technology Colleges providing free education.

2 'Setting' involves grouping children by ability across classes for a specific subject, as distinct from 'streaming', which pertains to all subjects. Using evidence from OFSTED inspections, the practice of setting in primary schools was recommended by HM Inspectors for the three core subjects (OFSTED, 1999). However, a recent study of 6,000 pupils at 45 secondary schools that had received good OFSTED inspection reports raises doubts about the wisdom of this advice. Although the research suggested that setting in maths could raise the attainment of more able pupils, the effect was small and at the cost of less able pupils. Overall, children in sets did not do better academically overall, while those in mixed ability groups had higher self-esteem (Ireson *et al.*, 1999). This supports a recent analysis of 20 research studies in the UK and United States that suggested ability-grouping has no significant effect on studentsí performance (Sukhnandan and Lee, 1998).

Part II

LOOKING AT PARTICULARS

Chapter 3

Target Setting, Inspection and Assessment

Derek Shaw

Previous policy

The Conservative Government's interest in the school curriculum was driven by a concern to make schools accountable. Pupil attainment was monitored through national tests, called Standard Assessment Tasks (SATs), at the end of Key Stages 1 to 3. The presumption at that time was that where a school's performance was exposed to public scrutiny, market forces could be relied upon to bring about an improvement; alternatively, the school would simply 'cease to trade' through loss of parental confidence. These arguments have been well rehearsed elsewhere (Bowe *et al.*, 1992). OFSTED (the Office for Standards in Education) was set up to inspect schools on a regular basis; initially this was set at every four years, but was reduced to six for the second cycle, though more frequently for schools with weaknesses.

Towards the end of the administration, proposals were made to extend the scope of Government direction. In 1995 Gillian Shepherd, Secretary of State for Education, launched the 'Improving Schools' programme and commissioned OFSTED to report on how the setting of targets could help schools to raise standards. The preface to the report (DfEE, 1996) indicates that the policy owes much to the National Targets for Education and Training originally promoted by the Confederation of British Industry in 1991 and supported by the then Department for Education (DfE). There is, then, a clear line of development of policy in this area that predates both the present and former governments.

Present policy

Overview

The principles underlying New Labour's policy decisions in this area were presented by the Secretary of State for Education, David Blunkett, in his Foreword to *Excellence in Schools* (DfEE, 1997). In noting that this was the 'first

White Paper of the new Government', he said it was 'about equipping the people of this country for the challenge of the future... [and]... about the Government's core commitment to equality of opportunity and *high standards for all*' (emphasis added). This ambition attracted universal support; the controversy that has ensued is not concerned with the goal but rather with the means by which it is to be realised.

The major development, signalled in Section 3 of *Excellence in Schools*, was to define specific expectations, or targets, which schools (singly and collectively, i.e. as an LEA) would be expected to achieve by levels and subjects. The *targets* would be set by reference to both national and local performance data, so that, in principle at least, schools would be set targets appropriate to their intake characteristics. This approach is called *benchmarking*. What is required, in the Government's view, is the dissemination of reliable performance data, which places *pressure* on low-performing schools to emulate their more successful peers. This is coupled with advice on effective teaching and learning approaches that will *support* schools in their endeavours. The principal players responsible for advising the Secretary of State in this enterprise are *OFSTED*, together with two new bodies, the *Standards and Effectiveness Unit* and the *Standards Task Force*.

Setting school targets

For some time now there has been interest in identifying factors that account for the common observation that some schools are 'better' than others. This has led to the burgeoning international interest in school effectiveness and improvement studies. The research appears to show that 'schools with similar intakes of pupils achieve widely differing results' (DfEE, 1997, 3.5) In turn, a welter of factors have emerged that have been associated with higher performing schools. Among these has been the effect on teaching and learning of the attitudes of the teachers themselves. The Government has this to say:

> One of the most powerful underlying reasons for low performance in our schools has been low expectations which have allowed poor quality teaching to continue unchallenged. Too many teachers, parents and pupils have come to accept a ceiling on achievement which is far below what is possible. (DfEE, 1997, 3.3)

The Government's policy is to demonstrate to teachers in low-performing schools and to the wider public that their pupils can achieve more. Performance tables expose the differences between schools; targets are the mechanism to lift expectations. Accordingly, since September, 1998, each school has been required to have 'challenging targets for improvement' for pupils aged 11 and 16 (DfEE, 1997, 3.12). Advice is supplied through Circular 11/98 (DfEE, 1998a). The responsibility for implementing the process is placed upon governing bodies, who must, annually, set and publish targets for future performance by their pupils. Each year, schools must publish both targets and actual performance for comparison, review targets in light of ongoing experience and determine what adjustments, if any, may be necessary to school planning to achieve their goals.

Initially, mixed levels of confidence were expressed by headteachers and LEAs in achieving the targets set, though David Blunkett and his two junior ministers had said they would resign if the Government's targets for literacy and numeracy were not achieved. A survey conducted for the National Association of Head Teachers (Tymms and Stout, 1999a) showed that only 49 per cent of heads believed they would hit their individual school targets, with small schools facing particular problems. Estimates from councils were little better, with 54 per cent of local authorities expecting to reach their Key Stage 2 targets in maths and 51 per cent in English in 2002. However, the responses suggested that, while LEAs were certain about the value of targets, heads were more circumspect (Tymms and Stout, 1999b). A key issue here was the contradiction between the DfEE's statement in Circular 11/98 that schools must feel ownership of the targets and another statement that schools would be put under pressure to change targets that the LEA or DfEE found unacceptable. Some schools had gone through this process clearly resented what one head called a 'bullying "big brother" approach'. A more fundamental difficulty arose from the fear that targets expressed as percentages of all pupils could encourage schools to concentrate on borderline pupils; percentages also made no sense for very small schools.

Baseline measurement

The Government made baseline assessment a statutory requirement in the Schools Standards and Framework Act, 1998. The initiative was not new and had been previously presented by the former School Curriculum and Assessment Authority (SCAA), since replaced by the Qualifications and Curriculum Authority (QCA). In his foreword to *Baseline Assessment: Draft Proposals* (SCAA, 1996a), Ron Dearing had commented:

> Finding out what children know and are capable of as soon as they enter the reception class is an essential element in being able to give them the education they need to progress quickly in those important early years.

Any initiative of this sort, worthy as it sounds, inevitably raises a large number of questions. *Baseline Assessment* showed an awareness of some of these, and specifically warned against too narrow a view of children's achievements, recommending instead that schools concentrated on all the areas of learning identified in another SCAA document, *Desirable Outcomes for Children's Learning on Entering Compulsory Education* (1996b). The concerns arising have focused on the emergence of an early years curriculum, geared to the National Curriculum, to the detriment of the education of very young children whose breadth of learning experience would be reduced and whose parents might become over-concerned with early achievement. Most seriously of all, there was a fear of the consequences of informing the most vulnerable children that they were failures during their earliest experiences of school.

Despite the criticism levelled at the 'Desirable Outcomes' initiative, evidence from the United States suggested it could be the way forward:

> A new report claims to have isolated effective strategies for raising the performance of students from low-income homes. Raising standards rather than 'dumbing down' the curriculum, increased learning time for basic English and maths, more on-the-job training for teachers and close monitoring of individual's progress are among the keys to success, it is claimed. The report, from the Education Trust, a Washington Foundation, collected data from 366 US elementary schools and secondary schools in 21 states that have succeeded in delivering above-average results in poor rural or inner-city areas. (Cornwell, 1999)

Recently, the Qualifications and Curriculum Authority has published details of a Foundation Stage for children aged three to six (*Early Learning Goals*, 1999), superseding *Desirable Outcomes*. The assumption is that a planned approach that integrates play and learning and combines education and care is in the best interests of all young children. Initial reaction from nursery and playgroup workers has been favourable. The Office for Standards in Education is now assigned to inspecting nurseries and playgroups as well as schools.

OFSTED

An approach that was piloted in the summer term of 1999 is the 'light touch' inspection. This is intended only for those schools (about a quarter) that can demonstrate sustained success through previous inspection reports and test and examination results. Other changes include a reduction in the period of inspection from five to two terms, ostensibly to save schools from unproductive preparation, and a sharper focus on classroom practice and progress made since the previous inspection.

Schools causing concern

In 1997, the Government introduced an 'early warning' system whereby schools that had failed OFSTED inspections, or were in danger of failing, would not be allowed to drift but placed on 'special measures', provided the verdict was agreed by the Chief Inspector. A school so categorised must draw up an action plan to address the key issues identified by the inspectors, though the LEA also has powers to appoint additional governors or even temporarily withdraw budgetary delegation. The LEA also has to provide the DfEE with an assessment of the school's ability to implement its action plan successfully. HMI then monitor the school's performance. After a maximum of two years, findings from a further inspection are used to decide whether the school should be allowed to continue or close. If the school has to close, a Fresh Start school can be opened on the same site. In the spring of 1999, for the first time more schools were being removed from special measures than were found to be failing. OFSTED (1999) has summarised the main features of schools that have been turned around effectively.

Schools causing concern but not failing overall can be categorised as having 'serious weaknesses' (in which case a procedure similar to schools in special measures is followed). Also, LEAs have a responsibility to issue a school in danger of failing with a 'formal warning' and to supply support with the aim of preventing failure.

The Standards Task Force

The remit of the Standards Task Force is outlined in *Excellence in Schools* (DfEE, 1997, 3.38):

- to unite the various educational interests in the new drive to raise standards;
- to be advocates, carrying the Crusade to every part of the education service;
- to advise the Secretary of State on the development and implementation of policies to improve school standards and meet the national targets for literacy and numeracy;
- to keep the Secretary of State abreast of good practice nationally and internationally.

The Introduction of the Task Force was surrounded by a good deal of politicking and it was presented as a minor triumph for the Secretary of State that, under his chairmanship, would be the joint vice-chairs of Chris Woodhead, the Chief Inspector of Schools, and Tim Brighouse, Director of Education in Birmingham. Whereas Woodhead had been identified, at least in the popular perception, with the 'naming and shaming' approach, Brighouse was seen as a champion of supporting schools and teachers and praising success. The Secretary of State, then, could claim that these appointments demonstrated his recognition of the strengths of each position.

Whether the move constituted a genuine attempt to reconcile opposing forces or, more cynically, was an attempt to placate voices in the teaching profession hostile to the Chief Inspector, we may never know. There is little doubt, though, that the uncertainty was always going to provide a hostage to fortune. It was no surprise that, when Brighouse resigned from the post in March 1999, there was immediate speculation as to the significance of his action. Doug McAvoy, general secretary of the National Union of Teachers, said: 'Professor Brighouse gave the Task Force an authority which will be hard to replace. His support for teachers is in stark contrast to that of the Chief Inspector', a view echoed in remarks by David Hart, general secretary of the National Association of Head

Teachers (*Guardian*, 19 March 1999, p.13). Geraldine Hackett in the *TES* observed that 'the most serious fallout is the recognition that there is a divide that cannot be bridged among education professionals. The Brighouse camp believes schools need to be nurtured and that 'naming and shaming' is not helpful (*TES*, 19 March 1999, p.1).

If we now review the remit of the Task Force, it is apparent that, far from 'uniting' interests, the divisions are in danger of being sharpened. Further, advice that the Task Force is expected to offer to the Government runs the risk of being seen as failing to recognise teachers' own concerns.

The Standards and Effectiveness Unit

The Standards and Effectiveness Unit is part of the Department's Schools Directorate and is charged with ensuring that all the partners in the education service contribute fully to the raising of standards. It challenges LEAs and schools about their endeavours in this direction, learns from their experience, questions their assumptions, and informs them about examples of best practice (DfEE, 1997, 3.39). It is staffed by a combination of civil servants and successful practitioners from schools, local authorities and other educational organisations.

Issues for debate

1. Problems with benchmarking

Setting targets that are appropriate for individual schools depends upon (a) the availability of reliable data about school performance, and (b) which 'school characteristics' are used to group schools as 'similar'.

The reliability of the national tests

The Government claims that 'We now have sound, consistent, national measures of pupil achievement for each school at each key stage of the National Curriculum' (DfEE, 1998a, 3.5).

In fact, there are significant difficulties with the reliability of the data on which we base statements about schools, and if this is unacknowledged we will experience difficulties, too, with the quality of the benchmarks. Given the extent to which the Government has supported Chris Woodhead's criticism of schools, one might expect them to listen when he addresses the issue of assessment through the SAT arrangements. In a speech delivered at the London School of Economics in December, 1998, he took a very sceptical view of the tests themselves:

> There are no reliable national curriculum tests. I have not got a lot of faith in them for three reasons. First, I am not sure the tests are the right tests. The concept of levels is a very vague one; we need standardised tests in literacy

and numeracy. Second, the tests have changed quite significantly over recent years so it is impossible to compare like with like. Third, a lot of individual tests are being administered in a creative way by some schools. (Reported in *TES*, 18 December 1998, p.1)

Woodhead is right to comment on the issue of 'levelness'. The levels relate to performance criteria. While this approach is described as criterion-referenced, there is an implicit norm-referencing present. For example, Level 4 was intended to represent the achievements of the average 11-year-old, and other levels were similarly related to age (DES/WO, 1988). Any changes of emphasis within (much less alterations to) the curriculum, lie uncomfortably with the concept of 'levels'. For further illustration there may be a genuine difficulty in equating (say) a Level 5 awarded in Key Stage 2 SATs with a Level 5 awarded at Key Stage 3. The endeavour is to examine a notional equal level of performance in differing contexts. This is central to an understanding of progress.

Comparison over time is always a problem for those monitoring performance. This arises for two reasons. First, the content with which the performance is demonstrated can change. A well-known concern is the way in which vocabulary comes in and out of fashion. Secondly, using the same test, when possible, is likely to result in 'teaching to the test', resulting in distortion of both the results of the test and the teaching to which the test candidates are exposed.

Problems were revealed in an embarrassing form in the summer of 1999 when it became known that the qualifying mark for Level 4 in the KS2 English test had been secretly lowered. David Blunkett was reportedly furious with this action by the Qualifications and Curriculum Authority since it laid it open to charges that the tests were 'fixed'. But the QCA defended its decision as a common procedure in educational testing: 'Because test questions must change every year it is impossible to set tests at exactly the same level, which is why we have to make these kinds of adjustments every year' (*TES*, 4 July 1999, p.6). Seamus Hegarty, the Director of the NFER, which devised the tests and had advised the QCA, said: 'It is preposterous to suggest that there is any kind of fiddle going on. It emerged from our pretesting that the 1999 test was significantly harder than last year's. There is no conspiracy, this was just a straightforward annual technical adjustment' (p.6) – a view later vindicated by an independent enquiry chaired by Jim Rose, Director of Primary Inspection at OFSTED (Rose *et al.*, 1999).

Three weeks after the Chief Inspector's comments, the Chief Executive of the QCA, Dr Nick Tate, wrote to the *TES* with a strong defence of the Authority's practices. He concluded:

Establishing the national tests has been a difficult process and there is always room for improvement. But it is in large measure because of the tests that we know as much as we do about the widely varying performance of schools. The tests have played a major role in raising expectations. A striking feature of the current educational scene, for which schools deserve huge credit, is the new determination to improve on past performance, and to keep on doing so year on year. This shift would have been difficult to achieve without the information the tests provide. (Letter to *TES*, 8 January 1999, p.20)

In the same issue of the *TES* (p.6), Seamus Hegarty also responded:

I emphatically reject Mr Woodhead's critique. He is wrong when he says the tests are unreliable. He is wrong when he implies they are not standardised and he is wrong when he rejects the possibility of making comparisons across years.

For good measure, he added: 'If the chief inspector's strictures were to be applied to his own annual reports, one wonders what weight would be attached to the numerous comparative judgements contained in them.'

In fact, the procedures followed in setting national tests involve a series of rigorous stages, which have recently been set out in detail by Quinlan and Scharaschkin (1999) of the QCA. They point out, however, that a major problem is the many and often contradictory purposes of the national tests – to provide both formative and summative assessment information for individual pupils, to supply the basis for comparisons between schools, and to identify progress in meeting targets. The USA uses different instruments for different purposes, as do many other countries. However, the Rose inquiry did ask for a thorough review of the purposes and procedures of the tests. Such a review is currently being carried out, but in September 1999 the QCA announced improvements to the marking procedures of tests that are based on the revised National Curriculum from 2003.

As regards the actual administration of the tests that Woodhead criticises, teacher representatives, predictably, complained about being insulted. However, without having to assume that pressured teachers might resort to underhand methods to improve their school's profile, there may still be occasions when they stray beyond the recommended administration procedures in supporting children during the test situation. Most teachers are likely to be familiar with the discomfort of replying 'I can't tell you that', to the innocent enquiry of one of their pupils. It runs against the grain of supportive classroom relationships. There is a basic tension between making the testing arrangements objective and maintaining minimal intrusion into classroom practice, especially, perhaps, with the youngest children, not least because they may raise stress levels for individual pupils. As June McKerrow, Director of the Mental Health Foundation, has commented:

Thirty years ago, we would have been appalled at the idea of SATs. Children need time to mess around; they don't need to be over-organised and they certainly don't need to be put through seven hours of testing at 11, especially when they place no value on any social skills.

We have many phone calls from anxious parents about the stress their children are under, but not the slightest nod of recognition from the Department for Education that SATs are a problem. Indeed, there has been talk of introducing them for an even younger age group. (Reported in *TES*, 20 July 1999, pp.2–3)

What is apparent here is that while there is general agreement about matters that may promote difficulty, there is rather less agreement about how successfully these difficulties are being dealt with. Unless they are resolved, the edifice that is being erected will be unsafe, particularly for those schools most likely to suffer adverse judgements. Readers might like to contemplate the following extracts from a letter Professor Colin Richards wrote to the *TES* (23 October 1998, p.19):

> Before another bout of panic sets in following the publication of the 1998 national test results for 11-year-olds consider the following: the results do not enable any judgements to be made about changing overall standards in English or maths since the tests used relate to only part, rather than the whole, of the national curriculum requirements in those subjects.
>
> Second, the extent to which the tests adequately reflect those areas they purport to assess is questionable. Your readers need to be satisfied that all the important aspects of maths or English are adequately represented and tested by the items used. I suspect many will not be satisfied.
>
> Third, there is ample research evidence that any changes in test wording, content or administration between one year and the next render invalid any year-on-year comparisons. The 1997 and 1998 tests in both English and mathematics differ significantly in both wording and content. Thus comparisons are invalid. The Government, DfEE and QCA need to recognise that no year-on-year comparisons are possible, and thus no proof that national targets in English and mathematics have been met (or not met) unless exactly the same tests are administered in exactly the same way to comparable cohorts of children.

Richards went on to say that there was 'a simple and relatively cheap alternative to the folly, anxiety, unreliability and invalidity that characterise the current assessment regime':

> First, to record trends over time and to see how far government targets are being met, exactly the same tests should be administered each year in the same way to a nationally representative sample of 11-year-olds, not by their class teachers, but confidentially by outside testers. Statisticians would determine the size of the sample, but it would probably number in the low thousands rather than the huge cohorts currently and expensively subject to national tests.
>
> Second, to give parents the information many want (as opposed to the 'level-type' information many don't understand), the QCA should commission short, standardised tests related to 'basic' reading, number and, ideally, oracy skills and require schools to administer these and report the results to parents on an annual or less frequent basis.
>
> These two procedures would enable the Government to monitor standards over time and parents to receive information on how their children are performing in those three basic areas. It would also save a huge amount of

money and remove an enormous source of anxiety and pressure from primary teachers.

Criteria for grouping schools

What factors should be taken into account when deciding which schools should be grouped together for benchmarking purposes? To date the tables provided by QCA in documents (known as Pandas, derived from Performance and Assessment) have included very few criteria. All schools are differentiated on the basis of the percentage of pupils on free school meals (FSM) in recognition of the effect of social deprivation on educational achievement. At Key Stages 1 and 2 there is a second criterion concerning the proportion of children for whom English is an additional language (EAL). The result is a set of six tables. The first five are for schools where fewer than 50 per cent of the children have EAL, and the proportions of children on FSM are less than 8 per cent, 9–20 per cent, 21–35 per cent, 36–50 per cent and over 50 per cent. The sixth is for schools where the EAL figure is over 50 per cent. Within these tables school performance is represented by the proportion of children achieving some level (for example Level 2 at KS1) on a number of indicators. By comparing their own performance scores with these figures, schools are able to see whether they are performing below, in line with, or above the national average.

In general terms this approach has credibility, but there is some difficulty over the apparently arbitrary nature in which the cut-off points are chosen. For a 200-pupil primary school, the presence of an additional two children in receipt of FSM could move the school from one category to another, and, in doing so, move the school's reported performance from (say) average to above average. Additionally, since the great majority of schools fall within three of the six tables, the apparent recognition of variation in school circumstances is much less than it might appear.

Another factor is known as 'mobility'. This refers to changes in schools' rolls caused by children whose school careers are fragmented by change. Among such children are the many from refugee families who have arrived in British, and especially London, schools in recent years. The extent of the problem is illustrated by a study of the London Borough of Hackney (Alston, 1999), where one in five of seven-year-olds has not been at the same school for the full KS1 curriculum, one in three of 11-year-olds has not been at their school for the full four years of Key Stage 2, and typically more than a quarter of the GCSE cohort joins their school after the courses have already begun. The study found that 'mobile' children were more disadvantaged than the general school population, and so there is a double-bind situation: the school needs *additional* help to meet exceptional need, but will be judged as *less* successful than other schools, based on its achievements. No account is taken of this in the benchmarking structures. Janet Dobson (1998), who is currently undertaking research in this area, has drawn attention to the absence of official recognition of the problem:

There are no national statistics on the subject, so it tends to be ignored. This is unfortunate for the schools concerned. It is clearly absurd to judge the quality of education in a school on the basis of test or exam results without knowing about its pupils' mobility. An inner-city school with poor achievement in literacy at key stage 2 may be a failing school. It may, equally, be a good school which regularly loses its high-achieving pupils through outward movement to the suburbs, while replacing them with children who have language or learning difficulties. Without the statistics, who knows?

Hackney may well be among the authorities that are most affected, but it is schools in depressed areas that are often nearest to the precipice when judgements are being made.

For discussion
What should be taken into account if we are to make credible like-with-like comparisons of schools? What modifications, if any, should be made to the present system?

2. The value-added debate

There has always been disquiet at the possibly misleading significance of assessment data when presented 'raw'. The Task Group on Assessment and Testing (TGAT) had commented on the matter much earlier:

> The general problem is that a school's 'performance' can only be fairly judged by taking account of many aspects of its work and of many factors outside its control that affect its work. Performance in the national assessment will only be one element in this broad picture. So any report of assessment results should be part of a broader report covering many activities and achievements of the school, including information that the school may or should publish about its curriculum. (DES/WO, 1988, para. 131)

The Task Group discussed whether the results should be adjusted to take account of these factors, but recommended that such a course would be inappropriate. The difficulty was how to recognise the circumstances which affect schools' performance, primarily intake characteristics, while not 'excusing' low levels of achievement.

During the 1990s, a good deal of attention was focused on the possibility of monitoring the performance of a cohort of children as they progressed through the education system. Borrowing from a manufacturing model, the approach has been characterised as measuring the 'value added' by a school. The pattern of the SAT arrangements appears to fit neatly with this process. In principle, it would be simply a matter of noting the SAT scores of a group of children at the beginning and end of a key stage. One problem, however, is that, as explained in the previous section, school populations are not necessarily stable, while small classes and transient populations make the issue tricky for primary schools (not to mention the validity of the tests themselves).

Although schools may want a 'fairer system', this has not been universally seen as 'it'. The Government's attempt to introduce a value-added measure to secondary performance tables in autumn 1998, based on a pilot study (DfEE, 1998b), created an outcry from the heads' unions. Among the objections raised were the problems of compounding maths, English and science tests at Key Stage 3 and the fear that schools which had performed well at that point would be penalised since it would be harder to 'add value' to already good results. The pilot study report identified various technical problems but also such general issues as the need to make the value-added tables understandable to people with no technical background, the number and type of value-added indicators that people would find useful, and the question of mobility discussed above.

Apart from these worries, improvement scores can only be calculated for Key Stages 2, 3 and 4. In a model purporting to examine the accountability of the education service as a whole, the absence of KS1 would be a major shortcoming. As we saw earlier, the move to introduce assessment near the beginning of a child's education was presented as for the benefit of teachers in identifying and meeting children's needs – not for assessing the outcomes of the phase of education, and, hence, teachers' inputs. This latter perspective is of particular interest when the conduct and content of early education has become such a contentious set of matters.

For discussion
By what criteria should school improvement be measured?

3. OFSTED

Because inspectors are in our schools on a daily basis, OFSTED is equipped to inform and advise the Secretary of State about good practice and, hence, the development of the education service. That's the theory. Why, then, is there such suspicion of, and antagonism towards, both OFSTED and the Chief Inspector, Chris Woodhead?

The issue of the conduct of OFSTED, and the way in which its inspections are carried out was the subject of an inquiry carried out by the House of Commons Select Committee on Education, a group made up of backbench MPs drawn from all parts of the House. The Committee's report (House of Commons, 1999) concluded that the Chief Inspector should curb his intemperate approach and rely on evidence, not conjecture. The Labour chairman, Malcolm Wicks, said MPs had been presented with two OFSTEDs: the first was the calm, professional inspection of schools, the other 'about blood and thunder and guts and tears' and 'giants stalking the land and sacking people'. The problem with the second OFSTED was the impact it was having on morale, which could inhibit the drive to raise standards. The MPs suggested that Mr Woodhead should be 'concerned to improve morale and promote confidence in the teaching profession', and that required inspections be 'positive and purposeful'.

Predictably, Mr Woodhead rejected criticism of his personal style and the lack of accountability of the inspection service, arguing it was necessary for the message from inspections to be communicated with absolute clarity – a view that ministers supported. In her evidence to the Committee, Estelle Morris, the standards minister, rejected proposals to change OFSTED's structure, while David Blunkett remained unshaken in his conviction that Mr Woodhead was serving a useful purpose. Ministers also rejected the Select Committee's proposal for a board of commissioners to which the Chief Inspector should be accountable on the grounds that OFSTED's independence was important constitutionally.

Though Mr Woodhead is apparently exonerated in the eyes of the Secretary of State, there remain questions about the conduct of OFSTED inspections and their contribution to the Government's drive to raise standards. Among the severest critics are Carol Fitz-Gibbon and Nicola Stephenson-Forster (1999), who are particularly censorious about classroom observation:

> The aspect of inspection that is most expensive in inspectors' time, the most costly to schools in staff stress, and the least validated, is the practice of having inspectors sit in classrooms using classroom observation methods which have not been demonstrated to meet any level of quality standards and drawing unchallengeable conclusions which have yet to be subjected to proper scrutiny for their reliability, validity or sufficiency for the purpose of publicly rating an entire school. It is this part of inspection which should be immediately suspended pending the application of proper standards. (p.114)

These observations were effectively shared by the Chief Education Officer for Surrey, who told the Select Committee that 15 per cent of inspections in his authority could be inaccurate. Other criticisms relate to the effects on schools. A survey by the NAHT in which heads complained that inspectors' reports were riddled with errors, almost a quarter saying that grades awarded to teachers were for lessons they had not taught, while others said grades given to heads were different from those that teachers had been given in their interviews with inspectors (*TES*, 20 November 1998). Around 40 per cent of heads in the NAHT survey said there was an increase in staff illness in the two to three months after the inspection, and almost three-quarters reported increased disaffection and lack of motivation. A study by Cullingford *et al.* (1998) reported that pupils were much more likely to achieve five or more high-grade GCSEs in years in which their schools were not inspected, suggesting that OFSTED inspections had the effect of *depressing* secondary pupils' GCSE scores. OFSTED refuted the claim, but offered no explanation for the phenomenon that the research team detected.

These allegations call into question the professional competence of OFSTED inspectors. In the following extract, Tim Brighouse, Chief Education Officer for Birmingham, calls upon his own experience when his education service was inspected:

That OFSTED, even at its best, was capable of error and misjudgement has been brought home forcibly during Birmingham's own inspection. Its final draft reports so often bring to mind the characteristics of a poker-playing sixth former writing for a tabloid. 'Poker-playing' because they are unwilling to reveal their hand of evidence even when called; 'sixth former' because they often confuse assertion with argument and opinion with evidence and 'tabloid' because their use of language can sometimes be extravagant and exaggerated. ...OFSTED was bound to have these problems when, before Chris Woodhead was appointed, it recruited thousands of inspectors and trained them in a matter of days rather than using the year-long apprenticeship model tried and tested under HMI.

Inconsistency of judgement and variability of inspection outcomes were thus built in from the beginning. Despite the chief inspector's personal, persistent and heroic attempts to improve the quality of inspection standards by frequent edicts and reviews of the inspection framework, doubts remain. After all, you can only paper over the cracks in a faulty design so many times before its structural weaknesses undermine the confidence of those who depend on it. That has now happened with school inspection. (Brighouse, 1998)

However, an evaluation of OFSTED undertaken by Kogan and Maden (1999) suggests that 'parents and governors do not share, in anything like the same degree, teachers' discontent with OFSTED' (p.27). As the researchers point out 'it is important that reasons for this discrepancy of judgement are considered by schools if they are to secure changes in the [inspection] system' (p.27). There have also been allegations that teachers sometimes attempt to mislead the OFSTED inspection teams. In response to claims that schools have rented IT equipment, hidden disruptive pupils, 'fiddled' class records and even encouraged weak teachers to take a week off for the period of the inspection, David Willetts, then the Conservative education spokesman, proposed that heads be obliged to sign a certificate of authenticity to confirm that the staffing and equipment seen by inspectors were an accurate reflection of the school's resources (*Guardian*, 4 March 1999, p.6).

An alternative form of inspection, mentioned earlier, and intended only for those schools that can demonstrate sustained success, is the 'light touch' approach where there is a much shorter lead time with schools receiving only four weeks notice. The inspection team is much smaller and spends only two days, as opposed to five, in the school, and much less paperwork is required. On the face of it, there should be less stress for teachers – and less expense for the Treasury. Yet those experiencing the pilot study reported mixed reactions:

A. Inevitably, the inspectors could not spend as much time observing in the classroom. ...there was some concern about inspectors not sitting through entire lessons. ...less experienced inspectors could draw the wrong conclusion as a result.

Another key difference was the amount of paperwork inspected. ...This time they [the inspectors] turned down teachers' requests to read departmental development plans. ...the approach in these areas was necessarily a shade more superficial than in a traditional inspection.

On balance, though, [the school] favoured the new regime.

B. The light touch inspection may in some respects be easier for schools. But I think that the full inspection gives us more time to discuss and develop ideas with the inspection team. I would have preferred a full inspection myself. (Quoted by Mansell, 1999)

As a device for keeping in touch, the light touch inspection may have a place. It is difficult to see, though, how it might replace the full inspection. A recent report on a survey among 250 primary and 100 registered inspectors, published early in 1999, could present a way ahead. Both groups agreed that:

- inspection teams should also help and advise schools;
- follow-up visits by the registered inspectors should become established practice;
- the notice period before an inspection should be reduced;
- local authorities should be involved in inspection, as they were seen as an under-used asset;
- inspectors should have experience of teaching the National Curriculum and the phase they are inspecting;
- the inspection process should encourage schools to carry out self evaluations (Ferguson and Earley, 1999)

For discussion
Could or should OFSTED inspections be remodelled?

Further reading

Clarke, S. (1999) *Targeting Assessment in the Primary Classroom: Strategies for Planning, Assessment, Pupil Feedback and Target Setting*. London: Hodder & Stoughton.
Shorrocks, D. (1999) *National Testing: Past, Present and Future*. London: British Psychological Society.

Plus the following listed in the references:

Cullingford, C. (ed.) (1999).
Department for Education and Employment/OFSTED (1996).
Department for Education and Employment (1997): *see* Section 3.
Qualifications and Curriculum Authority (1999).

References

Alston, C. (1999) 'Moving spoils the picture', *TES*, 16 April 1999, 15.
Bowe, R. *et al.* (1992) *Reforming Education and Changing Schools*. London: Routledge.
Brighouse, T. (1998) 'In search of infallibility', *TES*, 27 November 1998, 15.
Cornwell, T. (1999) 'Achieving against the odds', *TES*, 21 May 1999, 2.

Cullingford, C. (ed.) (1999) *An Inspector Calls: OFSTED and Its Effect on School Standards.* London: Kogan Page.

Cullingford, C. *et al.* (1998) 'The effects of OFSTED inspections on school performance'. Huddersfield: Huddersfield University.

Department for Education and Employment/OFSTED (1996) *Setting Targets to Raise Standards: a Survey of Good Practice.* London: DfEE.

Department for Education and Employment (1997) *Excellence in Schools.* London: Stationery Office.

Department for Education and Employment (1998a) *Target-setting in Schools* (Circular 11/98). London: DfEE.

Department for Education and Employment (1998b) *'Value Added' in the 16–19 Performance Tables.* London: DfEE.

Department of Education and Science/Welsh Office (1988) *National Curriculum Task Group on Assessment and Testing: a Report.* London: DES/WO.

Dobson, J. (1998) 'Statistics are vital', *TES*, 2 October 98, 21.

Ferguson, N. and Earley, P. (1999) 'Expect the light-touch inspection to multiply', *TES*, 22 Janary 1999, 32.

Fitz-Gibbon, C. and Stephenson-Forster, N.J. (1999) 'Is OFSTED helpful?', in Cullingford, C. (ed.) (1999) *An Inspector Calls: OFSTED and Its Effect on School Standards.* London: Kogan Page.

House of Commons (1999) *The Work of OFSTED.* Fourth Report of the Select Committee on Education and Employment. London: Stationery Office.

Kogan, M. and Maden, M. (1999) 'An evaluation of evaluators: the OFSTED system of school inspection', in Cullingford, C. (ed.) (1999) *An Inspector Calls: OFSTED and Its Effect on School Standards.* London: Kogan Page.

Mansell, W. (1999) 'Inspectors who wear silk gloves', *TES*, 23 July 1999, 10.

Office for Standards in Education (1999) *Lessons Learned from Special Measures.* London: OFSTED.

Qualifications and Curriculum Authority (1999) *Early Learning Goals.* London: QCA.

Quinlan, M. and Scharaschkin, A. (1999) 'National curriculum testing: problems and practicalities'. Paper presented to the British Educational Research Association Annual Conference, Sussex. (http://www/leeds/ac.uk/educol/adcom/bera99.htm)

Rose, J. *et al.* (1999) 'Weighing the baby: the report of the independent scrutiny panel on the 1999 key stage 2 National Curriculum tests in English and mathematics'. London: Department for Education and Employment.

School Curriculum and Assessment Authority (1996a) *Baseline Assessment: Draft Proposals.* London: SCAA.

School Curriculum and Assessment Authority (1996b) *Nursery Education: Desirable Outcomes for Children's Learning on Entering Compulsory Education.* London: SCAA.

Tymms, P. and Stout, J. (1999a) *Target-setting at Key Stage 2.* Haywards Heath, Sussex: National Association of Head Teachers.

Tymms, P. and Stout, J. (1999b) 'Target-setting', *Education Journal*, September, 28–9.

Chapter 4

Curriculum Initiatives

Jim Docking

Introduction

The national strategies in literacy, numeracy and ICT (information and communication technology) will certainly stand as New Labour's principal responses to the standards debate. As we saw in Chapter 1, the debate is far from straightforward, but in the run-up to the 1997 General Election education underachievement was in the centre of the political arena. Among 16-year-olds leaving school, 12–14 per cent were not reaching Grade G in GCSE English and mathematics, and among 11-year-olds about the same proportion were below Level 3 in these subjects in the National Curriculum tests (see Note 1).

The standards debate was also fuelled by a highly controversial OFSTED report – the findings of which were later challenged by researchers at London University Institute of Education – that reading standards in London boroughs were woefully inadequate and that the solution lay in whole-class teaching and phonics (HMI, 1996). At the same time came evidence from international comparative studies that English pupils in both reading (Brooks *et al.*, 1996) and key areas of mathematics (Keys *et al.*, 1996) were achieving significantly lower standards than pupils in many other countries. All this prompted the Conservative Government and Labour opposition to believe that primary school teaching methods, which they presented as the reason for our standards not being higher, needed to undergo a sea change if the problem was to be addressed effectively.

Alongside concerns about standards in the three Rs was a growing awareness that the rapid growth in information and communication technology was having significant implications for teaching and learning. Employers were now requiring school-leavers to possess skills in ICT as well as in English and mathematics, and familiarity with word-processing, databases and the Internet were becoming essential tools in a world gripped by the ubiquitous computer. Yet if schools were to take this matter seriously, they would need special funding to purchase the necessary but expensive hardware and software. Not only that: a largely computer-illiterate teaching force would need to be offered suitable training opportunities.

Previous policy

During the four months before the end of its administration, the Conservative Government initiated pilot projects in literacy and numeracy. The National Literacy Project in 250 schools and 18 local authorities aimed to improve both the quality of literacy teaching in the classroom and the management of literacy at whole-school level. Detailed termly schemes of work were provided in phonics, spelling, vocabulary, grammar, punctuation, comprehension and composition. A parallel project in numeracy, which also eventually involved about 250 schools in 18 authorities, pleased the traditionalists in giving prime importance to whole-class mental arithmetic and the mastering of number bonds and multiplication tables before the introduction of written calculations. But it also emphasised the importance of high-quality teacher–pupil interaction, with all children in the class encouraged to participate in oral work.

Present policy

The National Literacy Strategy

In May 1996, while in opposition, the Labour Party had set up a Literacy Task Force, chaired by Professor Michael Barber, to recommend ways of raising standards of literacy in English primary schools over a 5–10 year period. Three months before the General Election of May 1997, the Task Force published a report urging the adoption of measures that had helped to raise standards in New Zealand and parts of Australia and the United States (Literacy Task Force, 1997). Using data from the 1995 national tests, the report noted that even among the most disadvantaged schools, with more than 40 per cent of children eligible for free meals, the percentage of children achieving the national standard by the end of primary school ranged from zero to 70 per cent. The Task Force proposed that the establishment of a national literacy strategy could reduce such disparity and enable four-fifths of all 11-year-olds to reach the national standard in English by 2000.

The statistical assumptions underlying the task force's proposals were immediately attacked by two leading educational statisticians, Harvey Goldstein at the London Institute and Carol Fitz-Gibbon at Durham University. They condemned the attempt to reduce complex educational data to brief descriptions that compared 'similar schools', arguing that you could only compare similar pupils, and that to do otherwise would be unfair to teachers and misleading to the public (*TES*, 20 February 1997). None the less, just two weeks after winning the General Election, the Labour Government set national targets for all 11-year-olds. Its literacy target was that, by 2002, 80 per cent would be reaching Level 4 in the National Curriculum tests, and 95 per cent by 2007. This compared with just 58 per cent of that age group that had reached the expected standard in 1996, and assumed a rate of progress of about 5 per cent a year for five years.

Given that Level 4 had been determined as the *average* that could be realistically achieved by this age group, the targets were certainly ambitious (Dombey, 1998). In October, indicative targets for each local authority were handed out in sealed envelopes during a National Literacy Strategy conference in London. Ranging from 70 to 90 per cent according to how well the 11-year-olds in the authority were currently performing, the targets were quite challenging considering that in some inner-London boroughs fewer than 40 per cent were reaching the required standard. Subsequently, every primary school was expected to work to its own targets, after negotiation with (and sometimes pressure from) the LEA.

The declared purpose of the National Literacy Strategy, implemented from September 1998, was to improve the life chances of youngsters by ensuring that primary teachers taught reading 'in line with proven best practice' (DfEE, 1997a, p.19). Based on the recommendations of the Task Force, but using materials derived from the Conservative's pilot projects, it has never been legally compulsory. The presumption, however, has always been that each primary school would follow the framework unless it was able to demonstrate that its own approach was as effective as the national model. Its chief feature, the Literacy Hour, marked a watershed in relations between government and schools, for now there was to be detailed central control over teaching methods, with time set for different activities. This was justified on the grounds that the guidance given to schools would end the uncertainty experienced by teachers as fashions changed in the teaching of reading: those teachers who needed it would now have a blueprint for improving their practice, while effective teachers would still be able to employ methods they had found to work well.

The Literacy Hour (DfEE, 1998a) is divided into four components: the whole class sharing a text together (15 minutes); whole-class work on phonics, spelling and vocabulary, plus grammar and punctuation for 7- to 11-year-olds (15 minutes); group and independent work (20 minutes); whole class review on what has been achieved (10 minutes). The training materials, circulated to all primary schools, give exhaustive treatment at 'word level' (spelling, vocabulary, handwriting and phonics), 'sentence level' (grammar, punctuation, style) and 'text level' (comprehension and composition of various types of writing). Ongoing assessment of pupils' progress and parents sharing reading with their children for 20 minutes a day are strongly recommended.

Every primary school was required to appoint a literacy co-ordinator and also a member of the Governing Body to take special interest in the school's implementation of the strategy. In a cascade arrangement to ensure everyone was properly prepared, national advisers trained more than 200 local consultants, who in turn gave training to the headteacher, literacy co-ordinator and literacy governor in each primary school in their area. Local authorities were expected to provide support for schools that needed it, intervening as necessary. To fund the literacy strategy, the Government committed £60 million for each of the first three years, and in 1998–99 also allocated grants amounting to £3,000 per school for new books. Additionally, £20 million from the Standards Fund was used to invest in additional classroom assistants to support pupils who would be taking their Key Stage 2 tests in 2002, the target year.

To build on the work in primary schools, there have also been drives to raise standards of literacy at secondary and adult levels. In 1998–99, the Government funded pilot schemes in 22 local authorities for developing strategies in the first year of secondary school. Building on this experience, all schools with Key Stage 3 pupils (aged 11–14) were expected from September 1999 to develop a whole-school approach to literacy. To help parents in their own literacy and show them how to help their children, the Government has supported a £1.8 million family literacy project, run by the Basic Skills Agency, in 64 local authorities.

A National Year of Reading was launched as part of the strategy in September 1998 to help raise expectations and change attitudes among parents, employers, libraries and the general community. The campaign was organised by the National Literacy Trust, which was established to enhance reading standards in the UK by working to establish new partnerships between local authorities, further and higher education, the media, business, the arts, and other organisations. With a Government grant and support from many companies such as Marks & Spencer and WH Smith, its message was incorporated into TV soap operas. David Blunkett, the Education and Employment Secretary, chose the set of *EastEnders* to launch the campaign with a storyline featuring 'hard man' Grant Mitchell reading to his baby daughter Courtney. *Brookside*, *Coronation Street, Hollyoaks* and *Grange Hill* also included episodes depicting reading problems, while TV advertisements showed fathers reading to their children. The following February, actors from *Brookside* joined Estelle Morris, the School Standards Minister, to launch over 800 'Brookie Basics' – a network of more than 800 adult literacy clinics.

In April 1998, and again in 1999, booksellers offered a £1 book token to every child aged four to 18 years through vouchers distributed to schools and some national newspapers. In December 1998, business support for the literacy drive was given a further boost when Walkers Crisps and the publishers News International started their Free Books for Schools campaign, allowing each participating school to receive up to 100 books at no charge.

In spite of being described as 'national', the Literacy Strategy has not been given the same thrust in Wales. The Welsh Office's guidelines (1998) are a low-key document and does not impose a single policy for the province. Instead, it welcomes a diversity of approaches (as long as these deliver positive results) and emphasises the importance of classroom teachers' creative and professional skills. There is no prescribed time allocated for the teaching of reading, though the literacy hour has been adopted in some local authorities and schools. However, as in England, there is a clear commitment to reaching the national target, and each LEA in Wales has had to draw up a literacy strategy in consultation with schools.

The National Numeracy Strategy

The national target for numeracy, announced by the Government soon after taking office in May 1997, is that 75 per cent of 11-year-olds should reach Level 4 in the National Curriculum mathematics tests by 2002. This compared with 54 per cent the previous year. (Stephen Byers, then the School Standards Minister, put the significance of the target in context when he told listeners to Radio 5 Live that seven times eight equals 54!) In January 1999, the Government announced targets for individual authorities. These varied from 70 per cent in Nottingham, then the poorest performing authority, to 97 per cent in Richmond upon Thames, the best-performing LEA.

The Government's Numeracy Task Force proceeded to operate in a similar way to its literacy counterpart (though a year behind), searching for best classroom practice both in this country and abroad. Professor David Reynolds, its chairman, was concerned about the performance of English pupils internationally (discussed in Chapter 1) and an admirer of the methods used in Taiwan and Switzerland. He was impressed by projects run in some local authorities, such as the London Borough of Barking and Dagenham, where teachers had set targets and followed detailed instructions for whole-class teaching, arranging children in a horseshoe to facilitate classroom interaction. None the less, at the outset Reynolds made clear that he was not in favour of any single method, a traditional 'back to basics' approach, or a slavish imitation of the strategies used in some other countries: 'We want to base our work on evidence, not on ideology or conjecture. ...We will not fall prey to the assumptions that because a policy appears to work somewhere else it will automatically work in a British context' (Reynolds, 1997).

Building upon the recommendations of the Numeracy Task Force, which in turn owed much to the work of the Conservative's National Numeracy Project, the National Numeracy Strategy (DfEE, 1999a) is thus less prescriptive than its literacy counterpart. For instance, the third recommendation in the Task Force's report (1998) did not impose a single strategy but advised heads and teachers to 'review their current practice and consider to what extent the teaching practices we recommend...suggest a need for change in their school' – though it did add that they should consult both the LEA and the regional director for the strategy. The report was also non-dogmatic about ability setting, warning that pupils in lower sets can become discouraged. It urged schools to provide for children transferring between sets and to use setting less as the range of attainment narrowed (see Note 2 on page 42).

It was also somewhat guarded in its recommendations on the use of calculators, arguing that their use by pupils below Key Stage 2 should be 'limited', employed as 'an effective tool for learning about numbers' but not as 'a prop for simple arithmetic'. But it was more prescriptive in its statements about whole-class teaching, and wanted more time given to oral discussion and mental arithmetic, especially in the early years – though it also stressed that such teaching must engage each child in the classroom interactively, not passively. It also assumed that all children at Key Stages 1 and 2 experience a daily maths lesson of 45 to 60 minutes (depending on age) in which pride of place is given to teacher questioning to encourage classroom interaction, with oral and mental work featuring strongly. It thus marked a shift away from workcards and published schemes, which encouraged children to work individually, towards maximising interaction between the whole class and the teacher. Regular maths homework and guidance for parents to help their children were other important features.

In March 1999, the Prime Minister and Carol Vorderman, the mental arithmetic wizard on the TV *Countdown* programme, launched the countdown to Maths Year 2000 to engage the whole community in the drive to raise standards. Family numeracy projects, aimed at parents and children with low numeracy skills, were set up by the Basic Skills Agency in around 50 local authorities. The Strategy itself got under way in September, supported by a grant of £55 million. Much of this money was used to pay for national training materials and an elaborate training scheme involving 300 numeracy advisers, recruited by local authorities to support schools in effective classroom practice, supplemented by skilled local teachers (known as 'leading mathematics advisers') to give demonstration lessons. About 15 per cent of schools, identified by their LEA, also benefited from intensive support, and extra money has been allocated to recruit more classroom assistants.

Information and communication technology (ICT)

According to the Chief Inspector for Schools, ICT has been the most poorly taught subject, and much of the investment in equipment is wasted because teachers lack confidence and have not been given the training to use it effectively (OFSTED, 1999a). Yet from the start the Government announced its determination to create a society where, within ten years, ICT had 'permeated every aspect of education', realising its potential to help children to learn languages, enabling able pupils to 'sit in' on university lectures, giving one-to-one assistance for pupils struggling with literacy, and providing opportunities for teachers to share best practice (DfEE, 1997a). In July 1997, Baroness Blackstone, an Education minister, announced to the Commonwealth Education Ministers' Conference in Botswana that the Government was regarding the development of children's skills in ICT as the fourth 'R' – 'as important as literacy and numeracy'.

A key initiative in furthering the ICT culture is the National Grid for Learning (NGfL), launched by the Prime Minister in November 1998 together with a 'challenge' paper that sets out how learners, business and the education services can contribute to the development of the Grid (DfEE, 1998e). Essentially, NGfL is a forum that links schools, colleges, universities, libraries, adult education institutions, nurseries and galleries to each other and to the Internet to create a 'connected society' (DfEE, 1997b), while a Virtual Teacher Centre offers resources for professional development and the classroom. The Government has committed over £1 billion for the development of ICT in education and learning by 2002. This includes funding to link all 32,000 schools in Britain to the Grid, for schools to buy hardware and software, to train teachers in IT skills and to enable them to acquire laptops with on-line connections, and to develop a network of 800 computer centres in libraries, colleges shopping centres, workplaces and other accessible venues.

The Government has also forged a deal with approved suppliers whereby schools, colleges and libraries can purchase new computer equipment at a fraction of the normal price. This may help to lessen the danger of a social 'divide' between schools that can rely on extra resources from parents and those that cannot. The intention is that by 2002 serving teachers should feel confident about ICT and competent to use it within the curriculum, while all school-leavers will have ICT skills. Teacher-training must now include the use of ICT in subject teaching, for which a national curriculum has been provided, and the award of Qualified Teacher Status is now dependent on demonstrated competence in this area.

Study support, extra tuition and homework

In further efforts to raise standards, the Government has developed a national framework for study support – a range of voluntary activities outside normal lessons ranging from breakfast clubs to summer schools. It believes that the success of this initiative lies in its diversity and the fact that pupils choose to participate (DfEE, 1998d). By the beginning of 1999, 4,400 after-school and summer-holiday initiatives had been set up, producing what Brunel University and Kids' Clubs Network (1999) have called a childcare revolution. The intention is that, with the help of funding from the National Lottery and New Opportunities Fund, plus support from LEAs, business and charitable organisations, a least a quarter of primary schools and half of secondary schools will have received assistance for such enterprises by 2002.

Following a recommendation by the Literacy Task Force, the Government set up its first summer schools as part of the National Literacy Strategy in August 1997. The philosophy is that summer schools should make an important contribution in easing transition from primary to secondary school, giving children a boost in ability and confidence and making learning fun and rewarding (DfEE, 1999b). The charity Education Extra (an organisation for promoting after-school activities) organised 50 schools for 1,500 11-year-olds who were falling just short of the national standard (Level 3 rather than Level 4 in English). The summer school programme has since been widened to take in numeracy, (DfEE 1999c) focusing on oral work to improve children's skills in mental arithmetic, while some projects are targeted at pupils from special schools, ethnic minorities or very able children. They often involve games, drama, sport, computers, and the services of guest artists, poets and storytellers, and there are sometimes special activities such as designing a newspaper or web-site and landscape gardening. Some projects give rewards such as outings to theme parks and football strips for those who make the grade.

In another initiative, the Government decided to improve the chances of 11-year-olds performing well in national tests by funding 'booster revision classes' in reading and mathematics for the middle and final years of primary education. The classes are aimed at those who have fallen behind in literacy and writing, and particularly at boys in an attempt to narrow the gender gap. Originally these were to take place only after school or at weekends and the school holidays, but the Government bowed to pressure from schools and the unions by allowing breakfast and lunchtime clubs.

Homework after-school clubs in primary and secondary schools are another feature of study support. The first pilot schemes were launched in September 1997 following evidence that, although 90 per cent of parents believed homework was important, almost half of all pupils in their last year of primary schools were not usually given any (DfEE, 1997a). More such centres have since been set up, offering not only facilities for supervised study, but extra tuition and access to computers. Study support centres have also been sponsored by Premier League and Division One football clubs at weekends and during school holidays. The clubs typically open for six four-hour sessions a week with programmes focusing on literacy and numeracy, sometimes with players involved. The Government sees the football connection as highly motivational and as an opportunity to raise standards in inner-city areas.

A few months before the General Election of 1997, the Conservative Government announced that it had commissioned research on the value of homework. But its thunder was stolen by Tony Blair, who used an interview in the TV *Breakfast with Frost* programme to expound his own belief that schools should be given official guidelines about setting children homework, a promise that he kept once in office. The guidelines (DfEE, 1998b) explain the purposes of homework in terms of 'developing an effective partnership between the school and parents and other carers in pursuing the aims of the school', 'consolidating and reinforcing skills and understanding', 'exploiting resources for learning at home', 'extending school learning', and encouraging older pupils 'to develop the confidence and self-discipline needed to study on their own, and preparing them for the requirements of secondary school'. At secondary level, homework is seen as important in developing the skills of independent learning that are 'vital given the importance for pupils in the future of life long learning and adaptability'.

The guidelines also state recommended amounts of time for homework from the age of 5. In Years 1 and 2, pupils should be given an hour a week, focusing on reading, spelling, other literacy work and number work. In Years 3 and 4, the recommended time is increased by half an hour, with the same focus as for younger children but also 'occasional assignments in other subjects'. In Years 5 and 6, regular daily homework of half an hour is recommended, with more scope for tasks beyond the basics. Once pupils reach secondary school, the daily amount is increased to 45–90 minutes in Years 7 and 8, 1–2 hours in Year 9, and 1½–2½ hours in Years 10 and 11.

The guidelines and an accompanying book (Weston, 1999) maintain that homework is most effective when a range of conditions apply. Teachers should treat homework as seriously as they plan lessons, placing it in the school's overall plan for learning, agreeing among themselves what range of tasks should be encouraged, and drawing up a written policy after consulting parents and pupils. They should also involve parents either in working directly with their children or ensuring that homework is completed, though it also helps if alternative study support centres are provided.

The guidelines are voluntary, perhaps a reflection of the Government's sensitivity to 'big brother' charges from the unions and Opposition spokesmen, but ministers have assumed that schools will come under pressure from parents to adopt them.

Issues for debate

1. Are the national literacy and numeracy strategies likely to raise standards?

In his address to the National Association of Head Teachers in 1999, Tony Blair, the Prime Minister, described the national literacy and numeracy strategies as 'our two most critical education policies of this Parliament'. But are there reasons for supposing that these strategies will in fact raise standards?

Starting with the literacy strategy, there are two distinct, if related, questions:

(a) Is the strategy's objective, in terms of 11-year-olds' performance in the national tests, likely to be achieved?

(b) More fundamentally, is the strategy appropriate in terms of helping children to become more literate? It is one thing for children to be successfully taught to pass tests in a subject, and another to help them understand what the subject is really all about.

On question (a), there is no doubt about the views of David Blunkett, the Education Secretary, Michael Barber, head of the Standards and Effectiveness Unit, and Chris Woodhead, the Chief Inspector of Schools. Blunkett has staked his reputation on the targets for 11-year-olds being achieved and has warned critics not to act as Jonahs by undermining the credibility of the targets, or the confidence of those who can make the strategy work work (DfEE News 256/99). Barber has tried to keep the strategy buoyant through a series of articles in the *Times Educational Supplement*, insisting that teachers and local authorities have 'risen with relish' to the challenge (Barber, 1999). A survey for the National Association of Head Teachers, however, suggested that only around half of local authorities and heads were confident that their schools would meet their English and maths targets by 2002 (*TES*, 4 June 1999).

Woodhead (1998) has defended the strategy with particular fervour. Answering criticisms that the guidelines were unduly prescriptive, he maintained that they were sensible because they saved schools seeking individual solutions to common problems: 'The notion of the autonomous teacher reflecting in splendid isolation on best professional practice is a romantic but highly dangerous myth.' As long as too many children leave schools with reading ages significantly below their chronological age, he said, the national strategy is 'less a Stalinist imposition, more a liferaft'. He also insisted that the official instructions were not dogmatic and inflexible and that teachers must use their professional judgement according to local circumstances: 'The last thing anyone wants is for 440,000 teachers to have to dance to the tune of the same draconian Napoleonic code.'

It is difficult to fault the aim of any programme that sets out to improve basic standards of literacy. In a national poll in 1999, four out of five heads said their teachers were positive about it (DfEE News, 193/99); and, for all its prescriptiveness, the literacy hour has given teachers fresh ideas about the teaching of reading and language. But many have suggested that the national strategy is too authoritarian and mechanistic. Brian Cox (1998), for instance, author of the 1989 Cox Report on the teaching of reading, criticises the strategy for its assumption that there is only one right way to teach children to read. Likewise, Jim Sweetman (1998) dislikes the imperatives of the strategy's objectives, presented, as he puts it, 'in tablets of stone' with an evangelical fervour that 'conspires to include believers and exclude critics'. In a similar vein, Henrietta Dombey (1998) is critical of 'a pedagogy of untried uniformit...[that] denies children's widely varying out-of-school experiences' (p.129). Because children come to school with vastly different experiences of literacy, she says, they may have different needs that a uniform approach cannot cater for.

The top-down flavour of the strategy has also been criticised on the grounds that it does little to address the problems experienced by some parents whose attitudes to schooling are crucial if standards are to be raised. Masud Hoghughi (1999) argues that families in disadvantaged areas who suffer from such factors as poor health, poverty, unemployment and weak links with their community, and whose members are therefore prone to anxiety and depression, are hardly likely to make supporting their child's teacher their number one priority, and the gap between the disadvantaged and other pupils is likely to increase. He calls on the Government to extend the ideas of its parent-orientated and multi-agency Sure Start programme for very young children to older pupils and their families. There have also been complaints that children with special educational needs were initially poorly catered for in the literacy strategy, and that the special guidance later issued (DfEE, 1998d), while helpful, was inconsistent in advice about the wisdom of separate or mixed groupings (Byers, 1999).

Apart from these considerations, question (a) can be answered with reference to changes in the national tests performance figures together with findings from the evaluation studies being completed by Her Majesty's Inspectorate for Schools and the National Foundation for Educational Research. In the first year of the Literacy Strategy, the percentage of 11-year-old boys reaching Level 4 (the 'national standard') in English increased by eight points from 57 per cent in 1998 to 65 per cent in 1999; the percentage of girls rose by three points from 73 per cent to 76 per cent. The results were best for the reading component, where boys were up 14 percentage points, prompting ministers to claim that the Literacy Hour was working and the gender gap was narrowing; but scores in writing had barely changed. However, according to a NAHT survey, the improvements may be at the expense of attention to the non-core subjects (*TES*, 8 October 1999).

As regards HMI evaluations, progress made over 18 months in 55 of the 250 schools involved in the pilot National Literacy Project suggested that the strategy was having a positive impact on schools overall, raising standards significantly above the progress normally expected of pupils (HMI, 1998a; Sainsbury, 1998). Compared with control groups, children in the pilot schools were also more confident about reading, enjoyed it more, and said they now needed less help. However, higher achievers and girls made faster than average progress, and children eligible for free school meals made less progress than others. Bilingual pupils who were fluent in English, but not those still learning the language, outperformed those who spoke English only, while those classified in census returns as Black African, Black Other, Indian and Chinese obtained significantly higher scores than those from other ethnic groups. There were no significant differences between the progress children made in different authorities, but progress was uneven among schools of similar intakes.

An HMI evaluation of the strategy's first year (OFSTED, 1999b) also reached mixed conclusions. The quality of teaching during the Literacy Hour had generally improved, especially in reception classes and Years 5 and 6. On the other hand, although phonics was now being given greater emphasis than earlier in the year, its treatment in Years 3 and 4 was too often unsatisfactory. Also, the teaching of writing needed to be given higher priority, an issue reflected in the Key Stage 2 test results and the specially commissioned tests in Years 3, 4 and 5 of the sample schools.

Question (b) is about the *concept* of literacy and the purposes of literacy teaching. Even if the literacy strategy is effective in helping children to master reading skills, does it, as Dombey (1998) asks, teach them a love of literature and all that literature can do to give their lives enhanced meaning and personal significance? Dombey notes how it is only after a long list of technical skills that the Framework mentions such features as enjoyment, imagination, and critical awareness. There is no sense, she writes, of the part literacy can play in children's emotional development, 'no sense of the lessons learned through the imaginative exploration of painful experiences in the company of gifted authors and artists' (p.130). While acknowledging the significance that the Framework attaches to classroom interaction, she notes that the teacher is not supposed to divert from the lesson's stated objectives, however interesting a child's remark.

None of this denigrates the crucial importance of reading skills, 'but unless children experience the richer meanings that literacy can give them, they are unlikely to become literate in the sense of making their own active use of literacy outside school as well as in' (p. 130). Such doubts are regarded by Michael Barber (1998b) as unfounded: 'The strategy has never been about merely functional literacy. It is about enabling as many children as possible... to have access to the wonders of the written word.'

Turning now to the numeracy strategy, the maths results for 11-year-olds improved from 1998 to 1999, with boys moving up 10 percentage points to 69 per cent, and girls 11 percentage points to the same level. Ministers attributed the change to the Numeracy Strategy which 70 per cent of schools had been using a year ahead of schedule. An evaluation based on visits by inspectors to about a fifth of the schools involved in the pilot National Numeracy Project, showed that pupils in Years 2, 3 and 5 had made significantly better progress than predicted in both mental arithmetic and written work during the first five terms of the project (HMI, 1998b). This was particularly heartening in view of the fact that the project schools had twice the national average of children entitled to free meals, a rough indictor of disadvantage.

Other findings were that the attainment gap between ethnic and gender groups was closed, pupils whose first language was not English started to catch up with other pupils, and pupils with special educational needs made progress that exceeded that made in control groups. On the other hand, the inspectors said that the project had not made any real impact in a 'small but significant minority of schools', where there was 'deep-seated weaknesses in leadership management and the quality of teaching', and LEAs would need to give these schools a much greater degree of support and intervention.

There is also evidence that numeracy projects with families are having some impact, reaching 'hard to reach' parents through community outreach workers, bilingual teachers and health visitors. Children who participated in 14 pilot programmes funded by the Basic Skills Agency in 1997–98 made greater progress than a control group, while the parents became more involved with their children's numeracy work at school and engaged in more number games at home (BSA, 1998).

Early evaluations of summer schools have revealed mixed success. The first summer schools for 11-year-olds in English or maths evidently led to significant improvements in children's attitude to learning but not always in actual attainment (Sainsbury *et al.*, 1998). In both literacy and numeracy, most children gained confidence in their abilities and enjoyment of the subject, reading more frequently and regarding mathematics as more relevant to their daily lives; but although standardised scores in mental arithmetic showed significant improvements, those in reading suggested no significant changes though teachers' assessment of children with special educational needs did demonstrate improvements in reading, writing and speaking and listening.

For discussion
Should the literacy and numeracy strategies be regarded as a saviour or as a strait-jacket undermining teachers' professionalism?

2. Is the Government's faith in the value of homework well founded?

In the summer of 1999, David Blunkett, the Education Secretary, publicly accused researchers at Durham University of suggesting that daily homework for primary school children is bad for you (Blunkett, 1999). What was all the fuss about?

The researchers in question (Farrow *et al.*, 1999) had asked 20,000 11-year-olds in 492 schools across 33 LEAs how often they completed homework in reading, maths and science, and compared what they said with the pupils' scores in the Key Stage 2 national tests. One of their several findings was that, even after controlling for ability and background factors, pupils who reported doing homework at least once a week obtained *lower* test scores than those who said they did it only once a month – though doing a little homework was associated with better scores than doing none at all. The researchers did not conclude that homework was bad for you, as David Blunkett said, but simply pointed out that their findings conflicted with the conventional view that 'more is better' and called for more research on this issue.

In fact, the value of homework for primary school children is far from clear in spite of the Government's insistence that 'there is enormous advantage in children spending regular periods of time...on different learning activities devised by schools as part of a homework programme which supports the work they do in class' (DfEE, 1998b, para. 2). In a review of more than 100 studies, admittedly mainly American, Hallam and Cowan (1998) agree that the value of homework appears strong at secondary level, but say it is less clear for younger age groups. In another recent English study, Margaret Brown found no evidence to suggest that nightly homework will raise standards in mathematics among primary pupils: what mattered was the quality of teaching (*TES*, 25 June 1999).

Michael Barber, Head of the Standards and Effectiveness Unit, however, insists that the official homework guidelines are based on the research evidence reviewed by Penelope Weston (1999), who also undertook a series of case studies and carried out a telephone survey of 141 primary and secondary schools. Weston concluded that homework is a valuable element in school learning in not only offering opportunities for children to practise what they have learnt but in developing their skills of information retrieval and analysis as well as the planning and management of time. However, her work was based on the perspectives of teachers, parents and pupils, not measured achievement. Another source, this time from Barber himself and some colleagues (1997), suggested a link between the amount of homework set in secondary schools and the incidence of 'excellent' ratings from OFSTED inspections. But this was based upon just 14 schools, and it assumed that the 'excellence' ratings were due to the extra homework and that OFSTED ratings can be equated with effectiveness (Goldstein, 1997).

Of course, much must depend on the type and quality of homework set. For instance, Hallam and Cowan, in their study referred to above, concluded that homework that revises previous work or prepares for future work seems to be more beneficial than homework related only to work going on concurrently in the classroom; and they noted that teacher expectations were one of the most decisive factors in motivating pupils to complete homework, which is often set hurriedly at the ends of lessons with too little time for clarification and questions. As we saw earlier, the DfEE guidelines (1998c) contain a checklist of 'good practice' which rightly emphasises that homework needs the same careful planning that good teachers give to lessons.

For discussion
Critically examine the Government's guidelines on homework (DfEE, 1998c).

Further reading

Beard, R. (1998) *National Literacy Strategy: Review of the Research and Other Related Evidence.* London: Department for Education and Employment.
Cowan, R. and Hallam, S. (1999) *Viewpoint: What do we know about homework?* London: University of London Institute of Education.

References

Basic Skills Agency (1998) *Family Numeracy Adds Up.* London: BSA.
Barber, M. (1998a) 'Don't expect to be ignorant and free', *TES,* 4 September, 17.
Barber, M. (1998b) 'Great expectations for literate future', *TES,* 27 November, 17.
Barber, M. (1999) 'Britannia flies the flag for better literacy', *TES,* 5 April, 13.
Barber, M., Myers, K., Denning, T. and Johnson, M. (1997) *School Performance and Extra-Curricular Provision.* London: Department for Education and Employment.
Blunkett, D. (1999) CBI President's Reception Address, 19 July. DfEE Website.
Brooks, G. *et al.* (1996) *Reading Performance at Nine.* Slough: NFER.
Brunel University and Kids' Clubs Network (1999) *The Childcare Revolution: Facts and Figures for 1998.*
Byers, R. (1999) 'The National Literacy Strategy and pupils with special educational needs', *British Journal of Special Education,* 26(1), 8–11.
Cox, B. (ed.) (1998) *Literacy is Not Enough: Essays on the Importance of Reading.* Manchester: Manchester University Press and Book Trust.
Department for Education and Employment (1997a) *Excellence in Schools.* London: DfEE.
Department for Education and Employment (1997b) *Connecting the Learning Society.* London: DfEE.
Department for Education and Employment (1998a) *The National Literacy strategy: Framework for Teaching.* London: DfEE.
Department for Education and Employment (1998b) *The National Literacy strategy: Framework for Teaching: Children with Special Educational Needs.* London: DfEE.
Department for Education and Employment (1998c) *Homework: Guidelines for Primary and Secondary schools.* London: DfEE.

Department for Education and Employment (1998d) *Extending Opportunity: A National Framework for Study Support*. London: DfEE.

Department for Education and Employment (1998e) *Open for Learning, Open for Business*. London: DfEE.

Department for Education and Employment (1999a) *The National Numeracy Strategy: Framework for Teaching Mathematics from Reception to Year 6*. London: DfEE.

Department for Education and Employment (1999b) *National Literacy Strategy: Guidance for Providers of Summer Literacy Schools and Key Stage 3 Intervention Programmes for Literacy in 1999-2000*. London: DfEE.

Department for Education and Employment (1999c) *National Numeracy Strategy: Guidance for Providers of Summer Numeracy Schools 1999*. London: DfEE.

Dombey, H. (1998) 'Changing literacy in the early years of school', in Cox, B. (ed.) *Literacy is Not Enough: Essays on the Importance of Reading*. Manchester: Manchester University Press and Book Trust.

Farrow, S. *et al.* (1999) 'Homework and Attainment in Primary Schools', *British Educational Research Journal*, 25(3), 323–9.

Goldstein, H. (1997) 'School performance and extra-curricular provision' (Review of Barber *et al.*, 1997). Reproduced at http://ioe.ac.uk/hgoldstn/home_rep.html

Hallam, S. and Callam, R. (1998) 'Is homework important for increasing educational attainment?'. London: Institute of Education.

HM Inspectorate for Schools (1996) *The Teaching of Reading in 45 Inner London Primary Schools*. London: OFSTED.

HM Inspectorate for Schools (1998a) *The National Literacy Project: An HMI Evaluation*. London: OFSTED.

HM Inspectorate for Schools (1998b) *The National Numeracy Project: An HMI Evaluation*. London: OFSTED.

Hoghughi, M. (1999) 'Families hold the key', *TES*, 12 February, 15.

Keys, W. *et al.* (1996). *Third International Mathematics and Science Study, First National Report, Part 1: Achievement in Mathematics and Science at Age 13 in England*. Slough: NFER.

Literacy Task Force (1997) *A Reading Revolution: How We Can Teach Every Child to Read Well*. London: The Literacy Task Force.

London Borough of Tower Hamlets (1997) *Getting Results*.

Numeracy Task Force (1998) *The Implementation of the National Numeracy strategy*. London: DfEE Standards and Effectiveness Unit.

Office for Standards in Education (1999a) *The Annual Report of Her Majesty's Chief Inspector of Schools*. London: The Stationery Office.

Office for Standards in Education (1999b) *The National Literacy Strategy: An Evaluation of the First Year*. London: OFSTED.

Reynolds, D. (1997) 'A cool look at the evidence', *TES Extra Mathematics*, II.

Sainsbury, M. (1998) *Evaluation of the National Literacy Project*. Slough: NFER.

Sainsbury, M. *et al.* (1998) *The Evaluation of the 1998 Summer School Programme*. Slough: NFER.

Sweetman, J. (1998). 'Gamble on the future', *TES*, 30 January, 21.

Welsh Office (1998) *Raising Standards of Literacy in Primary Schools: A Framework for Action in Wales*.

Weston, P. (1999) *Homework: Learning from Practice*. London: The Stationery Office.

Woodhead, C. (1998) 'All aboard the literacy liferaft', *TES*, 24 April, 13.

Note

1 GCSE is awarded on a scale from A* down to G. The National Curriculum results of tests for Key Stages 1 to 3 are reported in levels from 1 (the lowest) to 8 (the highest), with Level 4 representing the 'national standard' at 11 years.

Chapter 5

The Revised National Curriculum

Jim Docking

Previous policy

The National Curriculum, which formed the central part of the Education Reform Act of 1988, was a watershed in the development of education in England and Wales. For the first time, a common curricular entitlement and framework was provided for pupils aged 5 to 16 in maintained schools (it is not compulsory for independent schools). The curriculum set out what schools were required to teach in English, mathematics, science, design and technology, information technology, history, geography, music, art, physical education, a modern language in secondary schools and Welsh in Welsh-speaking schools. (Pupils were also to be taught religious education, although not as part of the National Curriculum.) The content of each subject was divided into four 'key stages' to cater for pupils at different ages:

  KS1: 5–7 years (Years 1 and 2)
  KS2: 7–11 years (Years 3 to 6)
  KS3: 11–14 years (Years 7 to 9)
  KS4: 14–16 years (Years 10 and 11).

Schools were provided with detailed programmes of study and attainment targets that defined the expected standards of pupil performance at each key stage and formed the basis for national assessments. Provision was made for some pupils, usually those with special educational needs, to be withdrawn from all or part of the curriculum.

Representing a triumph for those who had campaigned for schools to be more accountable and return to more traditional academic knowledge, the introduction of the National Curriculum was highly controversial. Its critics included some Tory supporters on the right who thought that it was inconsistent with the 'free market' education policies that the Government was also introducing to provide for competition between schools and customer (parental) choice. Others criticised the short period for initial consultation and the way the advice from critics went unheeded, the highly prescriptive grammar school subject-based framework, the excessive bureaucracy and the assessment procedures (Basini, 1996). Many also pointed out that a large number of important topics that did not fit easily into the subject framework had been left out, including personal, social and health education.

In response to this latter criticism, schools were recommended in 1990 to adopt five cross-curricular themes – economic and industrial understanding, health education, education for citizenship, environmental education and careers education. Sex education and careers education were added to the compulsory requirements in 1993 and 1997 respectively. In 1994, OFSTED published a consultation paper on spiritual, moral, social and cultural development. Two years later, the School Curriculum and Assessment Authority (SCAA) set up a National Forum on Values in Education, and 150 people from various walks of life tried to identify a set of core values, which they thought could command general acceptance and form a basis for personal and social education in schools (SCAA, 1996, reproduced in DfEE/QCA, 1999).

The National Curriculum was thus revised on a number of occasions but most of all after a major and painstaking consultation exercise conducted by Sir Ron Dearing in 1994/95. The mandatory elements were slimmed down to make the curriculum more manageable for teachers and the number of attainment targets was reduced. At Key Stage 4, more flexibility was given for options, with compulsory subjects limited to English, mathematics, science, design and technology, a modern foreign language, information technology and physical education. A five-year moratorium on other changes to the National Curriculum was guaranteed until 2000.

Present policy

Emphasising the 3Rs

In spite of the various revisions under the Conservative administration, the National Curriculum retained its original 'broad and balanced' conception in making it compulsory for pupils from 5 to 16 to study a wide range of subjects. Under New Labour, this requirement and the moratorium came under challenge in face of the Government's priority to boost standards in literacy and numeracy. In June 1997, on the same day that the TIMSS results for nine-year-olds showed English pupils to be lagging behind in mathematics internationally (see Chapter 1), Estelle Morris, the Schools Standards Minister, told a primary curriculum conference that the Government would be making interim modifications to the 10-subject National Curriculum at Key Stages 1 and 2. By freeing primary school teachers from the statutory obligation to teach the full programmes of study in all subjects and limiting OFSTED inspections of primary schools to the core elements, more time would be available for the priority literacy and numeracy hours.

Accordingly, in September 1998, primary schools were given greater discretion in what to teach outside the core subjects of maths, English, information technology and science. History, geography, art, music, design and technology and PE remained a compulsory part of the curriculum, but teachers were given greater flexibility in determining their content. The one exception was swimming, which was kept as a statutory requirement in the interests of children's safety in water.

Revising the National Curriculum

The Government's move to focus on the core subjects at primary level was a temporary measure, pending the review of the National Curriculum. When in April 1998 David Blunkett, the Education Secretary, asked the Qualifications and Curriculum Authority (QCA) to conduct this exercise, he laid down four conditions:

1. any changes should be kept to a minimum so that teachers did not have their attention diverted from raising standards;
2. skills in literacy and numeracy must be the prime focus of the review;
3. pupils' entitlement to benefit from a 'broad and balanced curriculum' should be retained while also allowing for greater flexibility and less prescription;
4. the new curriculum should provide for a coherent and manageable framework for education in citizenship and personal, social and health education.

As part of its review, and in response to criticisms that the purposes of the National Curriculum had never been spelt out, the QCA conducted an extensive consultation exercise in an attempt to arrive at a set of aims that would command general acceptance. The consultation included a questionnaire to all maintained schools, seminars with headteachers, business leaders, parents and others, and enquiries about educational aims in other countries.

At the same time, the Government set up a number of advisory bodies to counter the 3Rs thrust:

- *The National Advisory Committee on Creative and Cultural Education.* Chaired by Professor Ken Robinson of Warwick University, and with members including such public names as Sir Simon Rattle and Lenny Henry, the report *All Our Futures* (NACCCE, 1999) called for increased priority to be given to the development of students' creative abilities and for the distinction between 'core' and 'foundation' subjects to be removed. (In January 1999 the Government announced grants of £180 million from the Standards and New Opportunities funds to reverse years of underfunding for art, design and music in education and the decline of after-school music clubs and youth orchestras.)
- *The National Advisory Group on Personal, Social and Health Education,* chaired jointly by Estelle Morris, the School Standards Secretary, and Tessa Jowell, the Minister for Public Health. The Report (DfEE, 1999) (oddly called

Preparing Young People for Adult Life, as if 'young people' did not have any present needs) included recommendations that personal, social and health education (PSHE) should be included in the statement of the aims and purposes of the National Curriculum, that the role of PSHE in each subject should be made explicit, that a Code of Practice for PSHE should be developed, that PSHE should be included in OFSTED inspections and in initial teacher training and courses for serving teachers, and that the Government should work with Health, other departments, and the youth service to develop a partnership strategy and ensure a consistent approach to PSHE in addressing the needs of young people. (The Government also set up an anti-drugs strategy *Tackling Drugs to Build a Better Britain*. This is a cross-departmental venture aimed to reduce young people's use of, and access to, illegal drugs, reducing the levels of repeated drugs offences, and increasing the involvement of drug addicts in treatment programmes that have a positive effect on crime. Starting in 1999, £22.5 million from the Standards Fund was allocated over three years for training and curriculum development to promote drug education in schools and the Youth Service.)

- *The Advisory Group on Education for Citizenship and the Teaching of Democracy in Schools.* David Blunkett asked Professor Bernard Crick, his former tutor, to chair this group. (See 'Issues for debate' below.)

Apart from the views of these official bodies, numerous individuals and organisations offered their opinions about changes that were needed in the school curriculum and the role that the Government should play. The most radical view was taken by James Tooley (1998), who argued that the whole idea of a Government-prescribed curriculum was misconceived on the grounds that central intervention in curriculum planning was beset with two major problems. One was that nowadays the Government could not predict with any accuracy the changing needs of society and therefore the knowledge that children would require in the future. The second was that any curriculum imposed upon schools destroyed teachers' commitment to the curriculum, not least because whatever was prescribed was bound to be controversial. Tooley preferred neither control from the centre nor control by the teaching profession but what he called 'circumscribed professional control'. This would involve a market-led system, whereby professionals in individual schools determined the curriculum along with their partners (such as business, religious and community groups) and parents and students chose the school whose curriculum they liked best.

The majority of critics, however, accepted the imposition of a national curriculum but wanted changes made. At one end of the continuum were those wanting further slimming down to give an unmistakable focus on improving standards in the 3Rs. Thus when Chris Woodhead, the chief inspector of schools, addressed a conference for inspectors and education officers at Keele in July 1998, he said he wanted even greater flexibility in non-core subjects, and spoke against overloading teachers with other initiatives. Contrasting arguments were put forward by Sir William Stubbs, chairman of the QCA, who told the Keele conference that the millennium review must not compromise the principles of inclusion and entitlement enshrined in the National Curriculum – a condition David Blunkett himself had laid down when setting up the review.

Professor Robin Alexander was another critic of the 'focus on basics' view. In his address to a SCAA conference in 1997, Alexander noted how the original National Curriculum was formulated at a time when officialdom rejected the belief that pedagogy in the early years should be founded on knowledge of children's development and learning. While he accepted the new emphasis on the economic and employment functions of education, he also believed that primary education should not be regarded as simply a preparation for secondary school but should address 'the imperatives and needs of early and middle childhood'. The review of the national curriculum, he said, should give proper recognition to such matters as individual development, personal and collective morality, social justice and social cohesion, cultural issues and the needs and obligations of the citizen in a democratic society. He wanted a core that went beyond the 'basics', not a core plus other compulsory subjects as at present. Such a core, he envisaged, would include education in values and 'what is essential both for individual empowerment and social progress'.

There were also major concerns, such as those expressed by the RSA (Bayliss, 1999), that the prescribed content was not adequately meeting the needs of the twenty-first century, where skills such as problem-solving, making judgements and the use of computers and the Internet would become increasingly important, as would the concept of lifelong learning (see 'Issues for debate' below).

Clearly, with such diverse views, some compromise was inevitable. In particular, the QCA had to take account of numerous developments since 1988 that had changed the shape of the National Curriculum and to consider the balance to be sought in preparing pupils for the world of work and advanced technology, on the one hand, and nurturing the development of personal interests, the arts and social values on the other. In April 1999, it presented a consultation draft of a revised National Curriculum to the Secretary of State. Following a summer of further debate, the final version was announced in September and distributed to schools in November in preparation for its introduction in September 2000.

Essentially, the revised National Curriculum (DfEE/QCA, 1999) reflects minimal change while attending up to a point to the views expressed by the advisory bodies and some others:

- For the first time, a rationale for the national and school curriculum is supplied (see 'Issues for debate'), going some way to appease those who wanted a clear statement of aims.
- The importance of business, personal finance, and preparing pupils for their future working lives is given greater emphasis in an attempt to make the curriculum more relevant to the economic needs of the twenty-first century.

Information Technology remains compulsory at all key stages but has been renamed Information and Communication Technology.

- Concessions have been made to the traditionalists through a number of requirements, some of which smack of the Education Secretary's personal hand. These include: reading pre-1914 authors and poets; giving emphasis to key historic periods, individuals and chronology in British history; learning about capital cities, rivers and mountains and how to use maps in geography; and learning about traditional values and the importance of marriage and parenting in personal and social education. Religious Education remains compulsory, though still outside the National Curriculum. However, although PE remains a requirement up to 16, competitive games are no longer required for 15- to 16-year-olds, a disappointment to those who believe that team sports breed a team spirit; the new provisions of choice, however, were designed to increase participation in sport by those older teenagers whose dislike of team games leads to them reject healthy exercise.

- In interests of 'balance', the non-core subjects in primary schools are all restored, but in a slimmer form. However, the Government still expects priority to be given to raising standards in the basics, and the requirements for English and mathematics have been aligned with the national literacy and numeracy frameworks.

- By making the non-core subjects less prescriptive, schools are given more flexibility, while older students are given greater scope to shape the curriculum according to their interests and to engage in work-related learning. But the division between the non-core and core subjects remains, suggesting that there is still no parity of esteem among the arts, science and humanities, as the NACCCE group had hoped for.

- Citizenship is given statutory status in secondary schools from 2002 and is commended to primary schools, while PSHE is given more prominence through a national (though non-statutory) framework.

- A modern language in primary schools remains non-statutory, but guidelines are provided for Key Stage 2.

- Under subject headings there are suggested links with other subjects and with ICT.

Issues for debate

1. Values, aims and purposes

For all its faults, the National Curriculum has had a beneficial impact on children's education in certain respects. For instance, it has given primary school children a broader curriculum (even with the refocusing on literacy and numeracy) and it has encouraged teachers to think more carefully in terms of pupils' progression in their learning. But it has suffered from the lack of an overriding philosophy or vision, being based on the assumption that the best way forward was to impose on schools a specified set of subjects, based on the grammar school tradition. A detailed specification of each subject's content and expected learning outcomes was provided, but the rationale for these selections was never made clear. Instead, the 1988 Education Reform Act had talked vaguely in terms of 'a balanced and broadly based curriculum which... promotes the spiritual, moral, cultural, mental and physical development of pupils...and prepares such pupils for...adult life' (Section 1.2), a statement that was effectively repeated in the 1996 Act (Section 351). Not only did this say it all yet nothing, neither in the Act nor elsewhere was any indication given as to how the individual subject requirements might contribute to these overall aims.

As we saw earlier, the QCA was sensitive to these criticisms and carried out extensive consultations to ascertain a consensus view on what the National Curriculum should be for. The QCA then prepared a statement giving a rationale for the national and school curriculum which has been incorporated in the new documentation.

After defining the school curriculum as 'all learning and other experiences that each school plans for its pupils' and explaining that the National Curriculum is an important element in this respect, the statement outlines a 'broad set of values' to underpin the curriculum. These are: the wellbeing and development of the individual; equality of opportunity for all; a healthy democracy; a productive economy; a sustainable environment. These values are in turn followed by two 'broad aims' for the school curriculum:

Aim 1: The school curriculum should aim to provide opportunities for all pupils to learn and achieve.
This is unpacked in terms of helping pupils to:

- develop an enjoyment of, and commitment to, learning;
- encourage their best possible progress and highest attainment;
- develop their confidence and capacity to learn and work independently and collaboratively;
- equip them with the essential learning skills of literacy, numeracy and IT;
- promote an enquiring mind and capacity to think rationally;
- enable them to think creatively, solve problems and make a difference for the better;
- develop their physical skills and willingness to pursue a healthy lifestyle;
- contribute to their sense of identity through knowledge and understanding of their spiritual, moral, social and cultural heritages;
- encourage them to appreciate human aspirations and achievements.

Aim 2: The school curriculum should aim to promote pupils' spiritual, moral, social and cultural development and prepare all pupils for the opportunities, responsibilities and experiences of life.
The statement explains that the school should:

- develop principles for distinguishing between right and wrong;

- develop pupils' knowledge and appreciation of their own and others' beliefs and cultures and how these influence individuals and societies;
- pass on the enduring values of society;
- develop pupils' integrity and autonomy and enable them to become responsible and caring citizens capable of contributing to a just society;
- develop equal opportunities and enable pupils to challenge discrimination and stereotyping;
- develop pupils' understanding and respect for the environment at personal, local, national and global levels;
- promote pupils' self-esteem and emotional wellbeing;
- equip pupils to make informed judgements and decisions and to understand their responsibilities and rights.

Four 'key functions' of the National Curriculum are then identified:

- *Establishing an entitlement for all pupils*, irrespective of circumstances, 'to develop the skills, knowledge and understanding necessary for their self-fulfilment and development as active and responsible citizens'.
- Establishing standards – explicit expectations of learning and attainment and national performance standards, which can be used to set targets for improvement, measure progress towards targets and compare performance between individuals, groups and schools.
- Promoting continuity and coherence through a national framework, facilitating transition between schools and providing a foundation for lifelong learning.
- Promoting public understanding of the work of schools and a common basis for public discussion of educational issues.

On the face of it, this is a great improvement on the woolly statements in the 1988 and 1996 Acts. But two questions need to be asked. The first is a practical one: do the statements sufficiently inform a school's arrangements for teaching and learning? True, in addition to the general statement, the content of each subject is now preceded by a statement about the subject's 'distinctive contribution' to the curriculum, but this is not the case for each part of subject programmes. Without the presence of a rationale alongside individual elements in the curriculum, teachers may well shelve the statements of overall purpose.

The second point is more fundamental. White (1998b) argues that every citizen should have the right to participate in discussions about school aims because the concept of democracy entails the assumption that all should be able to affect the shape of society in the future. However, he sees a difficulty with the QCA's consensus approach, which, although rooted in democratic principles, is limited to determining facts about what people think. White therefore suggests that educational aims should be determined not by seeking a consensus view but through a consideration of the values implicit in the concept of democracy. The curriculum should thus be values-led rather than subjects-led. There is not space here to do justice to White's discussion; but his conclusion is that, for modern liberal democracy, a number of values are required, notably political equality, the promotion and protection of autonomous well-being, liberty of thought and action, civic concern for other people's welfare, and knowledge. This is not a definitive list, he emphasises, but simply illustrative of an approach that starts from a commitment to democracy and then asks what are the implicit values in such a commitment and what aims of education can be determined from this.

For discussion
Read White (1998b). Do you accept his proposal that the aims of a national curriculum should be based on a consideration of the values implicit in the concept of democracy rather than a consensus view? Would the outcome be very different from the QCA's rationale?

2. Citizenship

As we have seen, the question of 'balance' exercised the minds of the various bodies set up to advise the QCA on the shape of the National Curriculum. Here we deal with one aspect of this issue, citizenship.

Like PSHE, citizenship had been added to the National Curriculum as a cross-curricular theme by the Conservative Government; but, even more than PSHE, it had become swamped by other reforms and ignored by many schools. When the Labour Government assumed power, it made clear its belief that 'a modern democratic society depends on the informed and active involvement of all its citizens' (DfEE, 1997, p.63) and set up an advisory group under Professor Bernard Crick. The Crick Report (QCA, 1998) argued that citizenship would not be taken seriously if it was just peripheral to the central curriculum; instead, it must be regarded as a body of knowledge in its own right and given a specific place from the infant school onwards.

The Advisory Group's ambitious aims (para. 1.5) reflected their criticisms of 'the worrying levels of apathy, ignorance and cynicism about political and public life and also involvement in neighbourhood and community affairs':

> We aim at no less than a change in the political culture of this country both nationally and locally; for people to think of themselves as active citizens, willing, able and equipped to have an influence in public life and with the critical capacities to weigh evidence before speaking and acting; to build on and to extend radically to young people the best in existing traditions of community involvement and public service, and to make them individually confident in finding new forms of involvement and action themselves.

The Group considered that education in citizenship was so important that it should be part of the statutory entitlement for all pupils, occupying about 5 per cent of curriculum time. It did not want, however, to prescribe a content for citizenship education, or to impose a single way of teaching about politics, or to advise it whether it should be taught separately or as part of other subjects. Instead, it proposed that pupils' entitlement to education in citizenship should be in the form of 'learning outcomes' for each key stage – but 'tightly enough defined so that standards and objectivity can be inspected by OFSTED' (QCA, 1998, para. 4.3). These outcomes would be based on three strands of citizenship education:

1. *Social and moral responsibility.* Children learning from the very beginning self-confidence and socially and morally responsible behaviour both in and beyond the classroom, both towards those in authority and towards each other (this is an essential pre-condition for citizenship).
2. *Community involvement.* Learning about and becoming helpfully involved in the life and concerns of their neighbourhood and communities, including learning through community involvement and service to the community.
3. *Political literacy.* Pupils learning about and how to make themselves effective in public life through knowledge, skills and values (QCA, 1998, para. 6.7).

The Group also proposed that students be given guidance on moral values and personal development as well as opportunities to participate in school decision-making and voluntary activities in the community. These arrangements, so it was argued, would give schools flexibility in relation to local circumstances, allow different approaches, and guard against the dangers of ministerial interventions about precise content and overburdening teachers. And in recognition of the pedagogic problems of dealing with controversial issues, a section of the report provided guidance for teachers on this issue.

In welcoming the report, the Education Secretary expressed relief that the thrust of the recommendations were on citizenship in the pupils' community rather than on human rights and international relationships which, if over-emphasised, would amount to 'escapism' (DfEE News, 289/98). He quoted with approval the efforts of schools in getting primary pupils to draw up suggestions for dealing with litter in their local park and debating real issues such as this in the Council chamber. At secondary level, he commended schools where the Schools Council was central to the life of the institution and students devised strategies to combat bullying.

At one level, it is difficult to complain about these proposals, which are a much-needed corrective to the customary emphasis on traditional subjects or the skills and knowledge necessary in the pursuit of economic prosperity. In a critique of the Crick Report, however, John Halliday (1999), while welcoming many of the recommendations, argues that the Advisory Group failed to address three problems. The first two arise from the relationship of citizenship education to the overall framework of the National Curriculum. Many students, he says, will fail to feel engaged in citizenship work if it amounts to 'an enforced supplement to a tightly prescribed curriculum that privileges certain forms of reasoning' (p.45). In his view, it is a more flexibly structured curriculum that gives teachers the space to engage in activities that draw upon students' interests. There is also the practical problem about what part of the curriculum should be dropped in favour of citizenship education. Halliday senses the danger of schools jettisoning 'precisely those activities that actually enable inclusive participation in a liberal democracy through rigorous engagement with public modes of reasoning' in favour of 'lessons in values education...designed to inculcate a shared sense of "social and moral responsibility"' (pp. 44–5).

Thirdly, Halliday criticises the Report's assumptions about the extent to which schools can or should work within a framework of consensual values (which the use of the term 'learning outcomes' reinforces). As he rightly points out, 'People may readily agree on a list of what appear to be obviously good and general values such as tolerance and human dignity until those values contradict their own deeply held personal and particular beliefs about abortion, animal rights and the distribution of material resources for example' (p.46). Drawing on the work of philosophers such as Rawls and Ackerman, he identifies different positions that one might take up to deal with this problem, and concludes that citizenship education should not try to search for a super-set of moral principles that can apply across all cases. This is because:

> there is an essential indeterminacy about moral life which implies neither moral objectivism nor relativism but confidence to make room for the *development* of moral judgement. The idea that institutionally sanctioned statements of general values can guide individual behaviour is dangerously wrong. (p.51, emphasis added)

We need to accept, argues Halliday, 'that practices contain their own set of moral principles' and that people should be encouraged 'to listen to the views of others with whom they disagree, to tolerate those views and sometimes to accept them even though they conflict with self interest'. What this means for schools is then clear: more genuine opportunities to understand and solve differences with others so that people 'come to see their common humanity without recourse to what could be a debilitating attempt to resolve what is common to all of them'. Referring to Lakatos' idea of 'touchstones' – common ground agreed by participating parties by which rival ideas can be evaluated – Halliday suggests that

> a curriculum for citizenship should be concerned to maximise opportunities to find 'touchstones' by inducting students into as many practices as possible so that they come to acquire those many forms of reasoning that enable participation in a democratic form of life. (p.53)

For discussion
Read the Crick Report (QCA, 1998) and sections of the revised National Curriculum on citizenship. What do you see as the strengths and shortcomings of this approach to citizenship education?

3. What should a National Curriculum look like in twenty years' time?

The revised National Curriculum is just that – a revision, not a radical rethink. But is it the kind of curriculum that is appropriate for the twenty-first century?

There are many views about this, but the one reviewed briefly here is that of the Royal Society for the Encouragement of Arts, Manufactures and Commerce. The RSA (the charity's misleading abbreviation) describes itself as 'an instrument of change, working to create a civilised society based on a sustainable economy'. The final report of its project 'Redefining the Curriculum' (Bayliss, 1999), was significantly entitled *Opening Minds* – the minds of politicians and others responsible for ensuring that the National Curriculum serves our long-term needs, and the minds of students growing up in a society of such substantial social and economic change.

The RSA's argument begins with the assertion that we are currently educating people for a world that is disappearing and that a radical reappraisal of the aims and purposes of schooling is essential. The present subject-based curriculum, it says, is outdated and its assumptions need challenging. This is not because subjects as such are irrelevant to people's education, but that their use as a *starting point* for curriculum design is not self-evident or necessarily in the interests of the students themselves: it is more, say the RSA, an instrument for the *producers* rather than the *consumers* of education. Furthermore, the present curriculum singularly fails to engage many young people, who see it as irrelevant to their needs and aspirations. According to a survey of over 10,000 12- to 25-year-olds in 1997, most young people believe that their schooling is failing to prepare them adequately for the future (Bayliss 1999, p.7).

In the view of the RSA, any real transformation of the curriculum must be underpinned by a shared understanding of what students need to learn to manage their lives and their work in a fast-changing world. These changes are not just economic (the impact of new technologies) but also social (the impact of family breakdown, changing attitudes to social relationships, social exclusion). These developments which make the world an increasingly complex place in which to live and work cannot be separated from the growth of the consumer society and knowledge economy and must therefore be addressed through a new vision of what students should learn. Further, such a vision needs to be shared with young people themselves and society in general, not just teachers, governors and parents.

For the RSA, the present domination of traditional subject content is so strong that 'the time for tinkering with the traditional curriculum is over'. What we need instead, it says, is a *competence*-led, rather than an *information*-led curriculum based around a series of competences necessary for learning, citizenship, relating to people, managing situations and managing information. Each of these would be unpacked in terms of more specific competencies with accompanying rationales so that the purpose of each part of the curriculum was made explicit to students as well as teachers and others:

> We want them to understand why every aspect of their education is important and why they are being asked to prepare themselves for adult life in a particular way; that their education is about both essential competences and developing their capacity to enjoy life and to value learning for its own sake. (p.13)

To illustrate, the report explains how a section on 'Competences for Managing Situations' might be presented in curriculum documentation. Under this broad heading, a number of related *individual competences* would be listed, such as 'understanding how to manage risk and uncertainty'. A *rationale* for this would be supplied, beginning 'The handling of risk and uncertainty is a feature, at some time or another, of the life of every individual. Everyone is faced, from a very early age, with issues of personal safety and comfort. Learning to understand the impact of risk and uncertainty on others and on situations is an important element of developing maturity.' Following the rationale, there would be suggested *learning outcomes*, such as the ability to recognise the existence of risk, hazard or un-certainty in different sorts of situations, to understand the difference between these, to make decisions about them including how to negotiate what level of risk is acceptable in different circumstances'. There would then be a set of *contexts* through which management of risk would be learned – the changing world, personal and social safety, safety and health in work, environmental safety, food safety, and financial risk and uncertainty. Each of these contexts would be connected to subjects such as history, English literature and language, geography, science and economics. Thus, subjects would still play a major role, but they would be used as a means to develop particular competences rather than ends in them-selves, while the purpose of *each aspect* of the curriculum would be made explicit.

The RSA sees clear implications in its proposals for teacher–student relations. Information and communication technology would be central in the learning process, making it more possible for learning to take place outside the classroom and lesson times, while the system would encourage students to take more responsibility for their own progress. Also recognised are implications for assessment and qualifications. Although there would be a place for summative assessment to record overall achievement at certain stages, the emphasis should be on formative assessment – recognising students' positive achievements and planning the next steps. Project work, work experience and 'extra-curricular' activities would have an important part to play. The 'bogus objectivity' of checklists would give way to the systematic collection of evidence, so that teacher assessment and observation of behaviours would have a stronger role than at present, and there could be a place for parent and peer assessment too.

Despite the attractions of relevance and coherence in this model, a number of problems would need to be faced. As the RSA acknowledges, because teachers are used to a subject approach, a decade at least would be required to develop and introduce a curriculum based on competences rather than subjects. The strategy therefore demands long-term planning; but this, argues the RSA, should be less of a problem once the vision is understood and shared. However, there are more fundamental issues not adequately brought out in the report. Although 'learning for its own sake' is seen as important, the approach as outlined seems overly instrumental, a feeling reinforced by the subservient way English literature is used in the illustrative examples, which also lack any reference to art and music or an opportunity to engage in discussion about moral values (except in the context of personal and social safety). The illustrative examples also look distinctly secondary-orientated, and more work needs to be done on implications for infants and juniors.

But at least we have here a critique of the inadequacies of the present National Curriculum to meet the economic and social challenges we are facing and a suggestion for an alternative approach that, with all its shortcomings, does endeavour to address the problem of student disengagement and systematically ensures that each element of the curriculum is justified in terms of the overall aims.

For discussion

Read the report *Opening Minds* (Bayliss, 1999). Do you agree with the RSA that a subject-based curriculum is no longer fulfilling students' educational needs and that a competence-based curriculum is the way forward?

Further reading

Reports – *see* Bayliss (1999), DfEE (1999), NACCCE (1998) and QCA (1998) in references below.
Best, R. (ed.) (2000) *Education for Spiritual, Moral, Social and Cultural Development.* London: Cassell.
Marples, R. (ed.) (1999) *The Aims of Education.* London: Routledge.
O'Hear, P. and White, J.W. (1991) *A National Curriculum for All: Laying the Foundations for Success.* London: Institute for Public Policy Research.
White (1998a). See references.

References

Alexander, R. (1997) 'Beyond Basics', *TES2*, 13 June, 11.
Basini, A. (1996) 'The National Curriculum: Foundation Subjects' in Docking, J. (ed.) *National School Policy.* London: David Fulton Publishers.
Bayliss (1999) *Opening Minds: Education for the 21st Century.* London: RSA.
Department for Education and Employment (1997) *Excellence in Schools.* London. DfEE.
Department for Education and Employment (1999) *Preparing Young People for Adult Life: a Report by the National Advisory Group on Personal, Social and Health Education.* London: DfEE.
Department for Education and Employment/Qualifications and Curriculum Authority (1999) *The National Curriculum.* Handbook for Primary Teachers in England and Handbook for Secondary teachers in England. London: DfEE and QCA.
Halliday, J. (1999) 'Political liberalism and citizenship education', *British Journal of Educational Studies,* 47(1), 43–55.
National Advisory Committee on Creative and Cultural Education (1999) *All Our Futures: Creativity, Culture and Education* (the Robinson Report). London: DfEE.
Qualifications and Curriculum Authority (1998) *Education for Citizenship and the Teaching of Democracy in Schools* (the Crick Report). London: QCA.
School Curriculum and Assessment Authority (1996) *Consultation on Values in Education and in the Community.* London: SCAA. Reproduced at www.nc.uk.net/about/values.html.
Tooley, J. (1998) 'Towards a state-free curriculum' in Association of Teachers and Lecturers, *Take, Care Mr Blunkett.* London: ATL.
White, J. (1998a) 'What is a national curriculum for?' in Association of Teachers and Lecturers, *Take, Care Mr Blunkett.* London: ATL.
White, J. (1998b) 'New Aims for a National Curriculum' in Aldrich, R. and White, J., *The National Curriculum Beyond 2000: The QCA and the Aims of Education.* London: Institute of Education.
Woodhead, C. (1998) 'All aboard the literacy liferaft', *TES*, 24 April, 13.

Chapter 6

Early Years Education

Peter Jackson

Previous policy

When Parliament approved the Conservative Government's Nursery Education and Grant-Maintained Schools Bill in 1996, it brought to an end the practice whereby pre-school education, save for provision for children in need, was left to local government discretion. Instead, it offered parents vouchers for exchange at registered institutions that were subject to rigorous inspection over six areas of learning. The policy therefore had much in common with school policy. Parents were, nominally at least, able to exercise choice, funds followed pupils, pupils worked towards set goals, OFSTED published inspection reports, and so on. However, the voucher system lasted for less than a year. At the 1997 General Election, Labour replaced the policy it had derided as ideological, divisive, super-ficial, piecemeal and cheap, and introduced its own reform of early years provision.

Present policy

Local integration

The Early Years Policy is, as its name implies, wider than merely pre-school policy. Labour's central idea was that provision should involve both development and education. It maintained that welfare services for children between the ages of 0 and 5 should, where practicable and desirable, be integrated. Formerly, they operated separately. Special needs units, day nurseries, nursery schools and voluntary/private institutions were largely independent of each other. Fragmented information, poor communication and endemic professional rivalry badly affected provision for needy children, whether at home or in care. In the Labour Government's view, appropriate support for children's development and their families was impossible without movement towards integration of services.

Critical of the Conservative Government's 'high command' management style and hostility to local government, Labour insisted that solutions must start within the community. Initially, it called for separate education and childcare partnerships. The former included teachers, nursery nurses, playgroup leaders, heads of maintained and private pre-schools, parents, religious leaders and representatives of ethnic minorities. The latter ranged from heads of residential special needs homes to social worker teams and individual childminders. Both groups had to identify needs and plan provision. Later, these combined to become Early Years Development and Care Partnerships, or EYDCPs, charged with planning educational development and childcare provision from 0 to 4, according to national guidelines. The plans were submitted to their local authorities for approval and incorporation into their general Education Development Plans for the area (see Chapter 10). Examples of the guidelines were as follows:

AIM: Quality, free places for children aged 4, plus an agreed percentage for 3-year-olds by 2001/2

AIM: Quality affordable childcare for children aged 0–14 in every neighbourhood.

CHECKLIST (selection)

- involvement of parents and other family members
- a framework of qualifications for early years and childcare workers
- diversity of provision across private, public and voluntary sectors
- childcare for children with SEN or disabilities
- equal opportunities for families from different cultural, ethnic and religious backgrounds
- integration of education and childcare
- qualified teachers should be involved in all settings.

New Labour seeks to bring the British concept of pre-school education more into line with the Continental idea of *educare*. Insisting that for young children education and childcare are two sides of the same coin, it intends to bring these traditionally separate services together for the benefit chiefly of children and families in need. At the same time it wants to soften the worst effects of competition between nurseries for places by requiring co-operative plans under the co-ordination of local authorities.

National initiatives

Sure Start and Early Excellence centres

The idea behind the Sure Start and Early Excellence initiatives is to identify, reward and fund innovative co-operative projects involving different groups and professions concerned with the early years. Aimed at areas of social need, *Sure*

Start targets social exclusion – the processes by which children are marginalised. The cross-departmental programmes complement the work of the EYDCPs, Children's Services Plans and Health Improvement Programmes, and link with other Government initiatives such as the National Priorities Guidance for Health and Social Care and the New Deal for Communities. Sure Start programmes respond to particular issues such as debt, illness, crime and neglect to ensure that the following core services are delivered in an integrated and coherent way:

- outreach services and home visiting;
- support for families and parents;
- services to support good quality play, learning and childcare;
- primary and community healthcare;
- special needs support.

The National Childcare Strategy monitors Sure Start, which has a target of 250 local programmes across England by 2002. The Strategy is accountable for the success of the individual programmes and their collective contribution to the support of children with multiple disadvantages. Its remit is extensive; it must:

- show how it tackles social exclusion, short and long term;
- promote early childhood development;
- support families in raising children;
- bring together existing services to good effect;
- analyse its own strengths and weaknesses;
- show how it empowers communities to help themselves;
- demonstrate its cost-effectiveness;
- itemise its long-term benefits.

Early Excellence Centres are embodiments of the integration of *educare* services, combining nursery education, childcare and other services for the under-fives. They involve children, parents, teachers and childcare professionals and have been well-received – so much so that the initial target of 25 by 2002 was met and extended in 1999. Individual centres differ greatly. Rural Cumbria, for example, has nursery schools, a community centre, a network of childminder support and training, and trained field workers for integrating education and childcare. Portsmouth, in contrast, comprises a special needs nursery with multi-agency support for local families, and includes training for parents and providers. Haven Centre extends the range of services at a nursery school that already has a day nursery, portage service and an integrated diagnostic SEN unit. The additions include a baby clinic, family support, parent and toddler group and adult training. Early Excellence Centres are achievements for innovative co-operation. They receive money and status from Government and are expected to stimulate good practice.

Class size

The White Paper *Excellence in Schools* (DfEE, 1997) promised that by 2002 no Key Stage 1 child would be in a class of more than 30. In fact, the current target is Year 2000. According to the Organisation for Economic and Cultural Development (1992–95), the UK's primary pupil–teacher ratio (PTR) is unusually high among developed nations, whereas at secondary level it is particularly low. In its examination of the class size issue and its relation to quality in education, OFSTED (1995) observed that this profile reflected traditional governmental priorities in education spending.

While pointing out that PTRs and class size are not the same, OFSTED drew attention to variations across the UK. A quarter of primary school classes exceeded 30 pupils, but not uniformly so. Inner London, in particular, had lower class sizes. Table 6.1 shows the distribution of class size in primary schools by type of area.

Table 6.1 Distribution of class size in primary schools

Type of area	Number of classes	Median	Lower Quartile	Upper Quartile	25% and under	30% and over
Inner London	1904	27	23	30	38	7
Outer London	4295	28	25	30	27	22
Metropolitan	10464	28	24	31	33	28
Shire non-rural	23078	28	24	31	32	27
Shire rural*	7675	26	21	29	47	18
TOTAL	47829	28	24	30	34	25

Source: OFSTED (1995), p.23

Figures are based on lessons in English, mathematics, science, geography and history, and are normally whole-class lessons. The total includes primary/middle schools but not nursery schools. It also includes schools for which LEA type was not available.
* Rural schools are defined as having only one secondary school within three miles.

Direct causal relationships between pupil–teacher ratios and achievement are difficult to establish, as the correlation between the low achievement of Inner London pupils and their low PTRs indicates. OFSTED (1995) noted that American research – notably the Student Teacher Achievement Ratio (STAR) experiment in Tennessee (Nye *et al.*, 1993) – found that while the reduction of class sizes to about 15 had lasting consequences for young children, especially the ethnic minority and socially disadvantaged, smaller reductions had little effect. OFSTED (1995) consulted its own inspection database with its statistics of actual class size and quality ratings. It concluded that:

- there was no clear link overall between class size and quality of teaching and learning – teaching methods, the use of classroom assistants and classroom organisation had a greater impact;

- however, small classes appeared to benefit children in the early years of primary education, children with special educational needs, lower attainers in secondary schools and pupils learning English as an additional language;
- the cost of reducing class size by one, two or three pupils was so high, and the likelihood of significant improvement in standards so low, that the money was better spent otherwise.

It recommended that, instead, teachers should adopt certain results of teacher effectiveness research, namely:

- planning well, setting and communicating clear objectives;
- taking pupils forward in new knowledge and/or skills and/or understanding;
- setting high expectations;
- holding question/answer sessions with the whole class, usually at the beginning or end of lessons;
- keeping tight reins on the time in lessons;
- providing clear explanation or instruction;
- providing tasks and exercises well matched to pupils' abilities.

The later National Foundation for Educational Research *Every Pupil Counts* (Jamison *et al.*, 1998) found that most Key Stage 1 teachers felt that reducing class size created a better *climate* for both teaching and learning. Teachers, it said, associated smaller classes with self-worth: they felt more in command; their motivation was keener; teaching seemed more fulfilling.

Although classroom climate and well-being are operationally hazy concepts for research, they are meaningful for teachers and parents. Lowering class size may have few direct consequences for increasing diversity or widening school choice (in fact it can restrict choice if popular schools have to turn away applicants once the threshold of 30 is reached because they cannot afford to employ another teacher), but it may help to restore confidence. Although both OFSTED and the NFER were relatively non-committal about the impact on *standards* of lowering class size, there seems good reason for undertaking what reduction is practicable.

Integration of inspection

The Office for Standards in Education has been central to the UK's educational reforms over the last decade. Although teachers dislike it, the inspection teams operate with increasingly impressive impartiality. They not only assess quality of provision but collect valuable registration and inspection data. Its published assessments are helpful to parents, and its data contribute to a rapidly growing and increasingly valuable resource for researchers and policy-makers. In 1999, keeping faith with its commitment to the harmonisation of education and care services, the Government extended OFSTED's remit to inspect the childcare and safety aspects of nurseries, playgroups and even childminders. This puts an end to the system whereby different teams, using different sets of criteria, inspect the same institutions. By moving responsibility for inspection (and thus also the destination of assessments and data) from local to national government, clear benefits for accountability ensue. First, the move clarifies the distinction between inspection and responsibility: the national agency inspects and evaluates while local childcare services take credit or blame accordingly. Secondly, it encourages the development of openness, in which professionals render account to non-professionals.

For too long, Governments pusillanimously allowed professions to police themselves, resulting in a depressing pattern of ineffectual inspection, question-able practice, crises and, occasionally, traumatic public inquiries. As a crucial function of society, child welfare belongs to the mainstream gaze. Although criteria differ between childcare and educational inspections, the *culture* of inspection – in terms of rigour, fairness, respect for evidence and impartiality – should be continuous. Over its short history, OFSTED has begun to develop such a culture, and childcare inspections should benefit.

Diversity of settings

Labour has continued the Conservative strategy of allowing voluntary and private educational settings access to funds while raising the standards they have to meet. The first OFSTED Report (1998a) on nursery inspections is instructive. Drawing on an impressive database (10,000 inspection notebooks, 40 inspection reports, a survey of 21 SEN institutions, 200 Section 10 reports, 17,000 lessons and inspections of 15,000 institutions by March 1998), it compared the achievements of different settings. Table 6.2 gives the results. Note the numbers of institutions inspected in each category.

Table 6.2 OFSTED verdicts on nursery institutions 1997–98

Type of provision	% desirable outcomes	% minor weaknesses	% poor
Playgroups (n = 5140)	49.0	49.3	1.6
Private nursery schools (n = 969)	74.3	25.0	0.6
Independent schools (n = 738)	86.3	13.5	0.1
Local authority day nurseries (n = 306)	67.6	32.0	0.3
Private day nurseries (n = 2109)	66.6	32.6	0.7
Others (n = 720), including M & H below	68.7	30.6	0.5
Montessori (n = 407)	75.4	23.8	0.7
High Scope (n = 171)	71.3	28.0	0.5

Source: OFSTED (1998a)

Analysis of achievement into curriculum areas revealed considerable variation. Although all settings handled personal and social development well, they varied considerably with respect to more academic areas – language and literacy, mathematics and knowledge/understanding of the world. Playgroups, in particular, found all three areas difficult. Overall, knowledge and understanding of the world were managed least well. Table 6.3 gives a statistical breakdown

Table 6.3 Percentage of institutions successfully promoting different areas of learning

Curriculum area	Play-group	Private nursery school	Independent school	Local authority day nursery	Private day nursery	Other
Personal and social development	83.5	87.5	89.7	94.1	86.9	91.3
Language and literacy	54.3	80.8	94.3	65.0	73.9	69.8
Mathematics	59.4	82.6	91.8	66.9	74.7	76.1
Knowledge/Understanding of the world	52.7	68.3	81.0	69.2	64.6	68.0
Physical development	77.0	72.5	80.4	82.3	78.0	80.2
Creative development	72.9	75.3	80.0	82.3	77.0	80.2

Source: OFSTED (1998a)

between the settings.

A second report (OFSTED 1998b) provided encouraging evidence of a marked increase in the quality of provision among those institutions in the first round that had displayed weaknesses needing urgent attention.

The Foundation Curriculum

Labour introduced baseline assessment in September 1998. Reception class teachers assess children by means of schemes approved by the Qualifications and Curriculum Authority, plus nursery records. The idea is laudable – it helps in planning individual work and measuring progress while also contributing to value-added statistics – but it centralises mathematics and language and literacy, a highly sensitive issue for some. This emphasis on mathematics and language in the nursery had received official blessing in the official consultation paper *Desirable Outcomes* on activities and outcomes for four-year-olds. This document, produced by the QCA's predecessor the School Curriculum and Assessment Authority (SCAA, 1995), avoided specifying *how* children should learn, concentrating on *what* they should learn. Even so, it drew a battery of criticism from early childhood educators, many of whom saw it as a national curriculum for the nursery.

To the framers of the curriculum, the SCAA proposals seemed reasonable. Owing to the diversity of provision, they regarded it as unfair and unscientific to prescribe one kind of nursery school methodology. First, the Government did not know what the best method was. Secondly, experiment might contribute an answer. With methods as different from each other as Montessori, Froebel, pre-prep and playgroup, the opportunity for comparison beckoned. Once curricular areas were specified, however, there was a basis for recording achievement and enabling effective inspection. As to the outcomes themselves, they should bear some relationship to the National Curriculum with which these four-year-olds would engage twelve months later.

In 1996, the Early Childhood Education Forum, a consortium of some 40 organisations involved in the care and education of young children, produced its own document on the nursery curriculum, *Quality in Diversity.* Its then chair, Gillian Pugh, declared that the Forum's report was based on five 'foundations' rather than 'outcomes':

- *Being and becoming:* effective learning begins with self-respect, feelings of personal worth and identity; it includes care of self, and the health and safety of the individual.
- *Belonging and connecting:* effective learning involves developing good relationships with other children and with adults, in families, communities and group settings; it involves learning to be a member of a child's own linguistic and cultural community group.
- *Being active and expressive:* effective learning includes contributing to others in various ways, learning when to lead and when to support leaders, learning to be responsible for self and others and to make appropriate choices in a group. Contributing and participating are motivated by a sense of belonging.
- *Thinking, imagining and reflecting:* in order to learn effectively, children build up their own understanding through the active processes of thinking, imagining and reflecting on everything they experience. These processes are crucial to real understanding and to positive attitudes to learning.

She comments:

This approach, which includes clear links into National Curriculum subjects, areas of experience as outlined by Her Majesty's Inspectorate and the High/Scope and Montessori curricula, seems far more appropriate to young children's learning than the proposals published by SCAA which reduce development to a low level and narrow band of outcomes and seriously underestimate young children's power and capacity to think. (Pugh, 1997, p.27)

Between the Forum's 'foundations' and SCAA's *Desirable Outcomes* there was indeed a gulf, one that OFSTED's 1998 report did nothing to bridge. As we have seen, the achievement in 'subject' areas of children in playgroups was significantly worse than that of children in more traditional settings. The Government's resolve that pre-school education should have a curricular foundation was not weakened by this news, as the QCA's *Review of Desirable Outcomes* (1999a) makes clear. There was to be a Foundation Curriculum to take children from the beginning of their third year to the end of their fifth year. This would align the UK with most other countries, where children begin school proper at six. The Foundation Curriculum specifies roughly the same areas as the SCAA document, but shows how the 'early learning goals' interleave with Key Stage 1.

The Government insists that curriculum objectives must underpin early childhood education. Early childhood organisations continue to protest against the academic nature of those objectives and the hidden curriculum of success and failure that, in their view, necessarily accompanies them. Yet in other ways, the

Early Childhood Education Forum's 1996 paper and the QCA's 1999 *Review* are complementary. Both, for example, back the idea of a three-year developmental curriculum, with links into the National Curriculum, and both give scope for children, including the most able, to find their levels of effective learning.

Details of the Foundation Stage, which have since been published in *Early Learning Goals* (QCA, 1999b), embrace:

- aims for the education of children aged three to the end of the reception year;
- a three-year foundation curriculum;
- early learning goals;
- curriculum guidance for schools and settings, including play, special educational needs, English as an additional language and the role of parents as partners.

The QCA guidance states that settings and schools should work closely with parents and carers to:

- foster personal, social and emotional well-being in all children, in particular by supporting their transition to a group/school setting and providing opportunities for each child to become a valued member of that group and community;
- promote positive attitudes to learning in all children, in particular an enthusiasm for knowledge and a confidence in their ability to be successful learners;
- enhance social skills in all children, in particular by providing opportunities that enable them to learn how to co-operate and work harmoniously, alongside and with, each other and to listen to each other;
- promote attention skills and persistence in all children.

Away from the controversial ground of the curriculum, there is considerable input and co-operation between the early childhood world and the Government, albeit by the Equal Opportunities Ministry, rather than the DfEE. To many outside entrenched positions, there seems the basis of a reasonable compromise between a humane and effective attention to *educare* alongside a knowledge-oriented (concepts, facts and skills) currriculum.

Issues for debate

1. Is such radical reform of early years provision necessary?

The Conservatives ran a minimalist pre-school programme. They devised a set of objectives for four-year-olds, gave out vouchers, invited providers to register, and then evaluated their achievement. It seemed altogether a carefully measured commitment. Labour's policy, in contrast, appears ambitiously comprehensive and interventionist. While its *curricular* programme is a reasonably consistent extension of previous practice, the rest differs radically. Rather than weakening local government, it has strengthened it; in place of the Conservative's sharp distinction between education and childcare, it has called for their integration.

Finally, Labour has demanded active and dynamic planning for childcare and education services at ground and local government levels. Is it justified?

Perhaps it is basically a social welfare programme, simply camouflaged as an education reform. If so, does it go far enough in tackling poverty, crime and neglect? On the other hand, if it is really educational reform then it is heavily biased towards the social disadvantaged and their families at the expense of the rest. Either way, there will be a bureaucratic shift in provision from the middle classes to the poor that will divert funds, focus on lower standards and increase controls. At the helm will be the Local Authority. Instead of insisting that local government should withdraw from what it cannot do well, the Government has increased its power and authority.

Nevertheless, the aim could be justified. For too long it has appeared both normal and reasonable to treat all under-fives equally despite the considerable minority of children and families who need extra help. To talk narrowly of 'education' is to miss the point that, for the under-fives, education is a part of human development. As on the Continent, we should think in terms of providing *educare*, because those children who lack proper nurture at home are in no position to thrive in school. Moreover, research claims that targeting early social intervention with appropriate developmental strategies is of net benefit to society in terms of later savings on the costs of welfare and crime.

Traditionally, health, social services and education have been separate functions of state. They have different staff, training, codes of practice, pay, conditions and status – little in common except the children for whom they act. (There are no agreed procedures even for screening out convicted paedophiles.) Children are sent to different and separate professional departments, each of which may compile basic information from scratch. Well-meaning referral is too often a one-way ticket towards ever-diminishing accountability and, where crime is involved, welfare can be overridden completely, as the cases of Mary Bell, Robert Thompson and John Venables vividly demonstrate. Children with single-category needs are rare.

Families still enjoy privileged status. Parliament treats them as basic units of society. Police are reluctant to intervene in 'domestics'; law-courts are even more wary. Power relationships within families are nobody else's business. Yet within them, young children are most at risk. Families change. They split, re-group, split again. New stepbrothers and stepsisters appear and stand in different authority relationships from natural brothers and sisters. What rights do new stepfathers have over acquired children? Rights within families are poorly defined, yet families are the chief shaping structures of young children's lives.

The Conservatives differentiated childcare and education and dealt with the latter as a schooling issue. Labour merged childcare and education and deals with the latter as a developmental issue. This, however, generates problems. Labour's policy for pre-school provision is the result of a collaboration between the Department for Education and Employment and the Equal Opportunities Ministry, and it shows. The day nursery is the dominant form of setting for Equal Opportunities. The problem is that beneath the rhetoric of the day nursery – an informal child-centred institution for socially disadvantaged children – lies the school-based curriculum. The result is that there will be an increasing tension between childcare/ development and education, perhaps even between the two departments of State. The DfEE suspects that informal teaching styles will be increasingly exposed as academically inadequate by OFSTED inspections, save for a few gifted teachers who can handle them well. The Equal Opportunities Ministry will resent the comparison, seeing day nursery work as primarily developmental. It is hard to escape the conclusion that the emphasis on development is misleading. Britain has the least developmental 3–8 schooling in the OECD. That may not necessarily be a bad thing, but it runs counter to the claims of the early years' reform.

For discussion

'Labour's reform of early years provision is the first and necessary stage in the long-term civilisation of Britain. Beside it, the Conservative Government's measure was little more than a glib fix of a problem of supply and demand.' Do you agree?

2. Will early years partnerships work?

Noting that the term 'partnership' presumes what it seeks, there are two issues in this question. The first is mutual understanding. Will these forums generate light instead of heat, co-operation rather than antagonism, empathy rather than indifference? The second is quality outcomes. If understanding is achieved, will that be sufficient to develop good quality educational and childcare structures?

Discourse in which it is normal to ask and answer questions is surprisingly absent among teachers and allied professionals. Multi-professional answerability is found in areas such as family therapy and special needs, but it is rare elsewhere. Partnerships cannot guarantee its development but they can provide opportunity to build up such a culture. If professions that engage with children under five do not meet regularly there is little chance of mutual understanding.

In addressing the question whether the partnerships will develop quality outcomes, it is useful to consider the known weaknesses of such an approach to planning. Recently, Paul Trowler (1999) reviewed ways of formulating policy. Conservative governments utilised, he said, a distinct top-down style, involving concepts such as authority, vision, clarity of objectives, lines of command, process-chasing, maintenance of morale, and so on. Labour strategy, in setting up the partnerships, favoured a bottom-up approach. Although Labour's approach has several strengths – democracy, relevance, self-motivation – it has weaknesses too. Representatives bring particular interests and defend them. Allegiance severely tests objectivity; roles limit the horizons of possibility; vision is confined. Mutual understanding swells in popularity, displacing implementation of policy. Moreover, since respect is vital to the concept of the partnership, there is a tendency to safeguard everyone's interests. For these reasons, there is a propensity to fudge, to discuss rather than decide, to go for compromise. It all bodes ill for quality outcomes.

'Partnerships' can embrace representatives from prep schools, alternative schools, ethnic minority groups, childminders' associations, children's homes, voluntary groups, and so on. Can such heterogeneity be reconciled? What sort of agreements and compromises would count as unworthwhile? If policy-plans demand priorities, values and preferences – and they do – are partnerships the way to do it?

Integration and co-ordination suggest networks and unification. Is greater integration of services simply a good thing? Of course, few favour poor communication, excessive confidentiality, internecine professional rivalry – but how far should integration go? When does integration yield diminishing returns? Expertise implies speciality, and that implies difference. Professions have different aims, skills and standards. Too much integration blurs the purpose of differentiation. And, why integration? What is it for? People who try to integrate scattered forces usually have a purpose, unless bureaucracy is an end in itself. Labour is vague on aims. The only certain outcome of its policy is that LEAs, discontent in the long Tory winter, have seen the glorious sun at last.

For discussion
'Getting professionals from different fields to talk together is not a policy but an excuse for one. Insisting that local authorities be involved simply institutionalises bureaucracy.' Do you agree?

3. Will the pre-school programme raise standards of education?

In the summer of 1999, both the QCA and OFSTED produced documents. Concerning its review of *Desirable Outcomes*, the QCA reported overwhelming support for a properly directed programme of activities. OFSTED, likewise, declared in its *Developments Since 1997–98* that the curricular underpinnings of nursery settings gave shape and structure to nursery education. As if commended by critics rather than Government appointees, the Minister, Margaret Hodge, announced:

> Having clearly defined outcomes and inspections has led to higher standards. The proposals for Early Learning Goals have previously been misunderstood. It is time to move on. OFSTED is absolutely right to point to the role of clear outcomes in ensuring high standards in nursery education, regardless of the provider or setting. (DfEE Press Release, No. 284/99)

Labour retains most of the agencies of its predecessor and behaves similarly. It names and shames teachers, schools and authorities that fail, usually in poor parts of the country. It showers praise, title and prestige on schools that excel. In between, most educators, in whose philosophy neither dunces caps nor gold stars figure, are harangued and exhorted. The curriculum is agreed, standards are set, teaching methods recommended. Teacher training is modifiable at Government whim. The task is straightforward: *improve standards*. Schooling is schooling is schooling. Yet young children's education here is different from that on the Continent. The Government's preferred term 'pre-school' as opposed to 'kindergarten' signals the difference. 'Pre-school' has a 'pre-curriculum' or now, extending into reception, a 'foundation' curriculum. There is school entry-level testing which inevitably concertinas back on to pre-school exit-level achievement.

Criticism of the Government's curriculum planning

On what does Labour's confidence rest? Not the judgement of the cream of developmental professionals – the heads of 16 of the 18 Early Excellence Centres that had been set up by May 1999. They responded negatively:

> Children under six should not be forced into formal learning of literacy and numeracy, but allowed to develop social skills and learn through play. ... The proposals would lower standards, hinder their work, damage children's development and increase the incidence of special educational needs by creating failures at five. (*Guardian*, 6 May 1999, p.7)

Nor does it draw comfort from research. In 1998, Channel 4 screened *The Early Years*. Based on work by Clare and David Mills (1998), the programme compared the UK approach with those of three educationally successful continental countries – Hungary, German Switzerland and Flemish Belgium. The researchers claimed that, after removing marked cultural differences, all three had similar approaches to the same simple aim: to prepare all children for formal school at age six or seven. Kindergarten education was highly structured, teacher-led, in classes of about eighteen. It avoided abstract concepts and encouraged discussion in small classes. All three countries gave attention to the following:

- attention, listening and memory skills;
- appropriate group behaviour;
- conceptual understanding (for mathematics);
- reading and writing skills.

Channel 4's recommendation was that controlled experiments should be established and evaluated so that the UK can proceed empirically rather than on principle. For a Government so committed to what it calls pragmatism it gives, so the company observed, curiously little attention to trial and error.

Counter-argument

It is worth noting three things, however. First, *The Review of the Desirable Outcomes* (QCA, 1999a) was published after the Channel 4 programme, and some of the latter's recommendations about collective discussion and activity methods were incorporated in the QCA document. Some of the criticism therefore misses the mark. Secondly, UK education has no need to be defensive about its best early years education. The finest teachers – formal and informal –

work creatively to help children develop and ensure curricular progress. That certain Continental ethnic regions (German-Swiss, Flemish-Belgian) currently enjoy high levels of performance in international tests of maths and science is of interest and should be kept under review.

Thirdly, the pre-school landscape in this country includes different educational settings and continuous evaluation. Since achievement in traditional categories of learning led Mills and Mills to the Continent for their research, then empirical evidence in traditional categories of learning in the UK should be given its due. Accumulating evidence can test the Government's belief that the informal approach is suitable only for gifted teachers.

So will the pre-school programme raise standards? It will be surprising if it does not. The long Foundation Curriculum offers balance, continuity and progression, allowing differentiation in children's individual programmes. Modifiable in the light of evidence it does, in some respects, represent an advance on National Curriculum thinking. Early Centres of Excellence already contribute to high quality practice among teachers, practitioners and others. The QCA's framework of qualifications for upgrading skills and authority is helpful. Sure Start supports children in need. Lower class sizes are promised. Finally, educational statistics are increasingly reliable. The signs are good.

For discussion
Evaluate *The Review of Desirable Outcomes* (QCA, 1999a) in the light of recent comparative research.

The future

From the child welfare perspective, integration of services – or a degree of de-fragmentation – is welcome, for co-operation and answerability between different professions are important. But if such integration is really for the benefit of childcare services, why should education be the medium of change? It is as if the day nursery were taken as the model of all forms of nursery settings. They seem destined to be bureaucratically united with childcare in the newly authorised local authorities.

From the educational perspective, integration of services must be seen alongside developments of curriculum, assessment and inspection structures. These permit varied settings of private and maintained, mainstream and alternative education; they provide increasingly impressive banks of evidence; they offer a lengthy, spacey new curriculum. Geared towards lower achievers, this curriculum will help to shift a substantial percentage into higher educational achievement.

However, the integration of services between the hitherto separate missions of education and childcare also brings a tension that the use of terms *development* and *partnership* cannot entirely dispel. The pursuit of higher educational standards is influenced by the academic achievements of the most able. Within rhetoric of individual competitiveness, the Government recommends pedagogic procedures and practices that appear to be associated with academic excellence. Such urgings are resented in the childcare tradition, where achievement is counted in terms of personal growth against a background of emotional deprivation. The true reconciliation that the integration of services cries out for will only come from the example of gifted early years professionals who find ways of helping children in need realise both their personal and their intellectual potential.

Further reading

David, T. (1998) *Researching Early Childhood Education: European Perspectives*. London: Paul Chapman.

Fthenakis, W. and Textor, M. (2000) *Approaches to Early Childhood Education*. Munich: University of Munich Press.

Penn, H. (ed.) (1999) *Theory, Policy and Practice in Early Childhood Services*. Milton Keynes: Open University Press.

References

Department for Education and Employment (1997) *Excellence in Schools*. London: DfEE.

Early Childhood Education Forum (1996) *Quality in Diversity: A Framework for Early Learning for Children 0-8*. London: National Children's Bureau.

Jamison, J. *et al.* (1998) *Every Pupil Counts: The Impact of Class Size at KS1*. Slough: NFER.

Mills, C. and Mills, D. (1998) *Dispatches: The Early Years*. London: Channel 4 Television.

Nye, B. *et al.* (1993) 'Class Size Research: From Experiment to Field Study to Policy Application' (STAR study). Paper presented to the American Educational Research Association.

OFSTED (1995) *Class Size and the Quality of Education*. London: OFSTED.

OFSTED (1998a) *The Quality of Education in Institutions inspected under the Nursery Funding Arrangements*. London: Stationery Office.

OFSTED (1998b) *The Quality of Nursery Education*. London: Stationery Office.

OFSTED (1999) *Developments Since 1997–98*. London: Stationery Office.

Organisation for Economic Development (1992–95) *Education at a Glance, Nos 1, 2, 3*. Paris: OECD.

Pugh, G. (1997) 'Early childhood education finds its voice, but is anyone listening?', in C. Cullingford (ed.) *The Politics of Primary Education*. Buckingham: Open University Press.

Qualifications and Curriculum Authority (1999a) *The Review of the Desirable Outcomes for Children's Learning on Entering Compulsory Education*. London: QCA.

Qualifications and Curriculum Authority (1999b) *Early Learning Goals*. London: QCA.

School Curriculum and Assessment Authority (1995) *Preschool Education Consultation: Desirable Outcomes for Children's Learning and Guidance for Providers*. London: SCAA.

Trowler, P. (1999) *Education Policy*. Eastbourne: The Gildredge Press.

Chapter 7

Special Educational Needs and Inclusion

Ron Letch

Introduction

The term 'special educational needs' was brought into general usage by the *Special Educational Needs Report of the Committee of Enquiry into the Education of Children and Young People* (DES, 1978), more commonly known as the Warnock Report, and subsequently the 1981 Education Act. Previously, a range of provision was made for children and young people who presented learning difficulties of one kind or another. Many mainstream schools made provision for 'backward' pupils, often in special classes or 'remedial centres' staffed by 'remedial teachers'. Where learning difficulties were particularly severe or children had physical or sensory disabilities they were placed in special schools. Children presenting severe behavioural problems, often described as maladjusted, were catered for at Child Guidance Clinics or special schools.

The Warnock Report sought to re-conceptualise the problem, and made a series of proposals as to how the needs of children could be better understood and met and how provision could accordingly be improved. The major proposal was to widen the concept of special education, which, the report suggested, was required by 'up to one in five children at some time during their school career' (DES, 1978, para. 3.17). This was generally understood to mean that 20 per cent of children have special educational needs at some time, though in many cases these would only be temporary.

This suggestion gave rise to much debate, but at its best it drew attention to the wide continuum of need from those with profound and multiple disabilities to those whose disabilities are transitory and are met by prompt and effective action. It also moved the debate from a *medical*, or deficit-based, model that often described children as imbeciles, feeble-minded and dull, educationally subnormal (ESN) or uneducable, to a *service* model of making appropriate provision to meet children's needs through focusing on school improvement. The report envisaged that the great majority of children with SEN would have their needs met in mainstream schools, but it also recognised that there would continue to be some children whose education would be provided in separate or, as some would describe them, segregated schools; these were estimated to be about two per cent of the school population.

The Warnock Report thus pointed to a way forward in providing for the needs of this diverse group of pupils with a complex set of needs. Like most innovations in education, however, it pointed to a direction in which to move rather than a series of actions that would resolve all the issues.

Previous policy

The Conservative Government sought to address the main issues of the Warnock Report in the Education Act 1981. The Act formalised the general thrust of the report by replacing 'handicap' with the concept of 'special educational need'. In doing so, it:

- confirmed the concept of a continuum of need;
- introduced a system for identifying children with SEN through individual staged assessment, culminating with a statement of SEN for pupils who needed special resources;
- placed a duty on LEAs to consider integration/inclusive education as a means of meeting a pupil's assessed needs.

A continuum of need

The Act stated that a child had a special educational need if he or she had a learning difficulty that required special educational provision (Section 1.1). A child was said to have a *learning difficulty* if

(a) he has a significantly greater difficulty in learning than the majority of children of his age; or

(b) he has a disability which either prevents or hinders him from making use of educational facilities generally provided in schools within the area of the local authority for children of his age. (Section 1.2)

Special educational provision was defined as:

provision which is additional to, or otherwise different from, the educational provision made generally for children of his age in schools maintained by the local education authority concerned. (Section 1.3)

In this way the Act encompassed all children with special educational needs from the most severely disabled placed in special schools to those receiving their education in mainstream schools alongside other children. The intention was to remove the distinction between the minorities described as 'handicapped' (the 2 per cent) and the 18 per cent mostly in mainstream schools. This marked a shift from a deficiency model of 'handicap' to a model of matching provision to need. However, the Act failed to address the wide discrepancies between provision in LEAs across the country and also the difficulty of linking resources to need.

Identification and staged assessment

The 1981 Act laid down procedures for identifying and assessing children with SEN and stated who should be responsible for these. It also laid down the point at which other professionals could be called in by mainstream schools to assist with planning appropriate learning strategies for children identified, and stressed the needs for early intervention and for parents to be involved and informed of the whole procedure.

The assessment procedure introduced by the Act was planned to progress through five stages. The first three were expected to be handled by staff in mainstream schools and to be appropriate to meet the needs of the majority of children with SEN. The learning needs identified in these stages were also expected to be met in ordinary schools, with appropriate adjustments to teaching and learning strategies plus the provision of additional support if necessary. Where the school was unable to meet the learning needs by making such arrangements, the fourth stage was invoked and a multi-disciplinary assessment made, with the LEA seeking the advice of medical, psychological and social services, as necessary. If it was then felt appropriate to do so, the LEA began the process of issuing a Statement of Special Educational Need, containing:

- an account of the child's special educational needs;
- an outline of the provision necessary to meet these needs;
- the type of school and perhaps the name of the school in which the child's needs will be met;
- an account of the child's non-educational needs (for example medical needs met by the health services);
- any non-educational provision to meet such needs.

However, it should be noted that progressing to Stage 4 does not mean that a statement must or will be merited (Stage 5). Whatever, the LEA's decision, parents have the right to appeal to an independent tribunal under the 1993 Education Act, and the tribunal's decision is binding on both parties.

Integration/inclusive education

The 1981 Act placed a duty on LEAs to secure that a child is educated in an ordinary school, subject to certain conditions:

- that the parents' views have been considered;
- the placement will be compatible with:
  - the child receiving the special educational provision he or she requires;

– the provision of efficient education of the children with whom the child will
be educated; and
– the efficient use of resources.

The implementation of this part of the Act has been hotly debated by a range of
interest groups. At one extreme there are those who feel that *all* children, irrespective of their degree of disability and need, have a right to be educated with their
peers in mainstream schools. Others feel just as strongly that such arrangements can
only disadvantage children's *educational* needs that are best met in specialist,
segregated facilities. This issue will be further explored later in this chapter.

SEN and the National Curriculum

The Education Reform Act 1988 introduced the National Curriculum and its
associated assessment plus measures to encourage competition between schools
– delegated funding, open enrolment and grant-maintained schools. The original
Bill made no reference to SEN, and it was only during the course of
parliamentary debate that a section was added concerning ways in which
schools could modify or 'disapply' the National Curriculum in certain cases. In
any case, it seemed to many that the concept of competition between schools,
plus the expectation that all pupils should follow a national curriculum and be
subjected to the national tests, was in conflict with the principles of the 1981 Act
that encouraged schools to address individual needs in the most effective way.
Some felt it would lead schools to press for Stage 4 assessment with prospects
of a statement of special educational need since this would be a way of gaining
additional funds for the school's budget.

Further developments

The Education (Schools) Act 1992 set up the Office for Standards in Education
whose remit is to improve standards of achievement through regular
independent inspection of schools. Special schools were included, and all
schools in the country have now been inspected at least once since OFSTED
was set up. Inspection reports are public documents and many special schools,
particularly those catering for pupils with emotional and behavioural difficulties,
have been strongly criticised.

In 1992 the Government published a White Paper *Choice and Diversity: A New
Framework for Schools* (DfEE, 1992a) and a consultation paper *Special
Educational Needs: Access to the System* (DfEE, 1992b). The outcome was the
Education Act 1993, which attempted to address some of the problems outlined
earlier in this chapter:

• It extended parental rights by creating independent tribunals to hear appeals.
• It attempted to speed up the statementing process by setting time limits for
each stage.

- It required the Secretary of State to issue a Code of Practice giving practical guidance to LEAs and schools on their responsibilities to children with SEN.

The Code of Practice on the Identification and Assessment of Special Educational Needs, issued the following year (DfE, 1994a), reaffirmed earlier arrangements and attempted to put right some of the problems that had arisen from earlier Acts. Part 1 of the Code sets out fundamental principles that are, in the main, based on the Warnock proposals:

- the concept of a continuum of need;
- maximum access to the National Curriculum for children with SEN;
- most children with SEN to be educated alongside their peers in ordinary schools;
- LEAs to be involved in meeting the needs of pre-school children;
- partnerships between children, their parents, schools, LEAs and other agencies is the key to purposeful assessment and provision.

Part 2 of the Code attempted to clarify the three school-based stages of assessment by providing a great deal more detail. The role and responsibility of the school's Special Educational Needs Coordinator (SENCO) was spelled out in detail, though this subsequently had the unfortunate effect of leading some teachers to assume that the SENCO's role exonerated them from any responsibility for special needs. Others have pointed out that the considerable demands laid upon SENCOs have not been matched by the time resource needed to carry out their duties effectively. The Code also gave school governors the responsibility to 'do their best to secure that the necessary provision is made for any pupil who has special educational needs' (para. 2.6). Greater clarity was offered on arriving at a decision to award or not to award a statement of need, and guidance was provided on the annual review of a statement. Significantly, statutory time limits for statementing were set out, but many LEAs found meeting these deadlines difficult and have been pressed hard to improve the percentage of statements completed in the eighteen weeks target period.

Present policy

Soon after their election in 1997, the Labour Government issued a White Paper *Excellence in Schools* (DfEE, 1997a), which was followed quickly by a Green Paper *Excellence for all Children: Meeting Special Educational Needs* (DfEE, 1997b). At the launch of the Green Paper, David Blunkett, Secretary of State for Education, summarised the Government's position:

> We want to see: basic problems tackled earlier and more effectively, more children with SEN in mainstream schools, and those in special schools not necessarily to be there throughout their school career; better partnerships

with parents, with schools and local authorities really involving parents in decision making. (DfEE News 333/9)

The Green Paper, which was a consultation document, addressed six main themes:

- high expectations of children with SEN;
- inclusion of children with SEN in mainstream schooling;
- support for parents of children with SEN and their involvement in decision making;
- value for money and shifting resources from remediation to prevention;
- more opportunities for staff development;
- provision for local partnerships.

It listed a number of ways the Government intended to ensure that children with SEN should share in raised standards through its policy of the pursuit of excellence. These included:

- greater emphasis on early identification and intervention with improved multi-agency co-operation and support;
- establishing early years development partnerships and baseline assessment;
- literacy and numeracy targets;
- target-setting for pupil performance in all schools including special schools;
- a reaffirmation of the importance of all pupils having access to the National Curriculum though recognising the need for the flexibility of access statements for a small number of pupils.

The role of parents of children with SEN was given prominence through highlighting three dimensions of parental involvement – choice, entitlement and partnership – with a promise to restore funding to assist parent partnership schemes. An extension of the supportive role of the 'Named Person', who gives the parents information and advice about their child's SEN, was also promised, as were improvements in appeal and conciliation procedures where disputes arise.

The Green Paper proposed to revise the Code of Practice, introduced by the Conservatives. Although the Code had been generally welcomed, it had also been criticised in a number of areas, including aspects of provision at the school stages 1–3. The vexed and sensitive issue of issuing statements was addressed even to the point of questioning whether statements were the best way of dealing with a particular level of needs. Of particular significance was the Government's commitment to inclusion and its support for the UNESCO 1994 Salamanca World Statement on special educational needs which calls on governments to adopt the principle of inclusive education and enrol children in regular schools unless there are compelling reasons for doing otherwise. The sensitivity of this proposal was recognised and a number of practical steps that might promote greater inclusion in mainstream schools of pupils with SEN were suggested. One consequence of increased inclusion is a decrease in the number of special schools. The Green Paper takes this on board and sees a developing role for those schools remaining: 'We will examine how special school staff can work more closely with mainstream schools and support services to meet the needs of all pupils with SEN' (para.13).

The Green Paper noted that access to SEN provision fluctuated across the country. It recognised that some of this variation was due to the difficulties of some smaller authorities not being able to provide for some pupils needing very specialised resources. In order to tackle these and other inequitable situations, the paper proposed the development of multi-agency regional planning for some aspects of SEN.

Mainstream schools play a major role in providing for pupils with SEN right across the continuum, but their success in carrying out this role varies considerably, as shown by OFSTED and Audit Commission reports. There are a number of reasons for this. As the Green Paper recognises, SEN co-ordinators, who play a central role in schools' policies and practices, are sometimes isolated because other staff are reluctant to get involved with special needs. *Excellence for All Children* therefore proposed there should be better professional development opportunities for all those likely to be involved in working with pupils with SEN. These included improvement in:

- initial teacher training and induction;
- in-service education for serving teachers and headteachers;
- providing national standards for SENCOs;
- providing opportunities for SEN specialist staff to increase their range of skills;
- introducing a national framework for training learning support assistants (LSAs);
- providing more opportunity for governor training; and
- seeking ways of changing the balance of work of educational psychologists (EPs) so that they can use their expertise as productively as possible.

One particularly thorny issue was tackled in the final chapter. Children with emotional and behavioural difficulties (EBD) as a group are often seen as the most challenging pupils to help in schools. As we shall see later under 'Issues for debate', this complex issue is related to the question of exclusions from schools and the Government's policy on social inclusion (DfEE, 1999). Chapter 8 of the Green Paper presents an overall strategy to tackle this problem, the main elements of which are:

- education policies for improving the achievement for all children combined with broader social policies to combat disadvantage;
- early identification and intervention;
- effective behaviour policies;
- strengthening the skills of staff working with pupils with EBD;
- a range of specialist support;
- wider dissemination of existing best practice; and
- encouraging fresh approaches in the secondary years.

Not surprisingly reaction to *Excellence for All Children* was mixed. Professor Alan Dyson, writing in the *Times Educational Supplement* (27 December 1997), generally welcomed the paper but was concerned that it did not sit too easily into the general education scene of competition, internal markets and naming and shaming. Others (e.g. Williams and Maloney, 1998) wanted to go much further than was proposed and to replace the statementing procedure altogether. Yet others vigorously attacked what they believed were proposals to weaken the legal framework since a number of safeguards that worked to the benefit of parents and children with SEN were in danger of being lost. Simmons (1998), for instance, feared a policy that would lead to a reduction in the number of children with statements, weaken LEA responsibilities to give details in the statement of provision that the child needs, and weaken the annual review process; she also criticised the requirement for SEN tribunals to consider not just a child's needs but an LEA's policies in relation to provision.

Some SEN practitioners, while generally welcoming much that the paper contained, felt that it lacked detail in some areas and dealt rather superficially with some topics such as inclusion. Nigel de Gruchy, General Secretary of the National Association of Schoolmasters Union of Women Teachers said in a interview for the BBC *Today* programme (22 October 1997) that although inclusion would be feasible for pupils with physical disabilities, inclusion for children with EBD could be a 'big problem', an 'absolute disaster' and bring 'untold misery' (quoted in Farrell, 1998).

In November 1998, the Government published its response to its consultations in *Meeting Special Educational Needs: a programme of action*. Introducing the action plan, Estelle Morris, the Schools Standards Minister, was careful to demonstrate that the Government was trying to respond positively to teachers' and parents' concerns about the future of statementing:

> Many parents of children with special educational needs, and organisations representing them, were concerned about the possibility of any reduction in the proportion of children with statements. We have listened carefully to what they have said. ... Over time we expect more parents to feel confident that their child's needs can be met without a statement. But we will not remove parents' rights to request a statutory assessment or statement. Nor will we remove the legal protection offered by statements (see Note 1). (DfEE News 510/98)

The action plan summarised the Government's SEN programme over the three-year period 1998-2000 and set out a number of commitments. These included additional resources of £60 million over the three years and a number of projects for further consultation and research. Key elements in the action programme include:

- *Improving support for parents and carers* by
  - providing early years education and childcare;
  - encouraging earlier identification of difficulties and appropriate intervention;

- setting up parent partnership schemes in all LEAs;
- developing conciliation services for parents in dispute with their LEA;
- involving children in the SEN process.
- *Improving the SEN framework* by
  - revising the SEN Code of Practice;
  - improving the guidance for Individual Education Plans (IEPs) that schools draw up to support children with SEN;
  - adapting the five stage model;
  - improving annual reviews of statements.
- *Developing a more inclusive education system* by
  - promoting inclusion in mainstream schools where parents want it and providing appropriate support ('a cornerstone of our strategy');
  - developing the role of special schools;
  - reviewing statutory provision;
  - improving arrangements for children with EBD.
- *Improving the knowledge and skills of SEN staff* including teachers, learning support assistants, educational psychologists and governors.
- *Improving partnerships of LEAs with other local agencies* by
  - extending regional co-ordination of SEN;
  - enabling more flexible funding between NHS and local authorities;
  - considering proposals to end the distinction between educational and non-educational needs and provision in statements.

The action plan received a cautious welcome, however, since many proposals are subject to further consultation, pilots and reviews before being finalised. At the time of writing, the Government is planning further SEN legislation, regulations and guidance to implement many of these suggestions.

Issues for debate

1. Inclusive education

The debate as to whether or not all pupils with special educational needs should be educated in mainstream schools with their peers continues unabated. As we have seen earlier in this chapter, successive governments have supported the principle of inclusion though no British government has gone so far as to make this a statutory requirement and close all special schools. Despite New Labour's argument that 'There are strong educational, as well as social and moral, grounds for educating children with SEN with their peers' (DfEE,1998, para.1), the Government strikes a note of reservation. In the same paragraph it states: 'Promoting inclusion in mainstream schools, *where parents want it and appropriate support can be provided*, will remain a cornerstone of our strategy' (italics added).

Bruce Knight (1999, p.3) defines inclusion as 'a concept which views children with disabilities as true full-time participants and members of their neighbourhood schools and communities'. In doing so, he cites the view of Stainback *et al.*

(1994) who state that 'the goal of inclusion is not to erase differences, but to enable all students to belong within an educational community that validates and values their individuality'. 'Inclusion' has largely replaced the term 'integration'. As Johnstone and Warwick (1999, p.8) note, 'integration' is seen by several writers 'as a process through which children are supported to enable them to participate in existing (largely unchanged) programmes in schools', whereas 'inclusion' 'suggests a willingness to restructure the school's programme in response to the diversity of pupils who attend'. But defining inclusion is one thing, justifying its policy is another. As Knight (1999, p.4) comments:

> While the concept of inclusion is logically and socially just, proponents of inclusion tend to make emotive statements such as 'inclusion is justified because all children can learn'. As Kauffman...suggests, these same people...need to clarify 'What can all children learn? At what rate? To what criterion of performance? With what resources? To what purpose?

However, Knight goes on to offer some very helpful advice on how schools might produce an effective policy on inclusion, and concludes: 'This ideal [of inclusion] can be achieved when schools restructure, set timelines, remain sensitive to individual student's needs and explicitly teach skills to students' (p.6).

John Wilson (1999) is even more impatient with what he sees as the ideological rhetoric put forward by governments and individuals such as Ainscow (1998) to justify inclusion, and suggests there is a paradox to be fairly faced:

> On the one hand, we have the feeling that it is wrong if people are left out of some community, are excluded, marginalised, unable to participate, not treated as equals or done justice to, in some ways are not full members of that community. On the other hand, we recognise that any community, social group or context of activity has its own aims and values. It exists *for* something, an orchestra to play music well, a cricket team to perform well on the field, a particular class to learn higher level mathematics etc.
>
> The clash between these two perspectives is that including everybody within some group seems inconsistent with fulfilling a group's purpose.
>
>   (Wilson, 1999, p.110)

Wilson supports the idea that schools should generate the feeling of 'inclusivity', but insists that 'putting all pupils in the same school is nowhere near the answer, if only because subcultures with a school may cut more psychological ice than the institution as a whole' (p.112).

Hornby (1999), after providing a useful summary of much recent and current thinking on the subject, also rejects the notion of inclusion for all children:

> It would therefore appear that the proponents of inclusion are deluding themselves, and perhaps others, when they argue that greater inclusion will lead to more effective education for children with SEN. Current policies of further increasing inclusion are particularly inappropriate at this time, since

the pressures in ordinary schools are having the effect of making them both less able and less willing to provide for pupils with SEN. (p.156)

Among the problems he cites is the relationship between the support teacher and the classroom teacher, which often falls down because of limited time for liaison.

Teachers, like many others, appear to have mixed views on the policy. According to recent evidence, most primary teachers believe that more, not fewer, children should be educated in special schools (Croll and Moses, 1999). The researchers also found, however, that when interviewed about special needs pupils in their own class, nine out of ten teachers said the mainstream classroom was the right place for them.

In its short pamphlet on inclusion, the National Association for Special Educational Needs states its belief that inclusion is a process and is not just about where children should be educated:

> Inclusion is not a simple concept, restricted to issues of placement. Its definition has to encompass broad notions of educational access and recognise the importance of catering for diverse needs. ... Inclusion is a process not a state. (NASEN, 1999)

For discussion

Is inclusion appropriate for all pupils? What are the implications for the other pupils in an ordinary classroom? If only some pupils are to be included how do you decide which ones? Could a special school pursue a policy of inclusion?

2. Pupils with emotional and behavioural difficulties

Pupils about whom teachers and others have the most problems when the issue of inclusion is raised are those with emotional and behavioural difficulties (EBD). The problem of arriving at an acceptable definition of EBD is recognised in DfEE Circular 9/94 *The Education of Children with Emotional and Behavioural Difficulties*:

> Emotional and behavioural difficulties lie on the continuum between behaviour which challenges teachers but which is within normal, albeit unacceptable, bounds and that which is indicative of serious mental illness. ... The distinction between normal but stressed behaviour, emotional and behavioural difficulties, and behaviour arising from mental illness is important because each needs to be treated differently. (para. 2)

Pupils with EBD not only exhibit behaviour arising from or caused by a wide range of difficulties, they also span the full range of ability found in mainstream schools. The response of the General Secretary of the NASUWT to proposals for the inclusion of such pupils in mainstream schools, reported earlier in this chapter, focuses on the concerns felt by some over this issue that inclusion for pupils with EBD could be a 'big problem', an 'absolute disaster' and bring 'untold misery'.

However, there is also a strong movement to tackle the dramatic rise in the number of pupils excluded from mainstream schools. Some of these pupils could be classified as having EBD, and some schools seem to be more successful than others in retaining and making effective provision for them. Ian Richards (1999) has studied the characteristics of schools that successfully provide inclusive environments for pupils with EBD. Like many others who have investigated this topic, he came to the conclusion that headteachers cannot simply 'include' such pupils without reviewing and changing a number of aspects of the school's work and life, such as timetabling and staff allocation. Not only do whole school behaviour and discipline policies, including policies on sanctions and rewards, need reviewing, the commitment of senior management to inclusion – and specifically to low exclusion – is essential. Richards' point is that in the schools where exclusion rates are low

> adults fight to give their children hope and the pupils know it. Adults understand, talk and work hard, not just on their subjects but for and about their pupils, about self-esteem and success. These adults and these schools want all their pupils to achieve academically, socially and behaviourally and plan flexibly for this. When things go wrong they do not blame, they rescue and re-plan. (p.102)

The Government is committed to reducing the number of pupils permanently excluded from schools, and help and guidance is provided in two recent publications: *Social Inclusion: Pupil Support* (DfEE, 1999) and *Principles into Practice: Effective Education for Pupils with Emotional and Behavioural Difficulties* (OFSTED, 1999). The first of these provides guidance to help schools reduce the risk of disaffection among pupils, bringing together 'good practice' on all aspects of schools' pastoral and disciplinary policies. The OFSTED publication is based on the findings from inspections of 40 special schools and units for pupils with EBD. It puts together the key features of these effective schools, and makes recommendations not only for schools but for Government, LEAs, inter-LEA and inter-agency cooperation.

For discussion
Read the guidance documents cited above. Is it realistic for most mainstream schools to cope with pupils who have emotional and behavioural difficulties? What objections might be raised to schools seeking to do this and how might these objections be met?

3. The role of special schools

Although the number of special schools has fallen in recent years (1,253 in 1993 to 1,164 in 1998 – a 7% decrease) there seems to be little question that such schools will have a distinctive role for the foreseeable future. The Green Paper devotes six paragraphs (12–17) to a developing role for special schools, which is picked up in the action programme: 'Special schools need to be confident, outward looking centres of excellence' (DfEE, 1998, para11). The Government is clear that the traditional role of special schools in providing specialist education will remain: 'But we shall maintain parents' rights to express a preference for a special school for children with special educational needs' (para. 9).

It has to be acknowledged, however, that the range of responsibilities for supporting teachers in the mainstream will be very demanding for both special and mainstream school staff. Some question whether it is possible to apply some of the teaching and learning strategies possible in a small special school, with its high adult–pupil ratio, in a mainstream setting. Knight (1999) warns that some mainstream teachers suggest they are being inclusive when they have not really changed from their previous practices. He refers to Fullan (1991, p.5) who discusses the notion of 'false clarity' to describe non-change: 'False clarity occurs when teachers believe they have changed but have merely assimilated superficial aspects into their current practice', a phenomenon that is sometimes described as innovation without change.

All this would suggest that the task of shifting the role of special schools towards assisting mainstream teachers to change their approach to accommodate 'included' pupils is a challenging one. It will mean a reappraisal of the skills and competences of staff in specialist schools to see how far these can be applied in mainstream situations. It will also mean planning appropriate ways for these teachers to teach other adults since most teachers are used to teaching children but not their peers. Maybe most of all, it will entail mainstream teachers being ready to change time-honoured practices. As Richards (1999) observes, adults need to 'avoid perceptions of inappropriate behaviour as a personal threat to their own status of power and examine these external signs for indications of cause' (p.100).

For discussion
What changes will there need to be for staff in special and mainstream schools if the concept of centres of excellence and outreach schools is to be achieved?

Further reading

The policy of inclusion is discussed in:

Ainscow, M. (1997) 'Towards inclusive schooling', *British Journal of Special Education*, 24(3), 6.
Allan, J. (1999) *Actively Seeking Inclusion: Pupils with Special Needs in Mainstream Schools*. London: Falmer Press.
Clark, C. *et al.* (1995) *Towards Inclusive Schools?* London: David Fulton Publishers.
Daniels, H. and Garner, P. (eds) (1999) *Inclusive Education*. London: Kogan Page.
Hall, J. (1997) *Social Devaluation and Special Education: The Right to Full Inclusion and an Honest Statement*. London: Jessica Kingsley.
Thomas, G. *et al.* (1998) *The Making of the Inclusive School*. London: Routledge.
Tilstone, C. (ed.) *Promoting Inclusive Practice*. London: Routledge.

The policy is criticised in:

Kauffman, J. M. and Hallahan, D. P. (1995) *The Illusion of Full Inclusion: A Comprehensive Critique of a Current Special Education Bandwangon*. Texas: PRO-ED.

Numerous articles on the issues raised in this chapter can be found in recent issues of SEN journals such as *Support for Learning* and *British Journal of Special Education.*

References

Ainscow, M. (1998) 'Exploring links between special needs and school improvement', *Support for Learning*, 13, 70–5.

Croll, P. and Moses, D. (1999) *Mainstream Primary Teachers' Views of Inclusion.* Reading: Reading University School of Education.

Department for Education (1992a) *Choice and Diversity: A New Framework for Schools.* London: DfE.

Department for Education (1992b) *Special Educational Needs: Access to the System.* London: DfE.

Department for Education (1994a) *The Code of Practice on the Identification and Assessment of Special Educational Needs.* London: DfE.

Department for Education (1994b) *Pupils with Problems. Circulars. 8–13.* London: HMSO.

Department for Education and Employment (1997a) *Excellence in Schools.* London: Stationery Office.

Department for Education and Employment (1997b) *Excellence for All Children: Meeting Special Educational Needs.* London: Stationery Office.

Department for Education and Employment (1998) *Meeting Special Educational Needs: A programme of Action.* London: Stationery Office.

Department for Education and Employment (1999) *Social Inclusion: Pupil Support.* (Circular10/99). London: Stationery Office.

Department of Education and Science (1978) *Special Educational Needs* (Warnock Report). London: HMSO.

Farrell, M. (1998) 'Notes on the Green Paper: an initial response', *British Journal of Special Education*, 25(1), 13–15.

Fullan, M. (1991) *The New Meaning of Educational Change* (2nd edn). Ontario: Ontario Institute of Studies in Education.

Hornby, G. (1999) 'Inclusion or delusion: Can one size fit all?', *Support for Learning*, 149(4), 152–7.

Johnstone, D. and Warwick, C. (1999) 'Community solutions to inclusion: some observations on practice in Europe and the United Kingdom', *Support for Learning*, 14(10), 8–12.

Kauffman, J. (1993) 'The effects of the sociopolitical environment on developments in special education', *Australasian Journal of Special Education*, 17, 3–13.

Knight, B. A. (1999) 'Towards inclusion of students with special educational needs in the regular classroom', *Support for Learning*, 14(1), 3–7.

National Association for Special Educational Needs (1999) *Inclusion: The Policy Context.* Tamworth: NASEN.

Office for Standards in Education (1999) *Principles into Practice: Effective Education for Pupils with Emotional and Behavioural Difficulties.* London: OFSTED.

Richards, I. C. (1999) 'Inclusive schools for pupils with emotional and behavioural difficulties', *Support for Learning*, 14(3), 99–103.

Simmons, K. (1998) 'Rights at Risk', *British Journal of Special Education*, 25(1), 9–12.

Stainback, S *et al.* (1994) 'A commentary on inclusion and the development of positive self-identity by people with disabilities', *Exceptional Children*, 60, 486–90.

Williams, H. and Maloney, S. (1998) 'Well meant but failing on almost all counts: the case against statementing', *British Journal of Special Education*, 25(1), 16–21.

Wilson, J. (1999) 'Some conceptual difficulties about "inclusion"', *Support for Learning*, 14(**3**), 110–12.

Note:

1 The incidence of statementing rose from 2.6% in 1995 to 3% in 1999 (DfEE Statistical First Release, 10/1999).

Chapter 8

14–19 and Lifelong Learning

Roger Marples

Previous policy

New Labour's policies relating to the education and training of 14–19-year-olds have to be located firmly within the context of the largely incoherent and, for the most part, reactive policies of the previous administration.

When they took office, the Conservatives were confronted with two phenomena that had enormous significance for this age group. The first was the alarming increase in youth unemployment that had been taking place during the 1970s; the second was the substantial rise in the number of those opting to remain in full-time education after the age of 16. In so far as there had been any serious debate about post-16 provision, it had tended to focus on the problem of how best young people might be assisted in the transition from school to work rather than on the specific qualifications then available. There were those who advocated a 'liberal education' for all, often construing attempts to 'vocationalise' the curriculum as a cynical attempt to introduce a discredited Secondary Modern curriculum for the less able pupil via the back door. Others, the 'new vocationalists', believed that while there may be nothing wrong with a liberal education, after around the age 14 there should be a real attempt to provide a measure of vocational relevance to the curriculum.

By 1979, with governmental acceptance of the Marshall Report (FEU 1979) and its advocacy of vocational preparation involving core skills, economic awareness, vocational courses and work experience, the more hard-nosed 'vocationalists' seem to have won the day, and in 1984 a new national pre-vocational qualification was created, the Certificate of Pre-Vocational Education (CPVE). Pre-vocational education was very much the dominating theme of the 1980s. The Technical and Vocational Education Initiative (TVEI) was launched in 1982, with over £1 billion of money allocated to schools, and in 1983 the Youth Training Scheme (YTS) began. While the former was a curriculum initiative involving technical and vocational education designed as a preparation for adult life, YTS was aimed at those who were unemployed during their first year after leaving school, providing opportunities to gain national qualifications covered by BTEC, CGLI and the RSA.

In spite of such initiatives, it was all too apparent by the mid-1980s that, as far as vocational education and training was concerned, Britain compared unfavourably with other countries (OECD, 1988). The principal obstacle to the attraction and retention of post-16 students seemed to rest with the qualification system itself. The existence of literally hundreds of qualifications with its inevitable duplication and lack of obvious equivalence, compounded the daunting situation confronting most 16-year-olds. It was not just that they were faced with a particularly rigid and inflexible dual track system leading, on the one hand, to conventional academic qualifications such as A-levels or, on the other, to a huge variety of vocational qualifications; it was that such a system had the undesirable consequence of forcing young people to choose between two radically different and highly specialised routes at an unnecessarily early age.

Once the choice had been made, it was impossibly difficult to transfer or progress from one track to the other, and it was far from clear how such a deeply divided system could possibly enjoy parity of esteem. The result was an important White Paper, *Education and Training for Young People* (DES, 1985), and the subsequent recommendation to set up a National Council for Vocational Qualifications (NCVQ). The tasks of the NCVQ included securing a comprehensive provision for vocational qualifications, the designing of a national framework for such qualifications (NVQs), and the specification of standards of occupational competence to meet the needs of employees.

The same period witnessed various attempts to reform the academic qualifications then available. GCSE, with its opportunities for course-work assessment and criterion-referenced grading, replaced O-level GCE and CSE in 1986. In 1987 Advanced Supplementary Levels (AS) were introduced; but in 1988 the Higginson Committee's recommendations that A-levels should be broadened to include five 'leaner' subjects than the more conventional three was firmly rejected on the questionable grounds that tinkering with A-levels would be a threat to the high standards of sixth form education. The debate about A-levels has since continued unabated, with opinion divided between those who wish to see their retention and those who would like to see them modified or abolished altogether. The issues are complex and we shall return to this shortly when considering the wider implications of the continuing academic and vocational divide.

Thus by the end of the 1980s, there existed a firmly entrenched dual track system – a largely unreformed academic track and the beginnings of a framework for national vocational qualifications (NVQs). The early 1990s witnessed a marked shift of policy. In 1991, a White Paper *Education and Training for the 21st Century* (DfE/ED/WO, 1991) was published, providing the debate with an altogether sharper focus. An impressive and radical report had been published the previous year by the Institute for Public Policy Research (Finegold *et al.*, 1990) advocating a unified and non-fragmented qualifications system, and this was to be followed by the National Commission on Education (NCE) in 1993 arguing for something very similar. Both of these reports are inspirational and well worth reading in their own right, but it is the White Paper with its *triple-track* national qualifications framework which set the agenda for the rest of the decade.

Reflecting the Government's concern over the number of students opting for the academic track which, it believed, was proving to be too easy in view of the amount of assessed coursework, the White Paper urged that more students should opt for the newly created General National Vocational Qualifications (GNVQs). The argument was that these would enable students to combine a general education with vocationally oriented courses, which should enjoy 'parity of esteem' with A-levels while maintaining the rigour of A-levels and encouraging a higher proportion of young people to participate in full-time education beyond the age of 16. The merits or otherwise of the triple-track system – (i) an academic track (A-levels), (ii) a broadly-based vocational track (GNVQs), and (iii) an occupationally specific track (NVQs) – has dominated debates about 14–19 provision for much of the 1990s.

GNVQs are meant to be sufficiently distinctive from occupationally specific NVQs to ensure that there is no confusion between them, that they are suitable for use by full-time students who have limited opportunities to demonstrate competence in the workplace, and that they enjoy equal standing with academic qualifications at the same level. They are modular in design and available at three levels – Foundation (Level 1), Intermediate (Level 2) and Advanced (Level 3). At each level, there are a number of units, some optional and some mandatory. GNVQs rely on a modified form of NVQ assessment methodology, which is outcome and competence based; but, unlike NVQs, their award does not imply that students are capable of performing competently in an occupation immediately on qualifying; rather, they will have achieved general skills and knowledge and understanding across a range of occupations. They are an alternative route to A-levels for those, often with lower grades at GCSE, who wish to continue in full-time education.

By 1996 more than 20 per cent of the age cohort were participating in GNVQs, although this figure does not represent more than a minuscule fall in the number of students opting for A-levels. Successful completion rates are substantially below those for A-level (Spours, 1995), which apparently has been largely due to the failure to complete one of the most notable features of GNVQ assessment, the portfolio. Portfolio assessment is both a strength and a weakness of the GNVQ in so far as it enables students to be more actively involved in their own learning while placing heavy demands on those responsible for record keeping. A more fundamental problem associated with GNVQs is their ambivalent status. One of their severest critics, Alan Smithers (1994), bemoans the fact that they have no syllabuses or subject matter and that they suffer from ambiguity of purpose, falling some way between the academic and the vocational and not succeeding in being clearly one or the other.

Smithers is also critical of NVQs on the grounds that they are only concerned with practical skills, it being unwarrantably assumed that candidates capable of performing specific tasks must have acquired the appropriate degree of knowledge and understanding. While NVQs continue to require virtually nothing in terms of general education, it would be naive to assume that they contribute significantly to opportunities for progression to either higher levels or to the alternative tracks. Furthermore, there are very real dangers in equating the immediate needs of employers with the long-term need for a modern workforce equipped with the high level skills required if Britain is to escape from what Finegold and Soskice (1988) have referred to as a 'low skills equilibrium', in which so many enterprises are staffed by a poorly trained workforce, including management, producing low quality goods and services.

In response to the shortcomings of NVQs, Modern Apprenticeships (MAs) were introduced in 1994 to meet the demands of all 16- to 19-year-olds opting for the work-based route, and they are now available in about 80 sectors. Open to people between the ages of 16 and 24, MAs are specifically designed to provide high quality training leading to NVQ Level 3. They are significantly different from the Youth Training Scheme in that national training organisations are directly involved in the MA curriculum. Research has shown that as many as 25 per cent of modern apprentices have started or completed A-levels (Unwin and Wellington, 1995). As commendable as this development in work-based learning is, however, it remains to be seen whether it will enjoy parity of esteem with A-levels or GNVQs.

By 1994 the triple-track framework was widely recognised as providing a hopelessly inadequate structure for meeting the needs of 14- to 19-year-olds. Like so much in relation to this age-phase it had, like topsy, grown as Government piled response upon response to the twin concerns of youth unemployment and widening participation in full-time education. The number of students failing A-levels continued at around 30 per cent, while GNVQs met with intense criticism not only for the low completion rate but for their complexity of design, narrow definition of core skills and the amount of bureaucracy associated with them. The uptake of NVQs had been lower than expected, especially outside government training schemes, and they continued to be perceived as having very little status. This, combined with the fact that a number of distinguished academics specialising in this area (Spours and Young, 1996; Raffe *et al.*, 1997) had been at pains to highlight the multitude of problems associated with a divided system, especially its inflexibility in terms of transfer across the tracks, its built in narrowness and lack of overall coherence.

By the mid 1990s the Conservative Government had, to its credit, begun to recognise the need to respond to the critics of the system as a whole and to those who wanted change made to vocational qualifications in particular. Gordon Beaumont was asked to review NVQs in 1995, but there is little in his report (1995) to assuage the critics who had serious misgivings about the view that occupational competence should be seen as the overriding criterion of successful work-based learning for this age group. Nor is it any wonder that a group of academics roundly castigated the report for failing to differentiate between the vastly different problems of providing effective vocational education and training for school-leavers, skilled craftspeople or graduates (letter to *Financial Times*, 17 January 1996). In 1996 John Capey undertook a similar review of GNVQs. His report (1996) was notable for its suggestions for simplifying the assessment methodology and rendering GNVQs closer to qualifications within the academic track.

The most significant and wide-ranging of the reports of the mid-1990s that addressed the problems facing the education and training of 14- to 19-year-olds was the Dearing Report *Review of Qualifications for 16–19 year olds* (1996). The Secretary of State at the time, Gillian Sheppard, charged Dearing with the task of devising ways to strengthen, improve and to encourage more coherence and breadth into the framework of 16–19 qualifications while maintaining the high standards associated with A-levels. Not only should new proposals build on the development of GNVQs and NVQs but participation and achievement should be increased and young people should be prepared for work and higher education. Given this remit, it is not surprising that, among 198 proposals, Dearing's concept of coherence was severely stretched:

- Not only did it include the retention of the three distinct pathways, it recommended that A-levels continue as firmly secure as ever, with a proposal that standards at A-level should be raised through special papers for more able students.
- However, the report emphasised that A-levels should be embedded in a system comprising four National Levels – entry, foundation, intermediate and advanced.
- Overarching all qualifications, Dearing called for two new qualifications – a National Certificate for a set number of passes at intermediate and advanced levels, and a Baccalaureate-style National Diploma to certify breadth and depth of study at advanced level. Each of these qualifications would require specific components at each level, namely core skills of communication, numeracy and IT.
- Vocational qualifications should have a greater rigour by renaming GNVQs 'Applied A-levels' and making greater use of external assessment.
- The NCVQ and SCAA (the School Curriculum and Assessment Authority) should be merged as a single national body for education and training to ensure common arrangements for quality assurance and to facilitate mixing and matching of courses.
- Youth Training should be relaunched with a system of National Traineeships to reward achievement in core skills and to lead to qualifications such as GNVQs and GCSEs.

Present policy

Taking Dearing forward

In addition to Capey, Beaumont and Dearing, New Labour inherited from the previous administration a whole culture of the value of market forces celebrating the fact that post-16 education and training is best carried out in a variety of institutions from schools to tertiary colleges and training agencies all operating within the context of the plethora of competing qualifications and validating bodies.

Only one week before the publication of the Dearing Review, however, New Labour in opposition had published its own policy statement *Aiming Higher: Labour's Proposals for the Reform of the 14–19 Curriculum* (Labour Party, 1996). The document listed the damaging effects of early specialisation entailed by the triple-track system, which it characterised as 'confusing, complex and fragmented' and stifling in the 'lack of opportunities for learners to combine different study options or transfer across separate courses' (paras. 3.20–1).

In the Introduction, David Blunkett acknowledged the problems of low participation and achievement rates, high drop-out rates, variable standards and restricted scope for broad-based study. There was a clear recognition that 'a coherent 14–19 curriculum was central to learning throughout life' and required flexible entry and exit points 'in which students can have their achievements recognised at different stages of progression' (para. 4.3). The document provided strong endorsement for those who wanted to see A-levels broadened as part of a programme for providing greater breadth of study to everyone in post-16 education and training.

There were also promises to upgrade and enhance vocational qualifications, to implement the major recommendations of the Beaumont review, and to strengthen education and training for those who enter the work-based route on leaving school: 'Every 16 and 17 year old in work should have a guaranteed training component as part of his or her job and it must become the norm for all those in the work-based route to undertake units of general education as well as specific vocational education' (para. 5.26). Once in office, they would bring existing qualifications under a single framework whereby students' achievements in any one or a combination of existing qualifications were recognised in a single overarching certificate at level 3, with advanced level education (vocational, academic or a mixture of the two) leading to the award of an Advanced Diploma.

Along with this there was approval for increased modularisation of learning programmes, the recognition of attainment in Records of Achievement, the development of a credit framework structure allowing leavers to gain and 'bank' recognition for attainment, the alignment of A-levels and GNVQ grades, the establishment of a database to facilitate the availability of modules, and curriculum guidelines and impartial careers education and guidance. There was also the promise to replace SCAA and NCVQ with a National Qualifications Council within which a Core Skills Unit would be established. Looking to the future, the Party defended a unified curriculum from 14–19 in which there was room for both core studies as well as opportunities to specialise. Such a curriculum would provide for community-based studies, active citizenship as well as preparation for parenthood and the development of knowledge and understanding of the world of work.

New Labour's Election Manifesto (1997), while containing no obvious policy change, lacked the missionary zeal of *Aiming Higher*. There was clearly a shift of emphasis reflecting the political climate of the time, with its focus on continuity and determination not to alienate the middle classes with anything smacking of a potential threat to A-levels. Little wonder then that the Manifesto signals no proposals whatever for coherence within 14–19 provision.

In October 1997, a few months after winning the election, Labour implemented a promise made in *Aiming Higher* by the creation of the extremely powerful Qualifications and Curriculum Authority (QCA), resulting from the merger of SCAA and NCVQ. Not only is the QCA responsible for the National Curriculum and its assessment, it also oversees the national qualifications framework as well as the development of occupational standards. In addition to building a coherent framework for the school curriculum and its assessment, the QCA aims to contribute to the raising of standards of attainment, to secure a rigorous system of regulation for national tests and qualifications, to enhance participation for all, and to promote lifelong learning. It is not surprising, therefore, that many people began to have high expectations of New Labour moving rapidly towards a unified system which would have been consistent with their policy proposals going back to at least 1992 (Labour Party, 1992).

What we were presented with however, was something much more cautious – the consultation paper on 16+, *Qualifying for Success* (DfEE, 1997). This presented a planned, staged approach to reform, with the intention of moving away from piecemeal change. The emphasis was on 'high and consistent standards across all qualifications' where there was parity of esteem, greater flexibility, a commitment to greater breadth combined with opportunities for specialisation, the need for all learners to attain high levels in key skills, the creation of positive attitudes, wider access to lifelong learning and the need to make a return to learning easier, clear progression routes in higher education, employment and further training, and a raising and widening of levels of participation, retention and achievement.

But the paper took the Dearing recommendations as its starting point, with a clear commitment to the retention of A-levels and GNVQs, while the narrowness of the former combined with the potential waste in terms of the numbers dropping out were recognised. In order to combat these problems, the consultation paper indicated New Labour's 'inclination' to support the Dearing proposals for the Advanced Subsidiary to represent the first half of a full A-level; and there was a limited degree of enthusiasm for modular A-levels, albeit with a strong emphasis on 'rigour' and 'standards'. As for GNVQs, much was made of what they should be called, while demonstrating a firm commitment to aligning them more closely with A-levels in terms of assessment procedures in the interests of comparable standards.

As a result of the consultation process, the Government now plans to introduce the following from September 2000:

- *A new three-unit Advanced Subsidiary (AS) qualification*, representing the first half of a full A-level and worth 50 per cent of the marks, with the aims of aiding the progression from GCSE to A-level.
- *New A-level syllabuses (called 'specifications')*, made up of six units, set at the same standard as current syllabuses and offering candidates the choice of linear (end-of course) or modular (staged) assessment, to the same standards in each. Whichever assessment option is chosen, candidates will have to demonstrate understanding of the whole syllabus through an element of synoptic assessment. They will be allowed to resit any module no more than once during their course and full-time 16- to 19-year-old candidates studying via a modular route will normally be required to complete their course within two years. Coursework will be restricted to a maximum of 30 per cent in most subjects in order 'to enable the awarding bodies to enhance the validity of the overall assessment regime without compromising on rigour'.
- *New 'world class tests'*, aimed at the most able students but designed to be more accessible than current S-levels.
- *A new Key Skills qualification* recording achievement in communication, application of number and IT, available to students on any programme. The relationship between these key skills and GNVQ will be changed so as to enable them to be both integral to all courses and separately certificated.
- *A revised GNVQ at foundation, intermediate and advanced levels* with a more rigorous and manageable assessment regime, and a new six-unit GNVQ at advanced level equivalent in size and demand to a single GCE A-level and graded on a similar A–E scale, with the possible introduction of a number of three-unit qualifications equivalent to a single AS (DfEE, 1999a).

What is left in the air is the status of those Key Skills excluded from the newly devised national qualifications, Improving Own Learning and Performance, Working with Others, and Problem Solving. While the QCA have been asked to suggest effective ways of promoting these wider skills as part of post-16 education and training programmes, they continue to be perceived, like so much else that remains unassessed, as having less significance than the others.

In her letter to Sir William Stubbs (Chairman of the QCA), Education and Employment Minister Baroness Blackstone sounds a cautionary note on the possibility of moving towards a unit-based credit system and the introduction of overarching certification. While acknowledging that the consultation process following *Qualifying for Success* indicated growing support for the exploration of such notions, she admits to difficulties 'both conceptual and practical' to which they might give rise and is sceptical about going further down this road without further examination on the part of QCA of the issues involved (DfEE, 1998a). Given New Labour's cautious approach to reform and their strong commitment to A-levels, as much for political reasons as any other, it is unlikely that they will be superseded by any form of overarching qualifications this side of the next general election.

Political expediency notwithstanding, New Labour was quick to recognise that Modern Apprenticeships and National Traineeships – the latter being launched in the spring of 1998 and designed as a higher quality replacement for YT – are, in themselves, insufficient to raise the quality of young people's training or to provide the basics for progression to higher levels of training or education.

Combating social exclusion

Since 1994 it has been New Labour's policy to combat welfare dependency and, since coming to power, it has been much more proactive in its attempts to tackle social exclusion and disaffection than its Conservative predecessors. In July 1997 the Government launched its £3.5 billion New Deal to get young people (aged 18–24) who have been legitimately claiming Job Seekers' Allowance for six months or more and the long-term unemployed into work. Since April 1998 such people have been entitled to a personal adviser who provides them with intensive help in terms of careers advice, basic education, basic social skills extending to problems associated with homelessness, debts or drug dependency. Such advice is the 'Gateway' to four New Deal options which are:

- a job with an employer with at least one day a week in education or training preparing for accredited qualifications;
- a job for sixth months with the Government's Environmental Taskforce, again with day-release education or training;
- a job for sixth months with the voluntary sector with day-release education or training;
- the opportunity for those who do not have the qualifications required for good employment prospects to take up full-time education or training on an approved course for up to one year including payment of benefits.

Those refusing to avail themselves of one of these options will have no fifth option. Refusal without good reason will lead to the imposition of benefit sanctions. Since its inception in 1998, 213,000 people have embarked on the New Deal and almost 58,000 young people have found jobs.

Additional strategies devised by New Labour to combat disaffection and social exclusion include:

- Investing in Young People Strategy (IiYP), outlined in *The Learning Age* (DfEE, 1998b). Geared to 14–19-year-olds it aims to: (i) increase the number of young people attaining a level 2 qualification, (ii) improve the quality and relevance of education and training, and (iii) ensure that all young people have the necessary skills for lifelong learning and employability;
- New Start, announced by Baroness Blackstone in March 1997 as a series of local projects set up to investigate and develop ways of tackling underachievement and social exclusion among 14–19-year-olds; it aims to

motivate and re-engage those of the age group who have both dropped out of learning or are at risk of doing so;
- policies to deal with exclusion, truancy, and disaffection, including Education Action Zones and Excellence in Cities.

In July 1999 the Social Exclusion Unit published a report entitled *Bridging the Gap: New Opportunities for 16–18 Year Olds Not in Education Employment or Training*, indicating that the most powerful predictor of unemployment at the age of 21 is non-participation for six months or more between the ages of 16–18. Moreover, such people are, by the age of 21, more likely to be parents, unqualified, untrained and at risk of depression and poor health. The Government's policy is designed to dovetail closely with the White Paper *Learning to Succeed: A New Framework for Post-16 Learning* (DfEE, 1999b) with proposals to ensure that young people stay in education or training, or work with a strong education/training component, until they are at least 18. There are four elements to this which are:

- a clear outcome to aim for by 19, to be called 'graduation';
- a variety of pathways to 'graduation' to suit the needs of all young people;
- building on the forthcoming Education Maintenance Allowance (EMA) pilots to engage the most disadvantaged groups, and a Youth Card to assist with transport and other costs; and
- a new multi-skill support service working with all young people, but giving priority to those most at risk of underachievement and disaffection, to support them between the ages of 13 and 19 through education and the transition to adulthood.

'Graduation' would require a minimum of level 2 qualifications (academic, vocational or occupational) involving the key skills of communication, application of number and IT as well as a range of options from arts, sports and community activity. There would be mechanisms for people who did not graduate by 19 to obtain equivalent recognition subsequently.

In his Foreword to *Learning to Succeed*, the Secretary of Sate, David Blunkett, states his determination to 'build on the best features of what we have at present, while seeking to remove the contradictions, conflict and incoherence which currently exists'. There is a ready acknowledgement that the present system fails a significant section of the community, that people with low skills and low qualifications are locked into a cycle of disadvantage, that education and training needs to be more coherent and accessible to both individuals and employers, that people need better advice and support as well as more flexible ways of learning, and that there are too many (and too many low quality) providers. The proposals for change, which are extensive and significant, are underpinned by a number of principles. These are:

- change should promote excellence and participation;
- employers should have a substantial stake in shaping post-16 education and training;
- systems must be learner driven and responsive to the needs of individuals, businesses and their communities;
- equal access to education, training and skills opportunities should be a priority, with equal opportunity in the mainstream of provision;
- people should have access to support in the form of good advice and guidance and, where appropriate, financial help; and
- accountability, efficiency and probity should be promoted at every level.

In order to improve standards and provide for greater coherence, the Government intends to establish, from April 2001, a new Learning and Skills Council for England (LSCE) with the responsibility for all post-16 education and training (excluding Higher Education), replacing the Further Education and Funding Council (FEFC) and the Training and Enterprise Councils (TECs). The LSCE will assume responsibility for:

- funding colleges;
- advising the government on the National Learning Targets from the National Advisory Council for Education and Training Targets;
- funding Modern Apprenticeships, National Traineeships and other government funded training and workforce development;
- developing, in partnership with local education authorities, arrangements for adult and community learning;
- providing information, advice and guidance to adults; and
- working with the pre-16 education sector to ensure coherence across all 14-19 education.

Two committees will advise the Council: one, the Young People's Learning Committee, will endeavour to ensure that young people's learning is geared towards both their employability and their personal development. Its advice will relate to A-levels, AS Levels, non-vocational and national vocational qualifications as well as other training provision. Its brief will also be concerned with ensuring the successful transition of younger people into the next stage of education, training and work. The other, the Adult Learning Committee, will examine ways of widening the participation and attainment of adults. The LSCE will operate through up to 50 Local Learning and Skills Councils (LLSCs) whose boundaries should fit with travel to work and study areas. At the heart of these new arrangements will be local Learning Partnerships in order to ensure that the system is fully responsible to local partners and community needs. As with the LSCE, employers will be the largest group on such bodies with Trade Unions and others having representation. Regional Development Agencies (RDAs) will have a key role in the planning arrangements for learning and skills; and it is intended that the link between RDAs and the LSCE, both at national and local level, should be a strong one. RDAs will work with local councils in order to assess how well regional skills are met.

In August 1999 the Government introduced a new support service aimed at preventing the 'disengagement' of young people from education and the world of work (estimated at 1 in 11 of the age group). A strategy called 'ConneXions' will try to ensure that the numbers of 16- to 19-year-olds in education and training are increased. Additionally, a new Youth Support Service based on the notion of personal advisers will, it is hoped, create a comprehensive structure for advice and support for all young people from the age of 13. The whole is designed to ensure a smooth transition from compulsory schooling to post-16 learning.

Underpinning these arrangements will be new rigorous independent inspection arrangements. These too are aimed at providing greater coherency by bringing together the inspection processes for young people in schools and colleges, including the Youth Service, through to the age of 19, all under OFSTED. In addition, a new independent Inspectorate will be created for post-19 provision in colleges, work-based provision for all ages, adult and community education and the University for Industry courses. Both inspectorates will have to work together where appropriate. As part of quality control the government wants the LLSCs to propose closing sixth forms that do not improve, and has asked the QCA to rationalise the number of qualifications on offer as well as promising to endorse new criteria for qualifications below degree level. In addition, the QCA will be expected to ensure that young people on work-based training take vocational qualifications covering the theory of their occupational area.

Lifelong learning

New Labour's policy on lifelong learning was outlined in a Green Paper published in February 1998, *The Learning Age: A Renaissance for a New Britain* (DfEE, 1998b). Its vision of learning's potential is inspirational in its recognition that a culture of learning is more than a means to enhance employment prospects. Lifelong learning is not only about empowerment; it is a significant factor in achieving personal autonomy and fulfilment. In its defence, the Government eschews any form of crude utilitarianism and reminds us that learning 'nourishes our souls (and) takes us in directions we never expected' (p.10).

The first chapter quotes with approval Bob Fryer who chaired a committee set up by New Labour's National Advisory Group for Continuing and Lifelong Learning, and whose report *Learning for the Twenty-first Century* was published in 1997: 'The country needs to develop a new learning culture, a culture of lifelong learning for all. It is essential to help...all of its people meet the challenge they now face as they move towards the twenty-first century.'

Non-participation was identified by Fryer as the problem, and he drew up a 10-point agenda for the development of a learning culture, including: the necessity for a government-established framework; a revolution in attitudes; simplified and integrated progression routes and pathways; effective partnership and collaboration; up-to-date, accessible and impartial information and advice; new technologies; and increased and re-directed funding. *The Learning Age* is, in large part, the Government's response not only to Fryer but also to another report published in the same year – *Learning Works: Widening Participation in Further Education*, commissioned by the Further Education and Funding Council (FEFC), the group chaired by Helena Kennedy. The report outlines an 18-point 'agenda for change' including various funding measures. *The Learning Age* endorses Kennedy's vision that further education will be at the centre of widening participation in order that the 62 per cent of the adult population of working age who do not have a level 3 qualification should recognise that this is the minimum to which they should aspire.

As well as acknowledging the potentially vast demand for education, the document recognises the obstacles people face such as time, cost, fear, ignorance and inconvenience, combined with the fact that they require better information and advice as well as the opportunity to study for qualifications relevant to their requirements. While it is clear that not everyone who learns either needs or wants a formal qualification, those who do so aspire must clearly understand what is on offer at every level from vocational qualifications at level 1 to postgraduate qualifications. The Report encouragingly proposes that a range of new entry level or 'starter' qualifications should be introduced to help those for whom foundation qualifications may be too daunting.

One of the most exciting proposals is the University for Industry (UfI), the aim of which is to connect those who want to learn with ways of doing so. One of its principal tasks will be to stimulate mass demand. The idea is to enable the public, private and voluntary sectors to make use of new technologies to make learning possible at a time and place to suit everyone – at home, at work or through learning centres where it will be possible to go and access UfI courses and materials. These will be located in places as familiar as the workplace, football clubs and shopping centres. In its early years it is intended that the UfI will focus on priority areas such as literacy and numeracy, ICT and the skills needs of small and medium-sized businesses, together with a number of specific sectors such as automotive components and environmental technology and distributive and retail trades. Based in Sheffield, it is due to be operational by 2000 and it is anticipated that 2.5 million will be benefiting from its services by 2002, taking much of the fear out of learning. To assist in this process a new national telephone helpline, Learning Direct, will be free, confidential and impartial.

In spite of the overwhelming case for a unit-based framework, *The Learning Age* adopts a cautious note and is unclear on specifics. It admits to the desire to see a 'National Credit Accumulation and Transfer System . . . and more "stopping-off points", separately accredited, during *higher* education' (para. 6.18, my emphasis) and 'it may be possible to develop within *further* education a system of commonly understood credits as currently happens with arrangements for access to higher education for adult learners' (para. 6.16, my emphasis).

However, if New Labour is serious about its commitment to developing a genuinely coherent system whereby anyone from 14 to old age may gain credit for what they have learnt – such credit being, in the words of the Fryer Report, 'portable, transferable and cumulative' – then it must give clear signals to the QCA, with whom the responsibility for the accreditation for qualifications clearly rests, to proceed towards such a laudable goal. *The Learning Age* is, meanwhile, depressingly backward-looking in the way it continues to distinguish between qualifications for 16- to 19-year-olds and higher education students, and it is little wonder that people remain confused when trying to steer their way through the minefield of the current qualifications framework. As Carole Scott (1998, p.16) says, 'Raising standards will be supported by ensuring that learning and assessment fit the needs and learning style of the students.' New Labour remains overly concerned with maintaining the standards and rigour associated with A-levels at the expense of the majority who continue to pursue less prestigious qualifications and, in too many cases, achieve far less than they might otherwise achieve.

Issues for debate

1. Problems associated with three separate pathways

As we have seen, the present triple-track system for 16+ comprises (i) an academic track (A-levels), (ii) a broadly based vocational track (GNVQs), and (iii) an occupationally specific track (NVQs). In their present form there is little opportunity for substantially larger numbers of the age cohort to successfully complete A-levels. Approximately only one-third of that cohort embark upon an A-level course, with almost 30 per cent of those who begin failing to complete it successfully. Again, a typical A-level student will follow a very narrow and highly specialised curriculum with no common or general education. This is a corollary of a system which allows for individual choice in preference to greater control of the curriculum once compulsory schooling has finished, and which all too frequently results in students pursuing a course of study lacking a coherent rationale.

While some students may combine their A-levels with the study of issues outside the A-level syllabus, the system provides for no opportunity for this to receive recognition in terms of credit accumulation. It is also unlikely that A-levels, as presently constructed, can possibly meet the demands of the large numbers of people wishing to participate in post-16 education; their highly specialised structure being incompatible with the increasing need for knowledge and skills across a much wider spectrum. Most damagingly, however, it is their very existence which is responsible for an undesirable knock-on effect on the educational opportunities for the majority of the age cohort who, for whatever reason, fail to embark on an A-level programme. It can plausibly be maintained that some form of general education should be available to *all* post-16 students, but this is unlikely to be a realistic goal at which to aim if A-levels continue as they are.

Michael Young (1997) has produced a useful summary of a series of attempts to reform A-levels from their inception in 1951 to the Dearing Report of 1996, and concludes by drawing an important distinction between A-levels as presently constituted and an Advanced Level curriculum. The latter, in marked contrast to the former, is not only 'a way of developing the knowledge and skills that young people are going to need in the next century', which entails building in 'the skills and knowledge (they) require as citizens, workers and parents'; such a curriculum would also have to 'develop specialist areas of knowledge and a way of linking a student's specialist studies to the aims of the curriculum as a whole' (p.52) – something which Young elsewhere has referred to as 'connective specialisation' (1998). Only by trying to conceive of subjects from the point of view of the curriculum as a whole, where knowledge is seen in a social, cultural, political and economic context, will we be able to overcome the restrictions resulting from the current academic/vocational divide and begin to develop a post-16 curriculum with breadth and flexibility, connections with specialist studies and academic and vocational studies, and increased opportunities for progression and credit transfer.

Numerous publications by the Post-16 Unit at the University of London Institute of Education have been at pains to rehearse the strengths and weaknesses of possible options to the three-track system, judged against the criteria of flexibility, breadth and coherence. The first option is to retain and improve the present triple routes. The second is to retain the three tracks, but provide some kind of overarching qualification framework with opportunities for students to mix various units from different pathways. The third option is to work towards the creation of a unified system of education and training with a core curriculum for all post-16 students, which, ideally, should be modular in form and allow for the possibility of credit accumulation and transfer within the context of a single qualifications structure.

The first option fares badly against the Unit's proposed criteria for obvious reasons. The present system is manifestly inflexible in allowing for students to combine courses of study from the various tracks, and the qualifications on offer are inherently narrow and over-specialised albeit in different ways. As with the tripartite system of secondary education established after the war, when it was assumed that there existed three different 'types' of youngster with recognisably different abilities, very similar assumptions underpinned recent post-16 provision for which the triple-track structure is ideally suited.

There is much in the Dearing Report which relates very closely to the second option especially in terms of Dearing's concern for greater flexibility, albeit within the three-track system. With the creation of a common qualifications framework it would be possible to provide qualifications which are unitised, each with a specific credit rating leading to the overarching qualification. This would allow scope for students to combine units of study from A-levels, GNVQs and NVQs as well as allowing students on each course to study units in common with their own credit rating. Such a provision would go some way towards improving breadth of study. But unless and until there is provision for a common core curriculum for post-16 students, combined with a system of learning which obviates the necessity to specialise unnecessarily early, the system would continue to lack overall coherence. The arguments for moving towards a third option – a completely unified system that would provide for flexibility, breadth and overall coherence – are thus overwhelming.

In his critical appraisal of the Dearing Review, Michael Young (1997) argues that these proposals do not fit neatly into what he and others have referred to as the 'framework' model' since 'existing qualifications can be awarded independently and thus the tracks are allowed to continue. On the other hand, the proposal for an Advanced Diploma provides an indication of what a Diploma within a unified system might look like (p.27). Dearing's framework refers only to four common National Levels within the existing framework of A-level, GNVQ and NVQ. Again, Dearing's recommendation to create the National Certificate and National Diploma as overarching qualifications do nothing to *replace* existing qualifications and thus are not as radical as that being suggested under the second option, namely, that all existing qualifications should be encompassed within a national framework with one title.

Young and Spours (1998) have spelled out in considerable detail what a unified system might look like. Underpinning the overall vision is, of course, the raising of standards, the changing demands facing young people in the twenty-first century, combined with the ever greater need for the recognition of the importance of lifelong learning. They refer to the necessity of a single system of certification with flexible entry points, credit accumulation and transfer and a single ladder of progression providing opportunities for young people on Modern Apprenticeships and other work-based routes, as well as those in full-time education. The curriculum in a unified system, if it is to reflect students' needs, must be one in which the academic/vocational divide is not enshrined. Not only will GCSEs need phasing out so as to enable students to progress up a single ladder at different rates, but the whole teaching and learning process must be based on the needs of individual students and not linked, as at present, to specific programmes.

For discussion
'The vision will need to be for a system that is inclusive of all young people, holds together their different needs and does not let these differences become a basis for new division' (Young and Spours, 1998). Do you agree with this vision? What are its practical and political implications?

2. An assessment of New Labour's policies for 14+

Pressure will almost certainly continue to build for a more unified and modular system in order to overcome the unnecessarily divisive English system. Scotland and Wales have gone much further in this respect, making it difficult to believe that New Labour, in its anticipated second term, will be willing to resist pressures for reform in England. The recent White Paper *Learning to Succeed* (DfEE, 1999b) provides some ground for optimism that New Labour is serious about its vision of a learning society and the need for greater flexibility where artificial barriers to credit accumulation and transfer are removed. Given New Labour's political expediency in its desire not to move too rapidly from the agenda set by the previous administration with its emphasis on voluntarism, market forces and institutional competition within 16–19 provision, the White Paper is no more than a step in the right direction.

If New Labour is concerned with standards, then it must concern itself with high standards for everyone, not just the preservation of an A-level 'gold standard' for a small minority. Where so many people are excluded by a system which emphasises methods of selection at the expense of opportunities for progression, and where the concept of high standards is unnecessarily restricted to raising attainment, the levels of achievement reached by so many will continue to fall way below what is both possible and desirable. If the Government is as serious about raising standards as it would have us believe, it would take more seriously than it does the need to increase them over all levels of achievement so that we can escape from a position of too many young people with low level skills and too little opportunity to partake in what is often referred to as a 'seamless link' between childhood and retirement.

It is to be hoped that the Learning and Skills Councils, in the support they provide to employers in terms of developing effective training plans and the creation of employee development schemes linked to Individual Lerarning Accounts (ILAs) (see Note 1), will contribute much to the modification of head-in-the-ground attitudes to the importance of education and training and the culture of voluntarism associated with it. In providing a strong link between the Learning Skills Council (LSCs) and Regional Development Councils (RDAs), the White Paper is a major step forward in the development of social partnerships in the context of regional devolution. But until a more coherent and less fragmented overall qualification system is devised, with opportunities for credit transfer, there remains justified grounds for scepticism of New Labour's ambitions to create a 'Learning Society'.

The stranglehold of A-levels will not go away, and if New Labour is serious about the rhetoric to be found in *Aiming Higher* and *Learning to Succeed* it will have to grasp the nettle which has bedevilled the system of 14-19 provision for far too long. The new Key Skills qualifications are symptomatic of a timid and backward-looking approach in so far as there is a piling on of yet more qualifications, within a divided and incoherent system, at the expense of addressing the issue of wholescale reform of all that is on offer to everyone aged 14+, including a fundamental reassessment of the nature and purpose of the GCSE within the overall system.

In their recent book on the subject, Ann Hodgson and Ken Spours (1999) characterise New Labour's current approach, which places a heavy burden of responsibility on individuals to access learning opportunities, as a 'weak framework'. This is because funds remain targeted towards certain groups, and divisions within the system are assumed to be overcome by the creation of overarching structures as opposed to their replacement with an entirely new system. They contrast this with a 'strong framework' approach. This aims to support individual empowerment by (i) 'modifying the behaviour of the education and training market by reforming key areas of the education and training system (e.g. qualifications and funding) to combat long-standing system barriers and divisions', (ii) encouraging everyone to participate in education and training 'by using state funding to provide permanent and balanced incentives for individuals and institutions' and (iii) 'devolving government power in order to strengthen regional and local collaboration to support the individual learner' (p.137).

A strong framework approach would be less voluntaristic than that associated with current programmes. There would be a greater role for government in terms of taxation policy, with legislation obliging employers to provide training. Funding would be more co-ordinated through, for instance, a Learning Bank instead of ILAs as currently conceived. The system of funding for *all* post-16-year-olds would be unified and less fragmented. A strong framework would also necessitate a single, unified and inclusive qualifications system from 14+ with credit accumulation and transfer, together with learning opportunities relying less on individual initiative (e.g UfI and ILAs), or incentives and sanctions in relation to welfare and benefit (e.g. New Deal and Educational Maintenance Allowances), but on a more co-ordinated approach relying on a strong local and regional network of access, guidance and progression routes underpinned by national qualifications with organisation and delivery being less competitive, voluntary and weak (Hodgson and Spours, pp.39–40).

Hodgson and Spours' book was produced before the White Paper *Learning to Succeed* which, as is likely, will go a considerable way towards strengthening local and regional networks, even if we continue to remain as far as ever from a unified national qualifications framework. But the authors are quite right to suggest that should New Labour win a second term of office it will need to address:

- the low skills equilibrium through the development of new social partnerships;
- the need for more developed structures and funding frameworks in order to provide a suitable framework for lifelong learning;
- the need for an 'all-through qualifications framework' in order to raise the levels of participation, achievement and progression, and
- the need to provide overall direction for the education and training system as a whole from 14+.

The need is obvious and the planning must begin at once. New Labour is, in many respects, moving in the right direction albeit far too slowly and with an occluded vision of where they ultimately wish to go.

For discussion

(a) Do you agree that what Hodgson and Spours call a 'strong framework' is needed if the Government is to create, as it wants, a 'learning society'?

(b) What implications has the concept of lifelong learning for schools?

Further reading

Halsall, R. (ed.) (1996) *Education and Training (14–19): Chaos or Coherence?* London: David Fulton Publishers.

Howieson, C. (1997) 'Unifying academic and vocational learning: the state of the debate in England and Scotland', *Journal of Education and Work*, 10(10), 5–35.

Marples, R. (1996) '14–19', in Docking, J. (ed.) (1996) *National School Policy*. London: David Fulton Publishers.

Pearce, N. and Hillman, J. (1998) *Wasted Youth: Raising Achievement and Tackling Social Exclusion*. London: Institute for Public Policy Research.

Raggatt, P. *et al.* (eds) (1996) *The Learning Society: Challenges and Trends*. London: Routledge.

References

Beaumont, G. (1995) *Review of 100 NVQs and SVQs: A Report Submitted to the DfEE*. London: DfEE.

Capey, J. (1996) *Review of GNVQ Assessment*. London: National Council for Vocational Qualifications.

Dearing, Sir R. (1996) *Review of Qualifications for 16–19 year olds*. London: SCAA.

Department of Education and Science (1985) *Education and Training for Young People*. London: HMSO.

Department for Education/Employment/Welsh Office (1991) *Education and Training for the 21st Century*. London: HMSO.

Department for Education (1995) *Review of 100 NVQs and SVQs: A Report Submitted to the DfEE*. London: DfEE.

Department for Education and Employment (1997) *Qualifying for Success: A Consultation Paper on the Future of Post-16 Qualifications*. London: DfEE.

Department for Education and Employment (1998a) *Qualifying for Success: The Response to the Qualifications and Curriculum Authority's Advice*. London: DfEE.

Department for Education and Employment (1998b) *The Learning Age: A Renaissance for a New Britain*. London: DfEE.

Department for Education and Employment (1999a) *Qualifying for Success: Post-16 Curriculum Reform*. London: DfEE.

Department for Education and Employment (1999b) *Learning to Succeed – A New Framework for Post-16 Learning*. London: DfEE.

Finegold, D. and Soskice, D. (1988) 'The failure of training in Britain: analysis and prescription', *Oxford Review of Economic Policy*, 4(3), 21–53.

Finegold, D. *et al.* (1990) *A British Baccalaureate: Overcoming Divisions between Education and Training*. London: Institute for Public Policy Research.

Fryer, R. (1997) *Learning for the 21st Century: First Report of the National Advisory Group for Continuing Education and Lifelong Learning*. London: NAGfCELL

Further Education Unit (1979) *A Basis for Choice*. London: FEU.

Hodgson, A. and Spours, K (eds) (1997) *Dearing and Beyond: 14-19 Qualifications and Systems*. London: Kogan Page.

Hodgson, A. and Spours, K. (1999) *New Labour's Educational Agenda: Issues and Policies for Education and Training from 14+*. London: Kogan Page.

Kennedy, H. (1997) *Learning Works: Widening Participation in Further Education*. Coventry: FEFC.

Labour Party (1992) *Opening Doors*. London: Labour Party.

Labour Party (1996) *Aiming Higher: Labour's Proposals for the Reform of the 14–19 Curriculum*. London: Labour Party.

Labour Party (1997) *Labour Party General Election Manifesto 1997: Because Britain Deserves Better*. London: Labour Party.

National Council for Vocational Qualifications (1996) *Review of GNVQ Assessment*. London: NCVQ.

Organisation for Economic Co-operation and Development (1988) *A Challenge to Complacency*. Paris: OECD.

Raffe, D. *et al*. (1997) *The Unification of Post-Compulsory Education: Towards a Conceptual Framework*. Unified Learning Project Working Paper 2, Post 16 Education Centre, University of London Institute of Education and University of Edinburgh Centre for Educational Sociology.

Scott, C. (1998) 'The Learning Age', *Adults Learning*, 9(8), 14–16.

Smithers, A. (1994) *All Our Futures*. Manchester: Manchester University Press.

Social Exclusion Unit (1999) *Bridging the Gap: New Opportunities for 16–18 Year Olds not in Education Employment or Training*. London: SEU.

Spours, K. (1995) *Post-compulsory Education and Training: Statistical Trends*. Learning for the Future Working Paper 7, Post-16 Education Centre, University of London Institute of Education.

Spours, K. and Young, M. (1995) *Post-Compulsory Curriculum and Qualifications: Options for Change* (Learning for the Future, Working Paper 6). Post-16 Education Centre, University of London Institute of Education/University of Warwick Centre for Education and Industry.

Spours, K. and Young, M. (1996) 'Dearing and beyond: steps and stages to a unified system,' *British Journal of Education and Work*, 19(3), 5–18.

Unwin, L. and Wellington, J. (1995) 'Reconstructing the work-based route lessons from the modern apprenticeship', *Journal of Vocational Education and Training*, 47(60), 337–52.

Welsh Office (1998) *Learning is for Everyone*. London: Stationery Office.

Young, M. (1997) 'The Dearing Review of 16–19 qualifications: a step towards a unified system?' in Hodgson, A. and Spours, L (eds) *Dearing and Beyond: 14–19 Qualifications, Frameworks and Systems*. London: Kogan Page.

Young, M. (1998) *The Curriculum of the Future*. London: Falmer Press.

Young, M. and Spours, K. (1998) '14–19 education legacy: opportunities and challenges', *Oxford Review of Education*, 24(**1**), 83–97.

Note

1 Individual Learning Accounts (ILAs) are part of the Government's package to help young adults save and borrow for investment in their own learning. Money directly (e.g. for an evening class) or indirectly (e.g. for meeting the cost of childcare to provide study time). To encourage people to open ILAs, the Government has announced a number of incentives such as discounts off the cost of courses and exemption from tax and National Insurance contributions.

Chapter 9

The Teaching Profession

Graham Welch and Pat Mahony

The education and training of teachers, for long the subject of professional discussion, is liable to change as our system of education, and its task in our society, also change and develop. In a healthy education service, this process is accompanied by a continuing professional debate which may be expected to lead to action by those responsible for shaping the policies and practice of the service. (HMI, 1983, p.1)

Introduction

Since these prescient words were written over 16 years ago, the world of education has been characterised by much 'continuing professional debate', with concomitant change and (arguable) development. Indeed, the last 25 years have been characterised by virtually constant change as different groups (both professional and political) have sought to create an education system that is best suited to their perceptions of the needs of the contemporary age. As a result, there has been an enormous increase in statutory legislation and associated document-ation, exemplified by Batholomew's *Law of Education* (a comprehensive record of Government legislation on education) increasing in size from one volume to three in the decade 1987–97 and now covering approximately 3,000 pages (Liell *et al.*, 1997).

The amount of legislation also provoked comment within the legislature, such as Lord Russell's, 'Well, my Lords, here we are again. We are debating the Second Reading of the 13th Education Bill in 14 years' and Lord Judd's enquiry as to 'whether there is now a constitutional requirement that there should be an annual Education Bill' (both comments in relation to the Education Act 1994) (Hinds, 1995, p.79). Both the volume and the prescriptive nature of this legislation can be seen as dramatically circumscribing teachers' autonomy, and has led critics to argue that teaching is becoming 'deprofessionalised' or 'reprofessionalised' despite the rhetoric of 'professionalism' contained in official policy documents (Ozga, 1995; Seddon, 1997; Lawn, 1997). This in turn has raised questions about the extent to which teaching has ever been a profession and whether it matters (*see* 'Issues for debate' below).

Previous policy

The period between 1979 and 1997 witnessed an increasing concern from Conservative governments to shift control of the school system away from the Local Education Authorities (LEAs), a trend that is continuing under New Labour. There was a move to devolve decision-making from LEAs to individual schools and their governing bodies, particularly in relation to finance, while (at the same time) ensuring that there was an explicit national policy framework set by central Government. In parallel, the control of teacher education was shifted away from Higher Education Institutions and LEAs to become increasingly tightly framed within centrally determined legislative policies. As a result, the Government's expectations of the teacher's role and what is defined as 'appropriate' professional behaviour by teachers became more and more overtly stipulated. As such, New Labour's educational policy on the teaching profession at the end of the twentieth century can be seen as a 'natural' and relatively seamless development of the policies of its Conservative (and Labour) predecessors. It is the nature of politicians to cast doubt on the efforts of their forebears and to promote themselves as having 'radical solutions' to the challenges of education. Yet, much of what is subsequently written in new policy documents has echoes of the past.

During the early 1980s, publications by HM Inspectorate revealed a tension in the debate about the rights of the teaching profession to determine its own affairs. On the one hand, there was a view that Government's role (if any) was to promote a healthy democratic debate about the nature of the *curriculum* (i.e. the opportunities for learning and 'what' is actually taught), rather than proscribing *pedagogical practices* (i.e. the professional nature of the teaching process, the 'how' of teaching):

> the broad definition of the purposes of school education is a shared responsi-
> bility [between 'schools' and the 'wider public'], whereas the detailed means by
> which they may be best realised in individual schools and for individual children
> are a matter for professional judgement. (HMI, 1980, pp.2–3)

On the other hand, perceived variations in teacher quality were attributed to weaknesses in initial teacher education:

> Notwithstanding the value of institutional [university, college, LEA] freedom in
> professional matters, and the value of variety and experiment in the
> curriculum of teacher education, there is a widely recognised need for agreed
> guidelines on the content of training, and for the guarantee of an acceptable

level of preparation in the subject or aspect of the curriculum which a teacher offers to teach. (HMI, 1983, p.3)

Since these words were written, successive Conservative governments (and now New Labour) brought forward legislation to make more and more explicit the nature of both pre-service training and, most recently, continuing professional development. The term 'standards' has featured strongly in recent times, referring sometimes to the academic achievement of school pupils, while at others being used to denote a criterial framework, specifications or competences which define what teachers should be able to do. In the first sense, the appeal to 'standards' was a key element in Sir Keith Joseph's Conservative Government policy paper to Parliament in March 1985:

> The Government's principal aims for all sectors of education are first, to raise standards at all levels of ability. … But the high standards achieved in some schools throw into relief the shortcomings, some of them serious, of the others. Nor are the objectives which even the best schools set themselves always well matched with the demands of the modern world. (DES, 1985, p.1)

Subsequently, the Conservative Government took action for 'high' as well as 'higher standards' through their focus on a number of areas including: embracing greater centralised prescription of the curriculum allied to reform of the examinations and assessment system; devolution of financial management to schools and a weakening of Local Education Authority (LEA) powers; the introduction of competitive quasi-market policies that exerted pressure on schools through published league tables of exam performance and inspection reports; open enrolment to deliver parental 'choice' and the re-introduction of differentiated schools. Each of these foci has been subject to subsequent legislation, such as the 1988 Education Reform Act that introduced the National Curriculum for schools from 1990 and Key Stage assessments in 1992 for all 7-, 11- and 14-year-olds. A similar agenda for change has underpinned the present Labour Government's statutory legislation on baseline assessment and the School Standards and Framework Act (both 1998).

These successive changes in policy directed at schooling brought parallel changes in the education and training of teachers as the move towards 'effective' schools generated a concomitant demand for 'effective' teachers. Teacher effectiveness was codified into 'Standards' (in its second sense) through developments that began in 1984 with a specification by the Secretary of State of the criteria for initial teacher education (ITE) courses leading to the award of Qualified Teacher Status (QTS) (DES, 1984). It has continued with New Labour's 1998 Green Paper on 'modernising the teaching profession' (DfEE, 1998a). Over the last 15 years, statutory regulations governing ITE courses alone have undergone six major revisions (by Circulars 24/89, 9/92, 14/93, 10/97, 4/98, 4/99).

Effective teachers for effective schools

These developments in teacher education need to be understood in terms of the imperatives emerging from the profoundly influential school effectiveness and school improvement movements. The key to 'effective' schools (defined largely in terms of academic performance) is seen as 'effective' teachers and leaders (Hextall and Mahony, 1998). As such, there is no disagreement between the former Conservative and the current Labour Secretaries of State (Shephard, 1996; DfEE, 1998a). The emphasis placed on 'effective' schools arises from a belief that they are crucial in the production of a labour force with sufficiently high levels of knowledge and skill to guarantee the competitiveness of the UK in the global economy.

Such a (utilitarian) belief is not without its critics. For example, using an interdisciplinary approach and drawing on international data, Ashton and Green (1996) devote an entire book to unpacking and challenging what they call the 'simplistic consensus' from which 'policy debates and much scholarly discussion begin' (p.3), namely that more and better skills necessarily lead to an improvement in a nation's economic performance. Secondly, from a recent project on school leadership, undertaken in Australia, Denmark, England and Scotland, empirical evidence supports the view that policy development is not simply a reaction to the supposedly deterministic imperatives of the global economy but that local cultures, histories and traditions play a significant part in the choices about how schools are organised and their purposes defined, what it means to be a teacher or a headteacher and who constitutes the 'we' making such decisions (Moos *et al.*, 1998).

Restructuring the welfare state

This is not to deny the role of supra-national bodies such as the World Bank and OECD in driving forward a restructuring of state welfare services in accordance with the principles of New Public Management (NPM) or 'new managerialism' (Smyth and Shacklock, 1998; Lingard, 1999). There has been a tendency to treat these transformations as though they were specific to the UK, but comparable developments in the delivery of public welfare services have been widespread among OECD countries. Broadly conceived, NPM has meant devolving or decentralising management of the public sector and remodelling it along the lines of 'best' commercial practice. Such practice involve an emphasis on leadership, explicit standards and measures of performance, greater emphasis on output controls (with resource allocation and rewards linked to measured performance), a break-up of large organisations into smaller units operating on decentralised budgets, introduction of competition (often involving contracts and public tendering procedures), stress on commercial styles of management (which replaces the former public service ethic) and stress on doing more for less (Hood, 1991, pp.4–5).

In the UK (though not elsewhere), the introduction of NPM was justified by questioning the motivations and efficiency of public sector workers. Education, in particular, has been seen as epitomising

> much that was seen to be wrong with burgeoning state power. It was construed as expensive, not self-evidently adequately productive, insufficiently accountable, monopolistic, producer-dominated, a bastion of an entrenched professional elite, resistant to consumer demand and, at worst, self-generating and self-serving. (Fergusson, 1994, p.93)

The increasing professional/managerial split in the public sector has been the subject of much discussion in the social policy literature. Particular attention has been given to the way that power has been seen as shifting towards managerial 'leaders' (in our case, the headteacher) and away from those (teachers) in direct contact with their 'customers' (pupils) (Clarke and Newman, 1997).

Within this wider context of education policy and public policy, the development of National Standards can be seen both as providing a centralised specification of 'effective teaching' and as the codification of relations between managers and managed. The National Standards can thus be understood as occurring within the centralisation/decentralisation linkage where 'policy steering' is achieved through much tighter regulation by the centre. As Hoggett (1996) explains:

> In virtually all sectors, operational decentralisation has been accompanied by the extended development of performance management systems. Such systems seem designed to both monitor and shape organisational behaviour and encompass a range of techniques, including performance review, staff appraisal systems, performance-related pay, scrutinies, so-called 'quality audits', customer feedback mechanisms, comparative tables of performance indicators, including 'league tables', chartermarks, customer charters, quality standards and total quality management. (p.20)

In this system, managers or 'leaders' become locally responsible for staff compliance and are given the means to reward 'preferred' teachers (Smyth and Shacklock, 1998).

Enter the Teacher Training Agency (TTA)

It is difficult to imagine that anybody could disagree with the belief expressed by all major political parties in recent years that 'good teachers using the most effective methods are the key to higher standards' (DfEE, 1997a, p.1). Such consensus probably ends at this point, however, for as soon as notions such as 'good teachers', 'effective methods' or 'higher standards' are defined, different viewpoints will emerge about the purposes, priorities and desirable ends of schooling and the best means of achieving them. In voicing some disquiet about the potentially negative impact of recent developments, we have no wish to fabricate some past golden age of teacher education (nor professionalism).

There were problems in the past, as indicated by HMI (themselves 'reformed' into OFSTED): 'Plans to achieve coherence in the work of tutors, teachers and students are still regularly frustrated, however, by the autonomy which tutors regularly enjoy in universities' (HMI, 1988, p.42).

As we have seen, the 1980s and '90s saw more than a decade of Conservative government interventions in the organisation and 'delivery' of ITE and professional development. When the Teacher Training Agency (TTA) was established in 1994, it was widely assumed that it would be predominantly concerned with Initial Teacher Training (as it had by now come to be called, although many professionals regard the term 'training' as antithetical to a professional career preparation and so prefer the phrase 'initial teacher education'). Its published purpose was 'to improve the quality of teaching, to raise the standards of teacher education and training, and to promote teaching as a profession, in order to improve the standards of pupils' achievement and the quality of their learning' (TTA, 1996, p.2). However, the Agency's functions were systematically broadened between 1994 and 1998 to the extent that it became difficult to think of any stage of teaching or area of teacher education which remained outside its remit.

At the core of its strategy was the development of a framework of 'National Standards'. These consisted of standards for the award of QTS, expert teachers (these were developed but never published), subject leaders, special educational needs coordinators, headteachers and special educational needs teachers.

Present policy

New Labour policies on teaching

In December 1998, the Labour government published a Green (consultation) Paper entitled *Teachers: Meeting the Challenge of Change* (DfEE, 1998a) which set out its proposals for 'modernising the teaching profession' according to the needs of the 'school of the future' that 'will often be a centre of lifelong learning' and which, coupled with the use of new information and communication technologies (ICT), requires a 'new professionalism' (pp.12–13). The Green Paper went on to say:

> The time has long gone when isolated, unaccountable professionals made curriculum and pedagogical decisions alone, without reference to the outside world. Teachers in a modern teaching profession need:
>
> • to have high expectations of themselves and of all pupils;
> • to accept accountability;
> • to take personal and collective responsibility for improving their skills and subject knowledge;
> • to seek to base decisions on evidence of what works in schools in this country and internationally;

- to work in partnership with other staff in schools;
- to welcome the contribution that parents, business and others outside a school can make to its success; and
- to anticipate change and promote innovation. (DfEE, 1998a, p.14)

Although this view of a 'modern teaching profession' is expressed in concepts which characterise New Labour policies and ideology, many of these ideas, as we noted earlier, were also central to the education policy statements from the former Conservative governments and provide an indication of how contemporary educational change is incremental in nature and rarely abrupt or radical (despite change of governments).

In a set of measures heralded as giving 'something for something' the Green Paper proposals include the introduction of a performance management system in which a restructuring of the profession, the introduction of annual appraisal and performance related pay are all underpinned by a framework of standards. To this end, a new 'standards framework' is currently being developed that is taking on a sharper significance in the restructuring of the profession and in the granting of reward. The new framework will consist of published standards for:

- the award of QTS (the first gateway into teaching);
- the induction period (the second gateway into teaching);
- a performance threshold (through which teachers will need to pass if they are to progress to higher salary levels);
- advanced skills teachers (ASTs); and
- headteachers.

It is envisaged that movement through the various positions within the structure will be accomplished by evaluation against the relevant standards, undertaken by headteachers, governing bodies, school leadership groups and, in some cases, with the assistance or ratification of external assessors (who will have been nationally trained).

General Teaching Council for England

Shortly after its election in May 1997, the Labour government announced its intention to establish a General Teaching Council for England. (There will be slightly different arrangements for the GTC for Wales; it is also worth noting that a GTC has been in existence in Scotland for some decades.) This intention was formalised within the Teaching and Higher Education Act, which became law in July 1998.

In his foreword to the 1997 Consultation, undertaken prior to the introduction of the legislation, Stephen Byers, then the Schools Standards Minister, laid out the basic thinking which underpinned the government's initiative:

There has long been agreement that a GTC is desirable. It will enhance the standing of teachers by giving them a clear professional voice, independent of government but working with us to raise standards. It will help restore the morale of teachers, who for too long have had too little say in determining the shape and future of their profession. It will celebrate the best of teaching, by drawing on the dedication and experience of those who have made teaching their vocation. It will be able to promote a positive image of teaching both within the profession and outside. It will bring together and reflect the interests of all those with a stake in ensuring high standards in teaching – parents, employers, higher education and the wider public as well as teachers. The GTC will take its place in our new national partnership to raise standards in schools.

Our aim is to set up a professional body which will encourage all teachers to play their part in the challenging programme of reform. ... The GTC must represent the highest professional standards and speak out where standards are not what they should be. We are not interested in a talking shop for teachers or a body to defend the way things are. An effective GTC must be an engine for change and a powerful driving force behind our new deal for teachers: high expectations and pressure to succeed, matched by support and recognition for achievement. (DfEE, 1997b, p.3)

The GTC, which starts operation in September 2000 with Lord Puttman as its Government-appointed Chairman for the first 18 months, comprises 64 members (11 elected primary teachers, 11 elected secondary teachers, one elected special school teacher, one elected primary head, one elected secondary head, nine union appointees, 17 from 'representative bodies', and 13 appointed by the Secretary of State). Its key responsibilities are to maintain a register of qualified teachers, discipline teachers for serious misconduct or incompetence, and advise the Government on issues such as the recruitment and supply of teachers, initial training and induction, and professional development.

The place of 'evidence' in professional action

One other key facet of New Labour's educational policy is worth noting because it offers an explicit basis for the professional action, rationality and critical reflection that should always be central to any debate about educational change in a democratic society. This is the 'evidence' base that determines proposed action by and for the profession, whether by individual teachers, schools, LEAs, Government departments, educational quangos or professional bodies. The case for 'evidence' and 'research' was stated simply by Sir Stewart Sutherland in his 1997 report on teacher education to the Dearing Inquiry into the future of Higher Education:

The purpose of teacher education and training should be to produce professional teachers who have the theoretical knowledge and understanding, combined with the practical skills, competences and commitment to teach to high national standards. ...From both the oral and written evidence presented to me, there does appear to be a consensus that teaching is, or should be, a 'research-based' profession. In other words, that the professional teacher should be one who has been trained and educated against a background of relevant and systematic research and has developed the critical capacities to use research findings as a basis for improving practice. (Sutherland, 1997, pp.4–5)

Subsequently, this notion of teachers' decisions being based on 'research' was reflected by David Blunkett, Secretary of State for Education and Employment, in his letter to the new Chair of the Teacher Training Agency (TTA), Professor Clive Booth: 'The best professions are evidence-based. ...I shall look to the Agency to make further progress in securing teaching as a more research-based profession' (TTA, 1997, p.31).

Accordingly, the TTA's Corporate Plan for 1998–2001 includes among its strategic objectives 'To help secure teaching as an evidence- and research-based profession', which has led to the awarding of a small number of annual Teacher Research Grants and proposals to disseminate guidance for teachers on using and conducting research.

Because education *is* contentious, it is essential that any 'evidence' being presented or used for educational policy and action (at whatever level) is open to scrutiny and analysis by others. Given the past two decades, in which successive Governments' teacher education policies have often reflected either their marginalisation or selectivity of research data, it will indeed be a radical change if research evidence is allowed to become more central to professional action.

Arguably, an 'evidence- and research-based profession' is likely to be in a much stronger position to scrutinize and critique the bases for Government policies that impinge on their professional action. Teaching could then be more likely to embrace one of the key features of a profession, namely 'a high degree of [appropriate] autonomy for the practitioner and the occupation as a whole' (Hoyle, 1990).

Issues for debate

1. Is teaching a profession?

There has been a long and sometimes fierce debate – fuelled by the prescriptive nature of recent education legislation – about whether teaching is a profession, a semi-profession or not a profession at all and whether this matters. Hoyle (1990, p.13) states that the criteria for a profession include:

a high degree of skill based on a body of systematic knowledge, a lengthy period of training, a high degree of autonomy for the practitioner and the occupation as a whole, a commitment – often expressed in a code of ethics – to the primacy of client interests.

The pervasive nature of the current official discourse of 'profession, professional, professionalism' raises questions about what this language is being employed to accomplish. There is no doubt that the language of 'professionality' carries significant historical, cultural, symbolic and personal power in England. The terms have come to function as 'hurrah' words in denoting a committed and responsible approach to doing one's work well; alternatively, to be called 'unprofessional' is to stand accused. This is not the case in other parts of Europe where the term 'professional' functions as a 'boo' word, associated with a peculiar brand of snobbery with roots in the development of the English class system, and where the appeal to 'professionalism' is taken to indicate an attempt by government to exert greater central control over teachers and teaching.

With regard to teaching in this country, there are particularly contentious elements within definitions of 'profession', at least in relation to its modern development which, as we saw earlier, take on a concrete significance in relation to the establishment of the General Teaching Council (GTC). Successive governments from the early 1980s have sought to challenge the basis of contemporary educational practices and have increasingly proscribed the autonomy of the practitioners, appearing to draw on George Bernard Shaw's dictum that the professions are a 'conspiracy against the laity' (Hoyle, 1990). Greater 'accountability', improved 'quality', higher 'standards', specific 'competences', strong 'leadership', increasing 'effectiveness' and better 'value for money' are just some of the terms that both the Conservative and Labour governments have introduced into the discourse of education as part of their justification for change and formal legislation.

For discussion
(a) Is teaching a profession or not, and does it matter?
(b) 'The time has long gone when isolated, unaccountable professionals made curriculum and pedagogical decisions alone, without reference to the outside world' (DfEE, 1998a). Why would a Government committed to an 'evidence-based profession' introduce its policy in such language? Is there any evidence to support such a statement by the DfEE?

2. The 'modernisation' of the teaching profession

At the time of writing, some of the detail of the proposals for the 'modernisation' of the teaching profession, as outlined in the 1998 Green Paper, are under intense negotiation. The Government seems both to have underestimated the scale of the responses it would receive to its consultation (over 41,000 responses) and to have glossed over the fact that most of the elements within its proposals have been emerging for some considerable time in the movement towards new public management or managerialism of the public services during the 1980s and 1990s:

We will be accused of being visionary and excessively ambitious. We plead guilty. After the years of drift, vision and ambition are surely what is needed. Creating a world-class education service was never going to be easy but that is what the economy and society of the future require. A modern teaching profession is central to this process. (DfEE, 1998a, p.19)

Whereas there has been overall support for proposals to provide better support, working conditions and professional development opportunities for staff, opposition to the proposals has been based on a range of issues concerned with the content of the standards against which teachers will be judged, the external factors that will be likely to motivate teachers and improve their work, the consistency and fairness of the proposed arrangements, and the overall value system embedded in the framework.

Are the standards against which teachers will be judged appropriate?
The content of the standards against which teachers will be judged has been the subject of intense academic debate. The Standards for QTS (TTA, 1998) are the first mandatory gateway into the profession and the most heavily regulated through ongoing annual OFSTED inspection of initial teacher education. QTS standards are viewed as particularly critical in shaping the professional orientations of new entrants to teaching and in providing the baseline on which standards for induction, performance threshold and advanced skilled teachers are built. Criticisms can be summarised as follows:

i. There is no explicit account of how teaching is being conceptualised, no indication that there are different representations of teaching, and no justification of, or rationale for, the particular account of teaching implicit in the QTS standards. New teachers and their tutors are being required to accept a version of professional standards without any account of the overall definition of teaching to which these standards belong (Mahony, 1999).

ii. Even if the account has not been made explicit, it is no surprise to find that the standards for QTS consist largely of achieving the subject knowledge and craft skills necessary to teach and assess the National Curriculum, thus depicting the new teacher as a technician rather than as a critical professional. (An interpretation that has currency in the imperative underpinning the standards framework is a demand for 'effective' teachers to 'produce' an up-skilled workforce that is able to enhance the nation's competitiveness within the global economy.)

iii. Teaching is also presented as an individualistic activity with no mention being made of the ability to work collaboratively with colleagues in countering the limitations of the 'egg crate school' where teachers are isolated physically and professionally (Fullan and Hargreaves, 1992). Although one standard refers to 'effective working relationships with professional colleagues' (TTA, 1998, p.11) these 'working relationships' are themselves in the process of being managerially restructured (Mahony and Hextall, 1998).

iv. The social and political contexts and purposes of teaching and learning are inadequately framed. If teachers are so essential in shaping the future, as the Government insists (DfEE, 1998a and b), then, arguably, their responsibilities extend beyond the narrowly vocational or economic. The standards, as currently defined, are seen as forming part of a 'dreary utilitarianism' that has come to characterise recent education policy.

v. Teachers' responsibilities in relation to equity issues are dealt with in an unsatisfactory manner. For example, the requirement that teachers have a working knowledge and understanding of anti-discrimination legislation does not satisfy even the most minimal account of what it means to work in non-discriminatory ways. The Macpherson Report, for example, makes clear that taking racism seriously involves radical scrutiny of everyday practices in schools rather than simply a knowledge of legislation:

Racism exists within all organisations and institutions, . . . it infiltrates the community and starts among the very young. Recent research in Cardiff showed that 50% of the racist incidents considered by the Race Equality Council involved young people under 16 years old, and 25% of these incidents involved children between the ages of six and 10 years. The problem is thus deeply ingrained. Radical thinking and sustained action are needed in order to tackle it head on . . . in all organisations and in particular in the fields of education and family life. (Macpherson, 1999, p.5)

Will the proposals help teachers improve their work?

In addition to concerns over content of standards, there is a range of criticisms directed at assumptions being made in the Green Paper about the external factors perceived as motivating teachers and enabling them to improve. There are fears that the demotivating effects for the majority of teachers of performance related pay will far outweigh the rewards for the few unless significantly more money is made available on a long-term basis to enable the majority to achieve the higher scales. Related to this are concerns that what motivates teachers is not simply money (though no-one has yet claimed that teachers could do with less of it). Even if self-interest were the over-riding motivator (rather than a professional commitment to doing the best job possible), it has been pointed out that the proposals may turn out to be self-defeating. Put bluntly, 'Why would I share my good ideas with you when you might use them to achieve faster progression through the system than me?' The concern is that good educational practice or innovative teaching, far from becoming shared among a school staff, will be seen as a personal commodity to be sold in the internal market of the school.

Will the system be consistent and fair?

A range of concerns has been expressed that the implementation of the system will be inconsistent and unfair. Although, at a common-sense level, it seems just that people who work harder should receive greater rewards, in practice there are a host of logistical problems (for example, over definition and evidence). Despite the apparent transparency of appraising staff against National Standards, in practice interpretation of the Standards means that judgement is always going to be a subjective process, grounded partly in the needs of the school as well as on the perceived talents of the individual teacher concerned. Australian evidence (Smyth and Shacklock, 1998) has indicated that those who 'succeed' are likely to be those in possession of 'valuable' (policy enhanced) skills, such as ICT capability. Leaving aside questions of favouritism or the tendency of managers to over-rate their own staff in an effort to retain them, those who have experienced the enhanced pay element of performance management seem less than sanguine about its supposed transparency. A recent letter to the *Times Educational Supplement* read:

> As someone who has worked under a performance pay system for the whole of the 1990s, I would reassure teachers that performance-related pay will be nothing as simple as a crude relationship between results and payments. Payments there will be, for some, but such is the complexity of PRP, no one will know why they did or did not get the money. (Letter from Keith Flett, *TES*, 23 July 1999, 16)

Related to this is the concern that those groups who have traditionally suffered discrimination within the labour market are likely to experience similar difficulty in negotiating the hoops and hurdles integral to the system being proposed. Speaking of the experience of performance management appraisal within the Civil Service, a person interviewed recently spoke about the social justice issues that had come to light and the ways in which unions had responded (see Note 1):

> 'And we...said, look we've got – statistical evidence. ...There is a strong case discrimination happening here, ...can you explain why this is actually happening? And they got some management consultants in, did this report and they identified yes, there is a problem, it's statistically significant but we don't think this was due to discrimination in the system. So we said, well what is it due to? Well we don't know. So it was like, they've identified there is a problem, they don't think it's caused by discrimination but they can't explain what it is. From my point of view that's completely unacceptable. There obviously is a problem and from our perspective the only factor that can account for it is the fact that you know, to do with gender and race. And that implies there is something in the system that is discriminating on those grounds...it all depends on the criteria that you use, how you measure performance, but it is a real minefield.'

Again, speaking of the opportunities for developing the professional capabilities necessary for promotion, another interviewee said:

> 'In terms of career progression...if you were in a school...it's quite a tiny community and that your reputation is made within that small community and...if they [senior managers] are coming with limited ideas about what a

black teacher is there for or can achieve or whatever, then it can be a very stifling environment, one where they are under-estimated, where their skills are specified or where their skills are kind of seen as only fit for certain types of jobs. ...[Black women and men] were saying again and again and again that schools were using them to discipline black children, to keep black children in check, to deal with parents, black ethnic minority parents, all those kinds of things. So that whether or not they were skilled in a wider sphere that was one difficulty.' [our inserts]

What is the value system that underpins the framework?

Finally, if performance management is to have a significance beyond the narrow question of performance-related-pay then the overall value system within which the whole framework is to be located needs to be spelt out. This also has to be something to which employees feel that they can express a commitment otherwise it will not succeed in motivating and encouraging their commitment. Within the private sector this value framework can (arguably) be limited to outcomes such as profitability, turnover or productivity. This is clearly not the case in the public sector generally and certainly not the case in education where the National Standards (subject to local interpretation) are intended to stand as proxy performance indicators. Speaking of performance management in the public sector, Marsden and French (1998) say:

> Determining the relevant dimensions of performance has been a major area of controversy across the public services as staff and their representatives have often argued that quantity is being stressed at the expense of quality. ...Deciding on valid criteria for performance measurement management is...much more than a simple technical issue, but one which relates to people's beliefs about the goals of the service they work for...a great many staff are strongly committed to a certain idea of public service, and there is much disagreement about the suitability of the targets chosen by management. (pp.5–6)

There are echoes here of Australian experience where Smyth and Shacklock (1998) describe how the professional discourses of teachers were often felt to clash with the managerially oriented way in which the standards for advanced skills teachers were couched. This leads us back to the question of whether teaching is a profession and whether it ought to be able to determine its own professional standards and on to a brief consideration of the role of the General Teaching Council (GTC) which, at the time of writing, is in the process of being established.

For discussion

(a) Peter Smith, General Secretary of the Association of Teachers and Lecturers, has urged teachers to avoid posturing and engage in 'a real and difficult debate about how we rethink how we reward the teaching profession' (*TES*,

17 September 1999, p.17). Discuss the implications of this 'rethink' in terms of the arguments presented above.

(b) How does your account of a 'good teacher' compare with the Standards for the Award of QTS?

3. The membership, powers and responsibilities of the General Teaching Council

Earlier (p.146), we quoted the beliefs expressed by a minister about Government thinking about the GTC initiative. Some brief clarification of two broad contextual features may help us to understand the significance of these statements.

First, while this is not the setting in which to enter into detailed history, it is important to know that decades of conflict and indecision have accompanied the GTC debate in England and Wales, accompanied by vigorous campaigning by teacher unions and a whole variety of educational and professional pressure groups (Sayer, 1993; Tomlinson, 1995). Previous endeavours have foundered on the twin rocks of political opposition from governments which have been unwilling to relinquish power and authority over such a significant occupational group as teachers, set alongside competitive struggles between teacher unions and professional associations over questions of status and relative weight of representation on a GTC. Echoes of both quandaries can be found in the current legislation.

Secondly, the GTC is being established alongside a number of other Government bodies responsible for teacher education. Both the legislation and official documents leave much of the interface between the GTC and the Government hazy. A number of key bodies have pointed out that the largely *advisory role* of the GTC contrasts strongly with the decision-making and/or control capacities possessed by, for example, doctors, engineers and members of the legal profession (General Medical Council, 1993; United Kingdom Central Council for Nursing, Midwifery and Health Visiting, 1998). If we take the most basic sociological definition of a profession (control over entry, establishment of a distinctive knowledge base, self regulation, responsibility for training methods, control over assessment of competence and certification), there is little basis for viewing the GTC as comparable with professional bodies in other occupational sectors.

Furthermore, there is a concern that there are some vital areas, such as the development of professional standards, where issues that might be regarded as falling quite properly within the remit of the profession are already being determined by the Teacher Training Agency (Ingvarson, 1998). If there is to be any meaning to 'professional ownership', then it is argued that there has to be greater influence on such matters by the appropriate professional body. However, schools and teachers, let alone wider constituencies, have figured very little in the TTA's own consultation process (Mahony and Hextall, 1997). Our argument is not that the GTC should represent or be answerable only to 'the profession', nor that it should possess autonomy over what are to count as professional standards for entry and subsequent progression. But, if it is to operate as a professional body, it needs to occupy a central place in the deliberative process, and not be given merely an advisory role on a par with a whole host of other bodies. Certainly, many would argue that the TTA and its ministerially appointed Board are no substitute for a properly established system of professional debate and decision-making, subject to appropriate mechanisms of transparency, accountability and political ratification.

The proposed membership (see p.149) largely reflects the major categories of practitioners, professional associations, employers and other representative bodies. There will also be approximately 25 per cent of the Council who will be appointed directly by the Secretary of State to achieve 'balance', fill gaps, 'ensure necessary mix of expertise, experience and personal qualities' (e.g. financial, legal, people with experience of running large organisations), to reflect 'wider public interest and bring fresh ideas' (DfEE, 1998b, p.20). However, no provision is made for ensuring the inclusion of marginalised groups or for addressing more general issues of social diversity. Such an omission fails to address questions about the form (or forms) of democracy that may be appropriate for complex and diverse societies at this point in time. There is also criticism that 39 of the 64 members will not be elected by or from teachers.

It could be argued that the debate has been dominated by professionally parochial concerns about representation, membership and powers which, while of vital significance to educational practitioners, have failed to engage with or even recognise, wider democratic issues that could and should be raised in discussions of educational governance. Beyond this insiders' perspective, there is a whole other debate which focuses on issues of accountability, public debate and inclusivity. Teacher education is not some obscure, esoteric matter. Teachers have a vital role to play in the formation of social relations and in the making of the kind of society envisaged for the future. Their training and employment are by no means insignificant elements within public sector expenditure patterns. Considerations such as these pose dilemmas about the new forms of representation and accountability that will best form the basis for democratic governance in the future. They also raise important questions about the nature and form of political accountability in this current historical, political context. As Ranson and Stewart (1994) say:

> Our current form of public accountability is inadequate or, more precisely, incomplete. It offers members of the public a particularly exiguous form of participation (periodic voting) which has been used to distance them from the polity. It establishes the polity as something out there, not something we as citizens are members of or believe we have any responsibility for. (p.235)

If increased participation is being proposed as a better alternative, then there are three different levels at which the representation of different 'voices' within the policy process are crucial:

- adequacy of representation on the policy making bodies themselves;
- sensitivity of the criteria, values and needs underpinning policy to the needs of different social groups;
- quality of policy outcomes communication and their rationales and the extent to which they both speak and listen to the responses of diverse, perhaps conflicting, bodies of interest.

In a society that takes democracy seriously, there are widespread legitimate interests in how teachers are themselves educated, in the content and purpose of their education, in who should be represented in these decisions and what values they espouse. These debates take us well beyond the confines of education policy, let alone the even more specific terrain of teacher education, but addressing such issues is vital if there is to be a sustainable public debate about 'effective' schooling.

For discussion
What roles should the General Teaching Council have and who should be represented on it?

Further reading

Hoyle, E. (1990) 'The teacher as professional in the 1990s', *NUT Education Review*, 4(1), 13–16.
Mahony, P. and Hextall, I. (1997) 'Problems of accountability in reinvented government: a case study of the Teacher Training Agency', *Journal of Education Policy*, 12(4), 267–78.
Smyth, J. and Shacklock, G. (1998) *Remaking Teaching: Ideology, policy and practice.* London: Routledge.

References

Ashton, D. and Green, F. (1996) *Education, Training and the Global Economy.* Cheltenham: Edward Elgar Publishing Ltd.
Bennett, G. and Meredith, P. (eds) (1998) 'Statutory instruments', *Education and the Law*, 10(4), 269–84.
Clarke, J. and Newman, J. (1997) *The Managerial State.* London: Sage.
Department for Education and Employment (1997a) *Excellence in Schools.* London: Stationery Office.
Department for Education and Employment (1997b) *Teaching: High Status, High Standards. General Teaching Council: a Consultation Document.* London: DfEE.
Department for Education and Employment (1998a) *Teachers: Meeting the Challenge of Change.* London: DfEE.
Department for Education and Employment (1998b) T*eaching: High Status, High Standards. The Composition of the General Teaching Council; A Consultation Document.* London: DfEE.
Department of Education and Science (1984) Circular 3/84 *Initial Teacher Training: Approval of Courses.* London: HMSO.
Department of Education and Science (1985) *Better Schools.* London: HMSO.
Fergusson, R. (1994) 'Managerialism in Education', in Clarke, J., Cochrane, A. and McLaughlin, E. (eds) *Managing Social Policy.* London: Sage.
Fullan, M. and Hargreaves, A. (1992) *What's Worth Fighting For in Your School?* Buckingham: Open University Press.
General Medical Council (1993) *Tomorrow's Doctors.* London: GMC.

Hextall, I. and Mahony, P. (1998) 'Effective teachers for effective schools', in Slee, R. *et al.* (eds) *School Effectiveness for Whom?* London: Falmer Press.

Hinds, W. (1995). 'The Education Act 1994 – the teacher training provisions', *Education and the Law,* 7(2), 79–90.

HM Inspectorate for Schools (1980) *A View of the Curriculum.* London: HMSO.

HM Inspectorate for Schools (1983) *Teaching in Schools: The Content of Initial Training.* London: Department of Education and Science.

HM Inspectorate for Schools (1988) *Education Observed 7: Initial Teacher Training in Universities in England, Northern Ireland and Wales.* London: Department of Education and Science.

Hoggett, P. (1996) 'New Modes of Control in the Public Service', *Public Administration,* 74, Spring, 9–31.

Hood, C. (1991) 'A public management for all seasons', *Public Administration,* 69, Spring, 3–19.

Hoyle, E. (1990) 'The teacher as professional in the 1990s', *NUT Education Review,* 4(1), 13–16.

Ingvarson, L. (1998) 'Professional development as the pursuit of professional standards: the standards-based professional development system', *Teaching and Teacher Education,* 14(1), 127–40.

Lawn, M. (1997) *Modern Times? Work, Professionalism and Citizenship in Teaching.* London: Falmer Press.

Liell, P. M. *et al.* (1997) *The Law of Education.* London: Butterworths.

Lingard, B. (1999) 'It is and it isn't: vernacular globalisation, educational policy and restructuring', in Burbules, N. and Torres, C. (eds) *Globalisation and Educational Policy.* New York: Routledge.

Macpherson, W. (1999) *The Inquiry into the Matters Arising from the Death of Stephen Lawrence.* London: Stationery Office.

Mahony, P. (1999) 'Teacher education policy and gender', in Salisbury, J. and Riddell, S. (eds) *Gender Policy and Educational Change.* London: Routledge.

Mahony, P. and Hextall, I. (1997) 'Sounds of silence: the social justice agenda of the Teacher Training Agency', *International Studies in Sociology of Education,* 7(2), 137–56.

Mahony, P. and Hextall, I. (1998) 'Social justice and the reconstruction of teaching', *Journal of Education Policy,* 13(4), 545–58.

Marsden, D. and French, S. (1998) *What a Performance: Performance Related Pay in the Public Services.* London: London School of Economics.

Moos, L. *et al.* (1998) 'What teachers, parents, governors and students want from their heads', in Macbeath, J. (ed.) *Effective School Management: Responding to Change.* London: Paul Chapman.

Ozga, J. (1995) 'Deskilling a profession: professionalism, deprofessionalism and the new managerialism', in Busher, H. and Saran, R. (eds) *Managing Teachers as Professionals in Schools.* London: Kogan Page.

Ranson, S. and Stewart, J. (1994) *Management for the Public Domain: Enabling the Learning Society.* London: Macmillan.

Sayer, J. (1993) *The Future Governance of Education.* London: Cassell.

Seddon, T. (1997) 'Education: deprofessionalised? or deregulated, reorganised and reauthorised?', *Australian Journal of Education,* 41(3), 228–47.

Shephard, G. (1996) 'Teachers make a difference'. Opening Address to the Joint OFSTED/TTA/SCAA Conference, London, March.

Smyth, J. and Shacklock, G. (1998) *Remaking Teaching: Ideology, Policy and Practice.* London: Routledge.

Stronach, I. and Morris, B. (1994) 'Polemical notes on educational evaluation in the age of policy hysteria', *Evaluation and Research in Education,* 8(4), 5–19.

Sutherland, Sir S. (1997) *Teacher Education and Training: A Study.* London: The National Committee of Inquiry into Higher Education.

Teacher Training Agency (1996) *A Strategic Plan for Teacher Supply and Recruitment: A Discussion Document.* London: TTA.

Teacher Training Agency (1997) *Annual Review 1997.* London: TTA.

Teacher Training Agency (1998) *Standards for the Award of Qualified Teacher Status.* London: TTA.

Tomlinson, J. (1995) 'Professional development and control: the role of General Teaching Councils', *Journal of Education for Teaching*, 24(1), 59–68.

United Kingdom Central Council for Nursing, Midwifery and Health Visiting (1998) *UKCC Handbook: Protecting the Public through Professional Standards*. London: UKCC.

Note

1. Substantial parts of this chapter are based on two ESRC projects undertaken by Pat Mahony and Ian Hextall. The first, *The Policy Context and Impact of the Teacher Training Agency,* ran from September 1995 until November 1996, and the second, *The Impact on Teaching of the National Professional Standards*, began in December 1997 and is due to be completed in March 2000. The interview extracts on pp.154–5 is taken from the former project.

Chapter 10

The Role of Local Education Authorities

Ron Letch

Introduction

As late as the mid-1980s, the educational system of England and Wales was described in a government publication as 'a national system locally administered' (DES/Welsh Office, 1985, p.1). While central government had overall responsibility, local education authorities (LEAs) enjoyed a large measure of control over the schools in their areas, managing their finances, determining spending priorities, devising local curriculum policies, appointing school staff and inspecting schools. Although the 1944 Education Act had put LEAs under the 'control and direction' of the Minister of Education, no minister before the 1980s chose to exercise such powers. Indeed, writing at the end of the 1970s, a leading writer in this field was able to say that 'there would be a first-class political crisis if this happened', adding that consultation and negotiation were the means that governments were both expected to employ, and did employ, in their dealings with LEAs (Dent, 1979).

Now, of course, all this has changed. During the 1970s, major questions about the effectiveness of education began to be publicly debated. The Black Papers on 'progressive' schooling, Prime Minister Callaghan's Ruskin speech on standards of schooling, and the William Tyndale School affair on the educational philosophy of a London primary school, all received wide publicity and debate, leading to changes in the educational scene and the way the system was administered (Riley, 1998). LEAs, whose powers were severely curtailed by the Conservatives, have now under New Labour been given a new lease of life, but they are, as it were, on probation and have been issued with a challenge: either they ensure that standards in their schools improve, or their powers will be taken over by other agencies (Riley *et al.*, 1999).

Previous policy

Under the Conservatives, changes in the role of LEAs were gradual but became focused in the Education Reform Act 1988 introduced by Kenneth Baker. This legislation brought into being self-regulated, centrally financed grant-maintained (GM) schools that had opted out of local control, while LEA schools were given powers of 'local management'. Both these measures greatly enhanced the independence, autonomy and accountability of schools. The same Act brought in the National Curriculum and open enrolment, virtually abolishing the powers of LEAs to influence what was taught in schools and to regulate school intakes. The corollary to these developments was the erosion of the powers and responsibilities of local authorities.

This marginalising of the local authority continued under the Conservative Government with speeches by Cabinet ministers suggesting that time was running out for LEAs. In 1991 Kenneth Clarke, at that time Secretary of State for Education, announced to the Conservative Local Government conference: 'I do not believe the day-to-day management of schools should be carried out by local education authorities'. At the same conference, Michael Heseltine, Secretary of State for the Environment, argued that if standards were to be improved education should be transferred from local authorities to central government.

A further blow came in the 1992 Education (Schools) Act, which removed from local authorities the power to inspect schools, and took away a significant part of the Rate Support Grant that paid for inspection and advisory services. The same Act created a new national inspection service, the Office for Standards in Education (OFSTED). Other moves shifted the fulcrum of power away from LEAs, as when responsibility for further education was transferred to the Further Education Funding Council in 1993–94 and the careers service was given to the Department for Education and Employment (DfEE) in 1994–95.

Despite the critical view of LEAs taken by the Conservative Government, there was a dilemma to be faced. Many of the reforms that had been introduced needed support and co-ordination at a local level. Gillian Sheppard, the last Conservative Education Secretary, introduced a White Paper that attempted to address this (DfEE, 1996). In this, the independence of schools was strongly reaffirmed, as was the responsibility of schools to generate their own improvement. However, the need for local authorities to provide advice, support services and sound databases to assist schools in setting their own improvement targets was also recognised, as was the role of LEAs as co-ordinators of local networks of schools, businesses and other local agencies. By encouraging a move towards networks, the Government believed it could bring about greater integration and coherence, thus redressing the emphasis on the independence of schools that some feared could lead to unhelpful isolation.

Present policy

In 1997 a new Labour Government came sweeping into power with a top priority of 'education, education, education'. It quickly set out its stall in a White Paper *Excellence in Schools* (1997), which described the LEA's role as essentially in terms of driving up standards:

> The LEA's task is to challenge schools to raise standards continuously and apply pressure where they do not. The role is not one of control. Those days are gone. An effective LEA will challenge schools to improve themselves, being ready to intervene where there are problems, but not interfere with schools that are doing well. (p.27)

Legislation followed with the School Standards and Framework Act in 1998, paving the way for a number of regulations and directives that the Government felt necessary to achieve its overriding intention to improve standards in schools.

The future of the LEA appears to be more secure under the new Labour administration, but any new security comes at a price. An article in the *Times Educational Supplement* on 13 March 1998 was sub-titled 'Local Authorities to be sidelined by new legislation'. In it, Don Foster, the Liberal Democratic education spokesman, was quoted as saying: 'The LEAs had been given to believe they would have a significant role, but when you look at the constraints it is, frankly, difficult to see how they will be able to fulfil it'. Stephen Byers, School Standards Minister, was also reported for his challenging statement that authorities did not have any God given right to run education.

The Government's demands on education authorities have come thick and fast. LEAs have been required to respond to a wide range of initiatives, often within a very short timescale. These include:

- Education Development Plans
- School Organisation Plans
- Asset Management Plans
- Best Value
- Fair Funding
- Education Action Zones
- Lifelong Learning Partnerships
- Admissions Forums
- Code of Practice: LEA–School Relations
- Excellence in Cities
- Children 'Looked After' by the LEA
- Social Inclusion and Behaviour Support
- LEA Inspections
- Bridging the Gap – post-16.

The work of compiling responses to these initiatives, together with the requirement to consult partners, has brought considerable pressure on LEA staff.

The Audit Commission has also played its part in reviewing the role of LEAs and speculating on their future. In January 1998, it published a discussion document *Changing Partners* in which advice was offered on ways LEAs could serve local education in the future. Writing in the *TES* shortly after the publication of the report, Greg Wilkinson, associate director at the Audit Commission, said:

> The stakes have never been higher. The Government has set demanding targets and has staked its credibility on their achievement. It will not look kindly on what it perceives as local authority failure. Therefore, authorities are well advised to treat the rumours of recent months as a wake-up call. (*TES*, 6 February 1998, p.9)

A further briefing paper *Held in Trust* was published in February 1999. Drawing upon the outcomes of LEA inspections and findings from research, the Audit Commission confirmed what it believed to be the new role of LEAs in the light of recent legislation:

- to provide leadership and direction for the local education service;
- to ensure that all children have access to education;
- to promote school improvement and high standards of education;
- to secure support services that schools need such as building maintenance, finance and personnel;
- to offer lifelong learning opportunities such as adult education.

The paper went on to offer 15 recommendations for LEAs to consider in terms of policy and direction, resource management and performance review.

Others who had a vested interest in the new Labour Government's reforming programme were also ready to add their voices to the debate on the future role of LEAs. In March 1998, David Hart, General Secretary of the NAHT, launched a swingeing attack on local education authorities. He insisted that many heads had little confidence in LEAs, which he said were guilty of 'a naked bid for power' in trying to regain control of pay bargaining and failing to consult heads over targets or action zone bids (*TES*, 20 March 1998). However, in a speech to the summer conference of the Society of Education Officers that same year, Michael Bichard, Permanent Secretary at the DfEE, concluded by saying:

> Now is the time for us to focus on what really matters. What really matters is raising standards, and if we are going to raise standards then we need confident, assertive, vigorous local authorities and I wish them well in the task. (Quoted in *Education Journal*, August 1998, p.6)

The means by which LEAs were to carry out the task of raising standards were contained in the plethora of Government initiatives listed earlier.

Education Development Plans

From April 1999, each LEA has been required to have in place an Education Development Plan (EDP), approved by the Secretary of State under the School Standards and Framework Act 1998. The plan covers a three-year period, subject to annual review, and is seen by the Government as the key mechanism for LEAs to meet their statutory duty to promote high standards in schools. LEAs were given clear guidance on what these plans must contain (DfEE, 1998a). Great emphasis was also placed on consultation with the local education community and, more specifically, on consultation and negotiation with schools on the pupil performance targets to be incorporated in the EDP. This requirement gave rise to some difficulties, as in many cases schools felt that the targets expected by the LEA were too high in relation to current performance. However, LEAs were confronted by the demands of the DfEE's Standards and Effectiveness Unit that the overall targets of the LEA should be high enough to allow the national targets to be realised by 2002.

Each EDP must contain a statement of proposals on setting targets, explaining how these are set, monitored and agreed with schools. It must also outline the Authority's school improvement programme, indicating the priorities for improvement to be addressed in relation to three key areas – pupils' standards of achievement, quality of teaching and quality of leadership. Additionally the EDP must contain an annexe with mandatory information based on an analysis of the needs on which targets and priorities are based. EDPs are a major source of evidence when LEAs are inspected by OFSTED and the Audit Commission.

Best Value

The Department for the Environment, Transport and the Regions document *Modernising Local Government: Improving Services through Best Value* (DETR, 1998) is intended for all departments in local councils, but it has significant implications for education, particularly when taken alongside EDPs and LEA inspections. The key themes of Best Value all stress public accountability:

- public consultation;
- service review;
- performance monitoring and measuring;
- strategic procurement of services.

LEAs are required to review their services (the majority of which are aimed at supporting schools), to assess their effectiveness, their value for money, and whether the authority is the best agency to provide them. How LEAs gather the evidence on which they base their judgements is a challenge they have to face. Schools are one obvious source of information on the value and effectiveness of services, but gathering this information requires well-organised systems of consultation and evaluation based on accurate and transparent information. It also requires sound comparative data so that services can be benchmarked against services provided by other authorities or agencies.

Fair Funding

In May 1998 the Government brought out its proposals for reforming the school funding system, *Fair Funding: Improving Delegation to Schools* (DfEE, 1998b), adding a further dimension to relations between LEAs and schools. The principles underlying the proposals were those included in other initiatives:

- *raising standards*;
- *self-management* – developing the concept of the semi-autonomous school;
- *accountability* – funding aligned with responsibilities;
- *transparency* – funding to be clear and comprehensive;
- *opportunity* – not to impose responsibilities schools cannot cope with;
- *equity* – equal treatment for foundation, community and voluntary schools, the three new categories;
- *value for money*.

The main proposals were to regulate the balance between central and delegated funding and the methods of distributing delegated funding. The new system, to be known as Devolved Funding, replaced the previous categories of Potential, General and Aggregated school budgets with two new ones – Local Schools Budgets (LSB) and Individual School Budgets (ISB). The LSB is the LEA's total revenue less non-school expenditure on adult/community education and lifelong learning, student awards, youth and under-fives. The ISB is what is left to delegate after the LEA central budget is removed.

The LEA's central budget is strongly linked to EDPs and Best Value. It covers four main areas:

- *strategic management* – running the Education Department;
- *access* – provision of school places, buildings, attendance;
- *support for school improvement* – preparing EDPs, monitoring and challenging schools through inspection and advisory services, implementing EDP programmes;
- *special educational needs (SEN)* – the Educational Psychology Service, statementing pupils, education otherwise than at school, support for pupils with SEN, preparation of behaviour support plans and pupil referral units.

Schools are now delegated 100 per cent funding for all services other than those listed above. This was intended to reinforce the concept of the self-managing school and the need for local authorities to ensure that their services were efficient and competitively priced so that schools would wish to buy them back. Some safeguards are built in to avoid schools having levels of delegation forced upon them that they do not want. In particular, the system of 'significant majority', prevents a minority of schools blocking the future of some services by voting not to take them up and hence make them financially unviable, disadvantaging the wishes of the majority of schools.

Responses to the original proposals were mixed, although The Education Network, Society of Education Officers and the Association of Chief Education Officers all gave them a cautious welcome. The National Association of Schoolmasters Union of Women Teachers took one of the strongest stances against the proposals (NASUWT, 1998). A number of GM schools also objected to some aspects, particularly the principle of equity, which meant a possible reduction in their budgets even though this would be matched by a reduction in their expenditure on services relocated in the LEA's central budget.

Education Action Zones

The Education Action Zone (EAZ) initiative was introduced in the Schools Standards and Framework Act 1998. In its guidance for applicants, the DfEE (1998c) described EAZs as test-beds for innovation that will drive up educational standards. Reaction to this initiative was very mixed. On the one hand, some saw EAZs as a Trojan horse, which would undermine the role of the LEA and local democracy. This was because each EAZ would have its own independent Education Action Forum and, where possible, private sector involvement. Each EAZ was to be made up of clusters of primary, secondary and special schools working in partnership not only with the LEA but also local parents, businesses and Training and Enterprise Councils. The partnership formed would involve a central role for business, and might also seek wider links with health or employment zones and with projects funded by the Single Regeneration Budget. Unlike its critics, however, the DfEE saw all this as enhancing the work of LEAs (DfEE, 1999a).

On the other hand, a number of groups welcomed the initiative with its funding of £750,000 per zone per year plus a further £250,000 in cash or kind from business. Zones also had priority access to a number of other DfEE initiatives such as specialist schools and the option of adapting the National Curriculum. They were also able to offer flexible contracts to attract 'outstanding educational leaders'. In the first round, these opportunities encouraged some 60 groups to apply for Action Zone status; 47 were taken forward for further consideration and 25 received ministerial approval in June 1998. A second tranche of EAZs was launched in 1999.

It is, perhaps, too soon to judge the success of these projects or their impact upon the role of LEAs. Critics still have their concerns but it will be some time before convincing evidence is available on which to judge the DfEE claim that EAZs will drive up educational standards. However, The Education Network published a review of the first wave of applications (*TEN*, October 1998). One of the observations made was that there seemed to be some confusion as to whether the initiative is mainly about innovation, tackling deprivation and social exclusion, or raising achievement. The reviewers also questioned how far applicants had gone in being innovative, particularly in relation to changes in the National Curriculum or in teachers' terms and conditions of service. It was acknowledged, however, that this reluctance to innovate might have been due to the tight timescale for submitting applications.

Code of Practice: LEA–School Relations

With so much government comment on partnerships, it is not surprising that New Labour felt bound to give some thought to the relationships that should govern LEAs and schools – particularly relevant in the case of GM schools returning to LEAs. The GM sector was very anxious to influence the final version of the Code of Practice since it wished to guard against losing the considerable independence its schools had enjoyed in their present status. Like all interest groups, it lobbied fiercely, and with some success. At the GM headteachers' conference in March 1998, Adrian Pritchard, managing director of the Grant-Maintained Schools Conference, told headteachers that Labour had done councils few favours:

> The role of the LEA envisaged by Government isn't as all-inclusive and all-intrusive as we might have feared. And where LEAs have become prematurely aggressive they have been knocked back. I have a very real sense that ministers don't have much confidence in LEAs as the vehicle for racheting up performance. (Quoted in *TES*, 20 March 1998, p.8)

Geraldine Hackett, reporting in the *TES* under the headline 'Code sets out Council's reach', wrote:

> According to Mr Byers [School Standards Minister], a delicate balancing act had to be performed in order that local authorities would have the powers...to confront the complacent and challenge the coasting. (*TES*, 27 March 1998, p.5)

She noted that early drafts of the Code had talked in terms of schools 'looking for safeguards against heavy-handed local authority powers of intervention and against interference in matters which are properly the school's own business'. She also drew attention to the concerns of chief education officers that earlier drafts had implied schools needed to be protected from LEAs.

Although the LEAs were concerned at the constraints being laid upon them by the code, one leading commentator was reasonably optimistic in believing that 'the foundation exists...for a significant step forward in establishing a new order – in which co-operation and collaboration replace competition and confrontation. That must be welcome' (Martin Rogers, *TEN Policy Briefing*, March 1998). When the final version of the Code of Practice came into effect in 1999, School Standards Minister Estelle Morris said:

All schools now have more autonomy than ever before. Local education authorities are having to adjust to their new role in raising standards and a new relationship with schools in their area. The Code of Practice on LEA–School Relations explains what LEAs should do to support school improvement – and just as importantly what they should not do. Along with EDPs and the new funding and inspection frameworks, the Code of Practice will define the role of a modern, effective LEA. (DfEE News, 163/99)

The Code sets down seven principles of a constructive relationship between LEAs and schools:

- All LEAs and schools should have raising standards as their overriding aim.
- Schools are responsible for their own performance and must be given maximum discretion to make decisions for themselves.
- LEA intervention should be in inverse proportion to success.
- The relationship between LEAs and schools must be based upon partnership and cooperation.
- Under-performance must not be tolerated: all schools should be successful or improving or both.
- LEAs and schools should aim to get and give maximum value for money in everything they do.
- LEAs and schools should avoid bureaucracy and imposing unnecessary burdens on each other.

The Code also describes how specific LEA powers and duties may appropriately be used, and gives examples of where their use would be inappropriate.

LEA inspections

The Education Act 1997 was the last of its kind passed by the Conservative Government. Among other things, it gave OFSTED the power to inspect LEAs and to invite the Audit Commission to assist in inspections. In practice, the Audit Commission has emerged as a partner in all inspections and may have an increasingly significant role as the requirements of Best Value (see above) begin to be applied. LEAs had already carried out work on external reviews of authorities and had, with the assistance of Eric Bolton, ex-Senior Chief HMI, developed and published a framework (ACEO, 1997) which was subsequently piloted in some authorities. None the less, OFSTED drew up its own framework and inspected 14 LEAs during the first year. As a result of this experience an amended framework was published for all future inspections (OFSTED, 1999). It is anticipated that all LEAs will have been inspected by the end of 2001. Although introduced by the Conservatives, the Labour Government has seized the powers of inspection as a major tool in its crusade to raise standards. Taken with EDPs, Fair Funding, Best Value and the Code of Practice, it provides a strategy of pressure and support to ensure LEAs deliver the goods.

As pointed out in the earlier part of this chapter, there was a price to pay for local authorities being brought back into a leading role in local education. The pressure on LEAs that receive unfavourable inspection reports can be dramatic, and the Secretary of State's powers of intervention are considerable where a report points to an authority's failure to support schools adequately. One of the first authorities to come under the spotlight as 'failing' was the London Borough of Hackney. The OFSTED report in September 1997 was scathing about the council's management structure and 'a failure of political will'. Despite the efforts of a new Director of Education and a 'hit squad' sent in by the DfEE with the agreement of the Authority, a follow-up inspection report published in February 1999 reported that many weaknesses remained. The Secretary of State, David Blunkett, said that he was 'minded' to direct the Education Director to contract out two services, which had been judged as particularly ineffective.

Events in Hackney then became the focus of some hard-hitting exchanges between the Local Government Association (LGA) and the DfEE. The LGA claimed that, according to newspaper leaks, ministers had already decided to contract out Hackney services before the OFSTED report was published. This was based on an earlier dispute with the Chief Executive of the Borough over the original inspection report. *The Local Government Chronicle* (12 March 1999) gave this dispute prime space with the bold headline 'LGA confronts Blunkett over LEA takeover threat'. The article opened with the dramatic sentence 'The LGA is threatening to take the Government to court if it strips Hackney LBC of its education service'. This low point in relations between the LGA and DfEE was further exacerbated by the rejection of a joint LGA/Development Agency bid to be included in the list of agencies licensed to provide services for authorities deemed to be failing. The Government, however, carried on with actions it believed were necessary if its claim that underperformance would not be tolerated were to be more than mere rhetoric, and eventually appointed Nord Anglia to run two key services.

This hard line was confirmed in June 1999 when the inspection report for the London Borough of Islington exposed OFSTED's perceptions of the LEA's weaknesses:

> The LEA is not adequately discharging its duties to support school improvement to secure suitable and effective education. The findings of this inspection...indicate that the LEA's support is inadequate and ineffective in most major areas. (para. 6)

This was followed by a list of 11 functions that were not adequately exercised. The Secretary of State responded to this damning report by announcing that private consultants would be sent in to arrange for most, if not all, the LEA's services to be put out to contract. Liverpool escaped a similar fate when the Government decided not to privatise services but instead to monitor closely progress made during 1999. Decisions about Haringey and Leicester are awaited.

Only a very few of the authorities inspected to date have received such critical reports with consequent action. Many reports have been positive, acknowledging the very effective work carried out by the authorities in supporting their schools. However, the relations between local and national Government remain fragile in some areas. In 1999, the Government published league tables of LEA budgets, castigating 44 authorities it claimed were failing to pass on increases in education funding to schools. Authorities were also accused of spending too much on red tape, and the Secretary of State announced that he intended to set limits on the amounts that authorities can spend on central services. The LGA's response was that the Government's figures were wrong, and they produced their own to prove it (*TES*, 25 June 1999). Attempts have since been made to address this lack of trust that often sours relations between central and local government. Discussions have taken place between the two parties to agree a protocol to govern interventions the Government deems necessary where a local authority service is found to be failing. At the time of writing, agreement has not been reached, but progress has been made (LGA Circular 211/99).

School Asset Management Plans

The new Government carried out a comprehensive spending review soon after taking up office. As a result of this, significant additional capital expenditure was made available in the schools' sector for the duration of this Parliament. In order to ensure that these funds are spent as effectively and efficiently as possible to raise educational standards, LEAs are required to prepare Asset Management Plans (AMPs) (DfEE, 1999c), consulting with schools and diocesan authorities over the assessments they make. In assessing existing school accommodation, AMPs must include information about:

- the *sufficiency of accommodation* – the need to add places because of population growth, remove places, reduce Key Stage 1 classes to no more than 30, and review land and property holdings
- the *condition of buildings* – the need to replace temporary buildings, improve claddings, roofs etc, replace boiler and heating systems, and address health and safety issues
- the *suitability of the accommodation* – the provision of libraries and learning resource areas in primary schools, updating science, technology and ICT facilities in secondary schools, and improving quality of external areas in all school.

The plans must also be arranged in four levels of priority.

It is envisaged that by December 2000, 90 per cent of authorities will have operational AMPs. One of their purposes will be to help the private sector develop partnerships with LEAs – yet another indication of the value the Government places on the involvement of the private sector through Public Private Partnerships.

Admissions Forums

The opportunity for parents to have a choice in the schools their children attend has always been a sensitive issue. After consulting with interested parties, the Secretary of State issued a Code of Practice on School Admissions (DfEE, 1999d), as required under the 1998 Schools Standards and Framework Act. One feature of this code merits particular mention. LEAs, together with other admission authorities, are required to set up Admissions Forums to be vehicles for consultation on issues arising from proposed admission arrangements. Membership must include relevant LEAs, school governors, headteachers, diocesan representatives, representatives from the Early Years Development Partnership, and special interests such as special educational needs and minority ethnic groups, local City Technology Colleges, and local parents. Where it has not been possible to reach local agreement on admissions issues, the Secretary of State appoints independent adjudicators, which have already required some schools to reduce their selective intake.

Behaviour Support Plans

It was the previous Government's Education Act of 1996 that placed a duty on LEAs to prepare a statement setting out their arrangements for the education of children with behavioural difficulties. This legislation came into effect under the present Government in April 1998.

Every Behaviour Support Plan (BSP) must include arrangements for providing advice and resources for schools for promoting good behaviour and discipline and for the education of children with behavioural difficulties (DfEE, Circular 1/88). They must include provision for children educated otherwise than at school and for assisting pupils with behavioural difficulties to find places at suitable schools, as well as making clear how the behaviour plan interacts with local policy for pupils with special educational needs (SEN). Requirements for consultation are detailed and wide-ranging. Those consulted must include: the headteachers and governors of all schools plus the principals of local FE and sixth form colleges and teachers in charge of pupil referral units (PRUs); representatives of local school staff, school-based support staff and their union representatives; representatives of local parents, health authorities, social services, the careers service, the local Training and Enterprise Council, local probation committees, voluntary bodies working with disaffected children and young people, and diocean bodies; the local Chief Constable and local magistrates.

The published plans must be widely distributed, with copies lodged at public libraries and other public places. They must also be available, on request, at a reasonable charge, and all parents of pupils assessed as having behavioural difficulties must be given the full plan, an extract or a summary. BSPs, like the other plans mentioned earlier, are scrutinised during the course of every LEA inspection.

Social inclusion

The inequalities in society, particularly in relation to disaffected young people and others who fail to benefit from educational opportunities, have been concerns that New Labour sees as having to be tackled at a local level. There are many agencies that need to be involved, not least local authorities through their education, social services and housing departments. LEAs are involved through their responsibility for special educational needs as well as the wider role of social inclusion. *Meeting Special Educational Needs – A Programme of Action* (DfEE, 1998d) includes a section devoted to developing a more inclusive education system. LEAs are required to publish information about their policy on inclusion in their EDP.

As explained in Chapter 7, inclusion of pupils with SEN in mainstream schools is a sensitive issue, which generates strong passions on both sides of the argument. Parents, teachers and voluntary agencies with particular concern for children and young people with SEN between them represent a whole range of attitudes, as the Government recognises:

> Promoting inclusion in mainstream schools, where parents want it and appropriate support can be provided, remains a cornerstone of our strategy. But our approach will be practical, not dogmatic and will put the needs of individual children first. We confirm that specialist provision – including special schools – will continue to play a role. (DfEE, 1998d, p.23)

The task of planning and putting into practice an inclusions policy remains one for the LEA. Balancing the wide range of interests involved, as well as providing the appropriate resources and training required, will challenge the most efficient authorities. Many will reflect on the cautious approach adopted by the Government and will proceed with care.

On the wider front, LEAs have a significant part to play in social inclusion. All approaches in providing pupil and parent support need to involve a number of agencies. The Education Welfare Service, educational psychologists, health workers, social services departments, child and adolescent mental health services, the youth service and voluntary agencies each make a distinct contribution. A multi-agency approach is therefore needed to meet the needs of young people who may be at risk, such as those with special educational needs, children in care, minority ethnic children, Travellers, young carers of children from families under stress, pregnant schoolgirls and teenage mothers. There may also be others permanently excluded from school or persistent non-attenders whose needs are best met through the involvement of a number of agencies. Many of the young people in these groups become part of the disaffected who fail to benefit from normal educational opportunities. LEAs have a key role to play in ensuring this network of concerned bodies is appropriately involved in tackling these issues (DfEE, 1999e).

The future

The DfEE *Code of Practice of LEA–School Relations* (1999b) and both the Audit Commission reports (1998 and 1999) all set out a clear role for LEAs to play. There is a downside, however, for alongside these new responsibilities must be seen the Government's aggressive approach to zero tolerance of underperformance and the consequences of failing to deliver. This changing culture is not easy for institutional organisations such as local authorities to face, particularly when the democratic context in which they exist is also changing. (DETR, 1998). There is a view among some in local government that the many new responsibilities laid upon them have not been matched by the powers and resources to do the job. Others point to a number of highly successful LEAs whose inspection reports have been glowing. By the time of the next General Election the picture may be clearer.

Issues for debate

1. Is there really a future for LEAs?

Both the last and present Governments have been ambivalent about the role of LEAs. As we mentioned earlier, Kenneth Clarke and Michael Heseltine appeared to be quite sure that time was running out for local authorities. It was only in 1997, when Gillian Sheppard offered LEAs a role in ensuring that schools were kept up to the mark, that some hope for the future was heralded. Although the new Labour Government has spelled out LEAs' role in raising standards, it has also been extremely demanding in its expectations. It has also been quite prepared for the private sector to take over some of the functions of failing LEAs, as can be seen in the outcomes of inspections of authorities such as Hackney and Islington. Patricia Rowan, a former editor of the *TES*, summed up the situation when she wrote:

> The Prime Minister and his advisers are ambivalent [about the role of local authorities], though by the time he came to power his predecessors had already battered local Government to its knees. The question now is whether Tony Blair will finish the job, or whether education authorities can still win the argument for plurality in general, or for their own survival in particular. The new threat to replace failing authorities with private or charitable companies, or even with more effective LEAs, drove home a message that wasn't just political window-dressing. (*TES*, 22 January 1999, p.23)

The Government has been prepared to 'name and shame' local authorities by publishing league tables of authority spending plans and highlighting bad councils that are holding on to too much resource for central services. The Government has also exposed councils whose EDPs it believed to be inadequate in showing that systems were in place to raise school standards. The Audit Commission, however, offers another side to the coin. Its latest publication *Held in Trust: The LEA of the Future* (1999) explores the recent history of local authorities and offers the optimistic view that there is a future for them in meeting the demands of the Government's recent legislation. But, they argue, cultural changes will be needed if they are to measure up to the challenge:

> LEAs face a demanding and rapidly changing environment. The challenges that they have been set present both an opportunity to grasp and a potential threat to their existence. Expectations of them are clearer than ever before, and LEAs need to devote considerable energy and thought to their key processes of policy and direction, resource management and performance review if they are to meet the challenge. (para. 104)

For discussion
Do you see a future for your LEA? Is it up to the challenge, and does it have the resources to do the job?

2. Is partnership rhetoric or reality?

The present Government has made much of the concept of partnership. The *Code of Practice – LEA–School Relations* takes partnership and co-operation as one of its principles of constructive relationships. It says that

> a constructive partnership between LEAs and schools will never be built solely on the assertion of legal rights and powers. It must be based on mutual recognition of the functions and contribution of each party. ... The principle of partnership is not limited to relations between LEAs and schools. It also applies to schools working with other schools, irrespective of present or past legal categories; and to LEAs working with local governor associations, dioceses, and many others as part of their local leadership and networking function. (DfEE, 1999c, para. 39d)

Such aspirations are very commendable but do face some difficulties in the light of some of the harsh criticisms cited earlier in this chapter. Partnership may seem rather a vain hope when one considers David Hart's accusation of local authorities' 'naked bid for power' and failing to consult heads over targets and action zones. There would appear to be a need to build confidence and trust between some LEAs and schools.

Successful partnership must rely heavily upon good communication and consultation procedures, the success of which are often influenced by the degree of trust between the partners. The Government has made much of the need for local authorities to consult with its partners on almost all aspects of its work, as, for instance, in the sophisticated mechanisms required for consultation on EDPs and behaviour plans. However, much tension has been created in some authorities when the rules of consultation have not been well understood, as over schools setting targets for improvement. Local authorities had to show that their targets were acceptably high to satisfy the requirements of their EDPs, which in turn had to be approved by the DfEE. Since school, EDP and DfEE targets are inextricably related, there have been some problems where schools and LEAs have not been able to agree on appropriate levels for school targets. These difficulties have been noted in a number of inspection reports and have led to schools dismissing the consultation exercise as a farce.

However, other developments such as Admissions Forums and School Organisation Committees seem to have produced much more positive results and have opened up a level of debate that has been widely welcomed. Early Years Development and Childcare Partnerships seem to have been equally successful, despite of, or because of, the wide range of representatives, and because their consultations usually lead to positive outcomes. In Chapter 11, Peter Jackson presents other views on this controversial area.

For discussion
What has been your experience of partnership and consultation in your LEA? What factors have contributed to their success or failure?

3. Can LEAs carry out their responsibility to raise standards while schools function to a large extent as autonomous and independent organisations?

We have seen how considerable changes have taken place in the relative roles of LEAs and schools during the last ten years. One of the ways that at one time LEAs could influence and direct the work of schools was through their inspection and advisory services. *At their best*, these services played a key role in the work of school improvement, although in some authorities they were less involved than in others. As we saw earlier, the 1992 Act removed the right of local authorities to inspect schools and set up OFSTED as a national inspection service. Many authorities chose to support advisory staff in training to become OFSTED inspectors. In so doing they hoped to earn income to pay for the posts they had lost and thus to retain as many such staff as possible. Many authorities also went into trading partnerships with schools so that services could be bought and sold, allowing advisory services to be kept viable. The outcome of these changes was variable. In many cases schools complained that when they wanted an adviser he or she was always out on OFSTED inspections. On the other hand, advisory teams claimed that OFSTED work gave them greater credibility with schools.

Many schools that had 'opted out' to become GM severed most or all of their contact with the local authority, sometimes through choice and sometimes because the local authority was unwilling to have links with schools that had chosen to leave the family. Whatever the reasons, many GM schools valued their new-found autonomy and the distant, 'light touch relations' with the central Funding Agency for Schools. Many GM schools have resented having to return to the LEA fold, albeit with 'foundation' status, enabling them to own their property and employ their own staff. For the majority of schools that remained with their LEA, Local Management of Schools had increased their independence by delegating to their control a large proportion of the education budget. The recent Fair Funding initiative, described earlier in this chapter, has taken this measure even further.

Thus we now have schools with a large measure of independence and autonomy, although paradoxically there is still tight control from central government through the National Curriculum, national testing, league tables and OFSTED inspections, while the Secretary of State has more central powers than any of his predecessors. The Government tends to see LEAs as its agent in administering the national agenda and achieving national targets, and it has placed considerable responsibilities on local authorities to promote high standards of education. At the same time, it is expected to pursue its role in partnership with schools and other agencies – not easy when in many authorities there needs to be significant culture changes and a better climate of trust with schools, particularly those which formerly held GM status and are now back as partners in the LEA.

For discussion
What experience do you have of school/LEA relationships in your area? How do you build trust in the present climate?

4. Does the LEA have a unique role as advocate?

There are always cases of individuals and groups in our communities who are disadvantaged or oppressed. Such persons may not always be the easiest to help as they might not conform to the standards and expectations of the communities in which they live. They may often find themselves in situations in which they need support, particularly when dealing with systems that appear bureaucratic. The LEA is often the body which can best serve such individuals and groups. The advocacy role of LEAs is often one of the most challenging, but the question needs to be asked 'If the LEA does not act as advocate, who else will?'

The Audit Commission picked up this theme in *Changing Partners* (1998), in which it said that one of the roles of the LEA is

> ensuring equity and an inclusive system of education in local schools and other institutions. Such a system will be based not merely on compliance with the statutory requirements around race, sex and disability discrimination. It will also be based on the interests of the difficult, the demanding (including children of exceptionally high ability) and the socially disadvantaged, and to prevent these sections of the community from being marginalized. (p.13)

This role of the LEA does not receive a great deal of attention in government publications other than in *Social Inclusion* (DfEE, 1999d). The role of advocate is not an easy one when the LEA is expected both to uphold and support schools and also to take seriously the case of the 'difficult parent' who harbours a grudge against the school. It is easy for a school's patience to run out with parents who, fairly or unfairly, have earned a reputation for being particularly awkward, not least when they refuse to recognise their child's unacceptable behaviour or condone the child's absence from school. Sometimes there is a role for an LEA officer to act as an intermediary to help bring parents and school together to work towards a resolution, particularly where the parents are not very effective at presenting their case. An LEA representative might also crucially act as an advocate on those occasions when a headteacher comes into such conflict with the chair of the governing body that the school cannot be run effectively. For such a role to be effective, it demands very mature relations between the LEA and its schools and other parties who may become involved in disputes.

For discussion

How important is the role of advocate for an LEA? What experience do you have of LEAs acting in this manner? Is it possible for an LEA to carry out this role successfully in the present climate where it may be brought into dispute with schools?

Further reading

Riley, K. A. (1998) *Whose School is it Anyway?* London: Falmer Press.

References

Association of Chief Education Officers (1997) *LEA Framework for External Reviewers*. ACEO.[1]
Audit Commission (1998) *Changing Partners*. London: Audit Commission.
Audit Commission (1999) *Held in Trust: The LEA of the Future*. London: Audit Commission.
Dent, H. C. (1979) *Education in England and Wales*. Sevenoaks: Hodder & Stoughton.
Department for Education and Employment (1996) *Self-Government for Schools*. London: Stationery Office.
Department for Education and Employment (1997) *Excellence in Schools*. London: Stationery Office.
Department for Education and Employment (1998a) *Education Development Plans*. London: DfEE.
Department for Education and Employment (1998b) *Fair Funding: Improving Delegation to Schools*. London: DfEE.
Department for Education and Employment (1998c) *Education Action Zones – Guidance for Applicants*. London: DfEE.
Department for Education and Employment (1998d) *Meeting Special Educational Needs: A Programme for Action*. London: Stationery Office.
Department for Education and Employment (1999a) *Education Action Zones*. London: DfEE.
Department for Education and Employment (1999b) *Code of Practice: LEA–School Relations*. London: Stationery Office.
Department for Education and Employment (1999c) *Guidance on Asset Management Plans*. London: DfEE.
Department of Education and Employment (1999d) *Code of Practice: Schools Admissions*. London: Stationery Office.
Department for Education and Employment (1999e) *Social Inclusion: Pupil Support*. London: Stationery Office.

Department of Education and Science/Welsh Office (1985) *The Educational System of England and Wales*. London: HMSO.

Department of the Environment, Transport and the Regions (1998) *Modernising Local Government: Improving Services through Best Value*. London: Stationery Office.

National Association of Schoolmasters Union of Women Teachers (1998) *Fair Funding: Improving Delegation to Schools – Response of the NASUWT*. London: NASUWT.

Office for Standards in Education (1999) *LEA Support for School Improvement*. London: OFSTED.

Riley, K. A. (1998) *Whose School is it Anyway?* London: Falmer Press.

Riley, K. A. *et al.* (2000) 'Caught between: the changing role and effectiveness of the Local Education Authority', in Riley, K. A. and Lewis, K. S. (eds) *Leadership on a Wider Scale: New Actors, New Roles*. London: Falmer Press.

Note

1. The Association of Chief Education Officers has no offices or permanent address or permanent secretary; the post rotates. The present secretary (November 1999) is at the Education Department in County Hall, Truro.

Chapter 11

Choice, Diversity and Partnerships

Peter Jackson

Previous policy

In its last twelve months of office, the Conservative Government continued its policy of strengthening central control while granting more freedoms to schools, effectively limiting the power of local government still further and piloting OFSTED inspections of LEAs. It introduced education vouchers for places at registered nurseries, whether maintained or not, and enlarged the assisted places scheme to include prep schools. It enabled schools to be more selective without having to gain central approval, and extended the financial powers of grant-maintained schools.

These measures of the 1996 and 1997 Education Acts blurred distinctions between maintained and independent schools. Public money supported the independent sector and the grant-maintained budget increased from £8.5 million in 1990–91 to £15 million in 1997–98. Maintained schools gained more discretion over their intake, enabling them to develop more autonomously than in the past, particularly towards specialism. Private schools queued for public funding.

Present policy

The Government's reform programme will touch every corner of the education world...every institution, every élitist practice and every shibboleth. I certainly hope so. And for this programme to succeed there needs to be coherence. Not simply an intellectual coherence, as policy is formulated, although that is welcome and necessary. But also coherence in its local implementation. This is what persuades me that we should set aside any lingering debate about whether or not LEAs have a role, and revert to the confident, assertive and vigorous work required to make the changes succeed on the ground. (Bichard, 1998, p.7)

Thus, the Permanent Secretary at the Department for Education and Employment welcomed the Labour programme. Alongside the new role for the LEA, the Government announced the abolition of the nursery voucher system, grant-maintained schools, the Funding Agency for Schools, the assisted places scheme and extended powers of selection. The aim, however, remained the same: raising standards. The command structure was similar: OFSTED, the Qualifications and Curriculum Authority, the Teacher Training Agency, the new Standards and Effectiveness Unit. The difference was the substitution of partnership for competition. In place of competing schools, there was now an infrastructure of committees, institutions and agencies managed by LEAs. Co-operation was sought within a system designed for competitiveness. Was this the third way?

Central government and schools

That New Labour's policy results in *more* diversity appears counter-intuitive. Yet, although grant-maintained schools, nursery vouchers and the assisted places scheme have been abolished, we now have greater freedom for schools in Education Action Zones, more specialist comprehensive schools, and the Excellence in Cities package. Closely associated with these measures are partnership initiatives.

Education Action Zones
Education Action Zones are promising. They are free districts where partnerships may cast off uniformity. Located in areas of rural or urban need, EAZ partnerships comprise clusters of schools – usually not more than 20 – working with LEAs, businesses, agencies and charities. They can use support initiatives, such as:

- specialist and beacon schools;
- early excellence centres;
- advanced teaching skills schemes;
- literacy summer schools;
- family literacy schemes;
- out-of-school hours learning activities;
- work-related learning;
- information and communications technology.

Action Zone partnerships each have a forum and a director. They can employ staff to work across several schools. They can use space and equipment flexibly. Crèches, for example, can be established for employees' children. They can deploy assistants to relieve teachers of administrative burdens and hire other specialists such as youth workers. They get up to £0.5m annually and are expected to generate more in money or expertise. Governing bodies may delegate some powers, including finance, to them.

The EAZ realises many of the thoughts in David Hargreaves' *Mosaic of*

Learning (1994). This influential pamphlet criticised the uniformity, bureaucracy and institutionalisation of schools, arguing that flexible, relevant and not necessarily permanent approaches to educating youngsters should challenge the existing stereotype. Action Zones, with their minimum, though renewable lives of three years, are the Government's creative response. They operate in areas of disadvantage in the first instance but have the potential to provide diversity and dynamism. The suggested time-span of three years is prudent however. Any innovations designed to combat established institutionalised thinking have to beware of waning enthusiasm and mental arthritis. Companies like Arthur Andersen and HSBC, already working with EAZs in Newham and Sheffield respectively, are reassured by time limits.

Excellence in Cities, Beacon schools and specialist schools

Closely associated with Education Action Zones is the *Excellence in Cities* strategy, announced in March 1999. This aims at improving the educational systems of selected cities by maximising the physical and human resources of the areas. It should help to counter the finding of OFSTED in 1993 that the policy whereby funds followed pupils resulted in financially poorer schools receiving less money, which widened educational opportunities gaps still further.

The EiC strategies are planned deliberately to transcend LEA boundaries, forcing authorities to co-operate. As with Action Zone partnerships, poor and depressed areas are targeted, especially large city estates. Ranges of expertise focus on specific problems, for example, school disaffection and transfer from primary to secondary schools. A strong feature of the strategy is supporting high-ability students, giving them access to inspired teaching and specialist facilities at colleges and learning centres. It comprises six investments (DfEE, 1999):

- advanced technology for City Learning Centres;
- additional specialist and beacon schools;
- new small EAZs;
- special programmes for the gifted and talented in all secondary schools;
- new learning support units to support disruptive pupils; and
- learning mentors for every pupil whose learning is being held back by non-school circumstances.

Included in the EiC strategy is the use of Beacons – schools of outstanding excellence prepared to share their methods with other schools and help to promote basic literacy and numeracy among adults. Five hundred Beacon schools are planned by September 2000, with at least a quarter within targeted city areas. Beacons outside depressed areas link with specified inner city schools. The idea is to share their know-how by such activities as:

- running seminars for teachers and governors from other schools; offering mentoring and consultancy; work-shadowing; providing in-service training;

- using the Internet to spread good practice;
- developing partnerships with Initial Teacher Training institutions, local schools and LEAs; releasing teachers to other establishments; supporting newly qualified teachers;
- preparing curriculum planning materials; video documentation.

Beacon schools, projected to rise to 2,000 by the year 2002, receive extra funding of about £30,000 in exchange for their partnership work. The concept is of the same family as the advanced teacher scheme and Early Excellence Centres. The burgeoning specialist school movement is particularly important for the able students who will stay as members of their own schools but use the facilities of specialist schools as appropriate.

Coming from the new Standards and Effectiveness Unit, the EiC strategy aims at school improvement rather than at diversification. Nevertheless, the net effect of a general improvement of poorer schools and greater opportunities for able students to develop individual pathways is to increase the pool of desirable schools, thereby enlarging parental choice.

Local government and admissions policies

During the Conservative years, some LEAs resisted the policy for schools to 'opt out' of their control and become grant-maintained (GM); others, such as the London Borough of Wandsworth, encouraged the decision. All returning GM schools, however (450 primaries, 650 secondaries), now have to fit in with the admissions policies of the LEAs.

Under the Conservatives, if comprehensive schools wanted to select more than 15 per cent of their pupils by academic ability, they had to gain Government permission. In contrast, Labour (under the Schools Standards and Framework Act 1998) stopped comprehensive schools from *introducing* selection altogether, and, where parents or other schools objected to existing selection, instructed adjudicators to end the practice where it currently existed. Indeed, if ten or more local parents object, adjudicators can force a school to abandon all partial selection. At the time of writing, appeals are under consideration in a number of authorities, and some decisions to restrict selection have been made. But even the new dispensation cannot demonise selection completely. Comprehensive schools need students in all ability bands.

There are clear implications for school choice here. Under the Conservatives, pupils most disadvantaged by high partial selection on academic grounds were low achievers who lived near popular schools. They had to travel to unpopular schools. Under Labour, high achievers living near unpopular schools will find themselves directed to fill up the higher streams. Labour's 'selection' scheme operates by offering 'able' students extra and specialised tuition at other schools while keeping them, nominally at least, on roll locally. As for schools, taking away their selective powers deprives them of an important means of shaping their own destinies.

The admissions policy will be regularised, at least across LEAs. What features should it have? Anne West and Hazel Pennell (1998), recently proposed a checklist. In their view, the admissions policy should:

- be transparent to all who use them;
- be equitable, so that pupils are not 'selected out' on social grounds;
- be predictable so that parents can assess their chances of success;
- be 'monitorable' for purposes of accountability;
- take account of the effect on neighbouring schools;
- enable pupils to attend nearby schools, if desired, for various specified reasons;
- enable pupils to attend the same school as siblings, if desired.

However, they warn that the admissions process must start from certain pre-requisites:

- there must be adequate information about choice – information centres and brochures are not currently standard practice;
- LEAs, not schools, should manage it;
- records should be retained for scrutiny and appeal, particularly where there is over-subscription;
- clearing-houses in large cities should end the practice of parents holding multiple offers;
- the procedure should be standardised across the country;
- application forms should seek information relating only to the admission criteria;
- academic selection records that can be scrutinised should be available;
- pre-admission interviews should be prohibited (since they cannot be scrutinised);
- aptitude tests should be eliminated (because aptitude in particular subjects is like academic ability).

A desire for fairness can, however, topple over into an ethical bureaucracy that effectively hands interpretative functions over to LEA officials. Critics of local authorities' records in managing education point to the slippage whereby co-ordinating functions of LEAs transmute into administrative, thence to managerial and finally to controlling functions over schools. The last two items of the list of pre-requisites may be justified but not self-evidently so. If, as the Secretary of State declared in summer 1999, the country will have one in four of its secondary schools designated 'specialist' by 2003, some operational sense will have to be given to 'aptitude'. To lump it in with 'ability within a subject' and thereby outlaw it as a selection criterion for a quarter of all secondary schools appears questionable.

Home–school partnerships

Home–school partnerships (DfEE, 1998), embodied in signed compacts, became compulsory from September 1999. They include:

- the curriculum and standards the school promises to deliver;
- the ethos it strives for;
- the attendance and behaviour it requires;
- the sanctions it has;
- the homework policy it operates;
- the parental involvement it expects;
- the meaning of the agreement.

The guidelines appear firm in their constraints on schools. For example, schools must not require financial contributions, nor, where there is religious disagreement, insist on school uniform regulations. The treatment of school and home, however, is not even-handed. The guidelines favour schools and reflect a 'Government-knows-best' point of view.

Of course, some parental practices worry educators, for example sending daughters abroad for weeks during term-time or refusing to send them to mixed secondary schools. The second of these is theoretically resolvable in the local education partnerships where the balance between mixed and single-sex secondary schools can be addressed. The first is less easy to deal with. Both, however, are potentially adversarial issues in which it seems proper for the Agreement to spell out the school point of view.

The treatment of issues concerning the achievement and behaviour of pupils and students is less satisfactory. Of course, parents contribute in some way to both – it would be impossible to demonstrate that they do not; but to declare them complicit is to blur accountability too much. School is the professional institution for which the parents pay. Pupils and students are – whatever their background – the youngsters the school is charged to educate. The degree of success or failure of the school is what should be held to account. The Agreement has the effect of making the school's responsibility for both the behaviour and achievement of youngsters rather less visible than it should be.

When the Agreement is considered alongside the battery of initiatives in such documents as Sure Start and Excellence in Cities, there is a discernible pattern of advice mingled with warnings. Parents should support the school behaviour and homework policies. There is 'help' in the shape of 'family' literacy remedial schemes for parents and children. For the parent on the dilapidated housing estate – so often the focus of this Government's concern – both the language and the sentiment it expresses seem at once condescending and admonishing. There are echoes of the 1970s' language of deprivation, with its emphasis on needs and parental inadequacy. Why is the balance tilted like this? What about absentee, uncaring, under-prepared or domineering teachers, dismal social environments, unyielding timetables, bullying and racism?

Vincent and Tomlinson (1997) have noted that the DfEE advice on home–school relationships includes 'an inherent social class bias, as most clauses are easier to fulfil if a family has particular cultural and financial resources. Gilborn (1998) uses the phrase 'new Puritanism' in arguing that the

Government 'seems intent on further reinforcing the disciplinary gaze of state agencies over parents and families'. Even if these reactions strike one as overly suspicious, and even if the compact has been revised in the more recent guidance, one can still ask why it should be a compact at all. Why should it not be a statement of the school's liabilities in the event that it fails to do what it tries to do? Should not the onus be on public institutions like schools, hospitals, care institutions, prisons etc. to come up to the mark?

Public–private partnerships

Hitherto, the private sector worked for the public sector. Under Public–Private Partnership (PPP, initiated by the previous Government), the two sectors co-operate. For example, one contractor builds a new school to the LEA's specification and then operates a range of specific services such as maintenance, heating and school meals on behalf of the LEA through a longer-term contract. The individual schools commit part of their budgets over the life of the contract and the contractor provides them with specified kinds and levels of services. School meals, technology centres and sports facilities are some of the projects already contracted.

There are different sorts of PPPs. The Private Finance Initiative is one in which the facility (a new school, for example) is built, maintained and owned by a private contractor and leased to a local authority. The Joint Venture scheme is for companies and public authorities together. Other forms of partnership cover partial (at least 10 per cent) contribution by a private company, such as the provision of a library or music block.

A more radical innovation is the company-run school or LEA. David Blunkett, the Education Secretary, at first insisted that privatisation was not on the agenda but later explained that he was bound by the principle of pragmatism: if there were signs of success, he would reconsider first principles. It is not yet clear, however, whether profit-making is officially approved. King's Manor Comprehensive School in Guildford, Surrey, will close in its present form in September 2000 and re-open as a voluntary-aided school called Kings College for the Arts and Technology. 3Es Ltd, its new owners, will have a majority on the Governing Body and can select from 10 to 15 per cent of students on aptitude. Its success, or otherwise, in turning round a failing school will have a marked effect on the school–business movement, affecting choice and diversity in unpredictable ways. Business has also moved into failing LEAs, with the firm Nord Anglia taking over the School Improvement Service and the Ethnic Minority Achievement Service in Hackney LEA following bad inspection reports. Hackney's neighbouring council Islington was identified in May 1999 as being in even worse shape. The *Guardian* covered the story for an unprecedented three successive days (17–19 May 1999), calling it 'the biggest privatisation yet seen in education'.

If these companies succeed, it is surely only a matter of time before such privatisation applies to non-failing institutions. Perhaps the future is anticipated in Tooley's observation: 'Consumers should be able to buy education from competing suppliers. We should no more expect to control it democratically than we control Tesco democratically. Only the children of the very poor should have education provided by the state' (*Guardian*, 20 April 1999, pp.2–3). Although Professor Tooley is a spokesman for the Edison Project, an American educational company, he is a long-term advocate of state withdrawal from education.

Alison Taylor (1998), however, raises pertinent issues about conflicts of interests and values in her Canadian study of a school–business partnership. She notes that the OECD encourages such partnerships and concedes that the practice can offer enticing short-term benefits, especially to public authorities at their wits' end. She cautions however that little is yet known about the long-term term disadvantages that might accrue from conflicts of values, interests and commitment.

Maintained school–independent school co-operation

Public–private partnerships that link maintained and independent schools are less controversial. They operate more at the 'co-operation' end of the partnership scheme than the contractual. Table 11.1, from a reply to an MP's question, gives an idea of current activity in this field.

This initiative is particularly important in helping to weaken old antagonisms between the state and independent sector, particularly in England, where most independent schools are located. Once the Labour Government establishes its credibility with the independent sector, reassuring it that the benignity it displays towards commerce extends to private enterprise in education too, co-operation will go much further. It is not simply that the best independent schools have facilities and specialised teaching that state students could benefit from; they also have long histories of distinctive individuality, something that the state system has almost systematically ignored. If the latter is now turning to its Beacon schools for good ideas, it may not be too long before it acknowledges the richness of practice in the independent sector and seeks to learn from it.

Table 11.1 Partnerships between maintained and independent schools

Lead organisation	Number of all applications	Successful applications	
		Number	%
Maintained school	179	38	21
Independent school	89	8	9
LEA	12	1	7
Others*	14	1	7
TOTAL	294	48	16.3

* Others = universities, charitable trusts, associations of schools.
Source: Education Parliamentary Monitor, 1998, Vol. 2, No. 10.

Issues for debate

1. 'The Action Zone is the Government's best idea for improving state schooling and widening diversity and choice'

The converse of the old adage 'if it works, don't fix it' applies to the idea of the Action Zone. It is a new attempt at solving a deeply rooted problem of chronic under-achievement. Each forum can set its own pay and conditions of service. It can depart from the anyone-as-long-as-it's-a-teacher approach to staffing, so that youth workers, sports coaches, communications experts, and medical people can contribute. It also permits variations on the National Curriculum and experimentation with new subject combinations such as art and technology, sports science, media and communication, as well as old ones such as classic languages. It has the weaknesses as well as the strengths of experiment, of course, but it has the supreme virtue of re-discovering motivation. Not least, it is a social idea. Schools, teachers, governing bodies, LEAs, school students themselves have to think wider and more reflectively. In principle, an Action Zone (which may in time develop both identity and name) can be an alternative to the LEA norm in areas that are successful.

For discussion
Is the Education Action Zone a Trojan horse destined to break up the state system?

2. 'Empowering LEAs is the Government's worst idea for improving state schooling and enlarging diversity and choice'

Taking the view that LEAs were complicit in the UK's abysmal educational standards, successive Conservative administrations marginalised them. In contrast, Labour asks: 'What more can schools, LEAs, OFSTED and the DfEE do to ensure everyone including parents plays their part in helping to raise standards?' (DfEE, 1999, p.6). For Labour, LEAs are part of the answer; for the Conservatives they are part of the problem. At the very least, Labour should have asked OFSTED to evaluate the performance of GM-type LEAs (such as Wandsworth) against the rest. To assume, without argument, that LEAs should be re-armed looks more like the payment of a debt than a publicly responsible decision.

Grant-maintained schools have been forced to rejoin the LEAs, which now withhold, on average, about a fifth of their former grant. Hammersmith and Fulham, for example, keeps £231 per pupil from the London Oratory for 'central administration, other strategic management, school improvement and non-specific grants' (O'Hear, 1999). Instead of defining their special character by embodying it in individual articles, schools have to follow instruments of Government guidelines. All maintained schools lose their ability to set up new selection arrangements, except to ensure a comprehensive spread of ability in each school and to maintain certain specialisms. They are subject to control over

funding. School staffs are employed by the LEAs. Secondary schools are expected
to 'set'; primary schools must have literacy and numeracy hours. LEAs implement
the class size regulations. With partnerships they make decisions 'about plans to
open new schools or to change the size or character of existing schools' (DfEE,
1999, p.1). Each of the 150 local authorities in England and Wales is drawing up
'at least 17 different plans at a cost in time and staff of more than 1,000 man-years'
(O'Hear, 1999). The outlook is not good for schools to develop autonomously,
and distinctly wintry for alternative schools.

For discussion
Will the re-empowerment of LEAs nullify the best effects of national educational
reform? (See also Chapter 10.)

3. Has educational choice for ethnic minorities such as the Muslims widened during the 1990s?

The Conservative Government tried to persuade church schools to opt out of LEA
influence. Had it succeeded, British education would be very different, since
roughly a third of all schools are church schools. In the end, it failed: only 8 per
cent of Roman Catholic and 4 per cent of Anglican schools became GM. Priscilla
Chadwick surmises that church schools stayed because they disapproved of the
ethics of the educational market in general and the funding of GM schools in
particular (their extra funding came at the expense of maintained schools from
the common pool). The result was a general presumption against opting out
unless there were compelling special reasons.

The 7,000 religious schools in the voluntary sector of England and Wales
provide for about 20 per cent of all pupils, yet only a handful – less than 30 –
are non-Christian, and most of those are Jewish. The largest non-Christian faith
community – Muslims – could, with good reason, believe themselves to be
currently discriminated against. From their perspective, the situation appears
indefensible. Either state-funding should be withdrawn from all Anglican,
Roman Catholic, Methodist and Jewish schools, or it should be extended to
Muslim schools on the same basis. Since the first alternative commands little
political support, the case for the second is strong.

The main opposing argument is that it would create an unacceptable diversity,
amounting to a society divided not by class, the old English disease, but by
religion or race or – to use the current emollient – 'ethnicity'. The difficulty with
this view is that the stronger the argument is held, the more powerful becomes
the case for abolishing public financial support for all religious schools. If
support for Christian schools with public funding remains solid and claims for
new religious schools are denied, then that is not only divisive, it is unjust.

At present, neither the Conservatives nor Labour deny Muslim and other
private schools the right to state-funding, but the conditions that applications
have to satisfy are severe – especially when the Audit Commission maintains that

there are far more school places than school students. Meanwhile, the religious prejudice at the roots of education in England and Wales continues.

An interesting recent variation on this dilemma appeared in the *Times Educational Supplement.* David Budge (*TES*, 10 October 1998) claimed that the pressure for change was more imaginary than real. The truth of the matter was, he wrote, that Muslims did not want their own schools. He quoted Geoffrey Walford (who had spoken at the 1998 European Conference on Educational Research) to the effect that only 2 per cent of Muslim children attended the 60 or so private Muslim schools. Such was the impoverished nature of most of these (with an average size of no more than 120 pupils) that very few realistic applications would be made. According to Budge, research in the early 1990s found that the majority of Muslims did not wish to send their children to Muslim schools. What relief this must bring to those who genuinely believed British education had a problem on its hands!

The difficulty with this 'solution' is that its logic is faulty. From the fact that few parents sent their children to those Muslim schools at that time, one cannot infer that they would not choose to send their children to a properly financed and maintained voluntary sector of Muslim-based schools, much as Christians do to theirs. Indeed, Muslim families often preferred to send their children to Anglican and Roman Catholic schools on the grounds that they had strong moral and disciplinary codes and that a large proportion of schools at secondary level were for girls only.

However, during the 1990s, the league tables clearly showed that voluntary sector schools were obtaining, on average, better results than their neighbouring schools. As a consequence, there was a dramatic increase in their popularity among parents not previously noted for their piety. The 1996 Channel 4 investigation in the Witness series ('School Prayers') examined how the appeals procedures worked at Canon Slade Secondary Church of England School, Bolton. In 1991, the minimum points score for admission was 13. In 1996, after two very successful performances in the league tables, it climbed to 31. Of the 410 applications, 240 had 31 points or more. By far the most important criterion against which points could be amassed was church attendance. Church attendance with a parent every week for four years gives 31 points. How could moral Muslim families justify, with a clear conscience, observance of such a practice?

Whatever may have been the research 'in the early 1990s' to which Budge referred, by 1996, Muslim children's chances of getting into church schools were much diminished. The fault is not Labour's – it is a consequence of the league tables and an upsurge of parental interest in this sector; but there is no remedy from Labour, nor none in sight. Opportunities for Muslim families continue to decline as educationally ambitious parents target the voluntary sector. Ironically, one of the few countries in the world with a liberal religious dimension to its educational system makes no room for families with strongly held non-Christian and non-Jewish beliefs.

For discussion

How should school choice for religious groups other than Christians and Jews be widened?

4. Will handing over management of schools and LEAs to business widen both diversity and choice?

So far, the Government has allowed businesses to bid for control only of failing schools and authorities. At present, the Government speaks with forked tongue over the question of profit-making. Once it admits the principle publicly, then it has no answer to charges of having assisted privatisation. If it continues to equivocate, however, businesses may soon lose interest in the experiment. Turning around a failing school or authority is very hard work indeed.

James Tooley, among others, cannot understand why governments drag their feet. If schools are managed to the satisfaction of pupils, parents and OFSTED, why should the companies not make a profit? In any case, the real test of whether business should be directly involved is not whether a company can bring a school or authority back to life. There are already examples of failure by respected senior educational management teams to do that. It is whether it can manage ordinary schools better than LEA officials, present Boards of Governors and senior staff. Justifiable popularity – that is, over-subscription plus praise from OFSTED – is a perfectly acceptable criterion.

In the USA, the Charter School movement has made considerable headway. By September 1999, 1,400 charter schools were operating in 34 states and Washington DC – about 1 per cent of the 80,000 public schools nation-wide. They are state-funded schools operated by educators, parents, community leaders, companies and others. Subject to the usual monitoring procedures, they are free from the normal bureaucratic and regulatory red tape, although if they fail to meet agreed standards they may be closed down. With the approval of the Superintendent, 10 per cent of Washington DC's students will be enrolled in Charter schools in 1999–2000, providing, as she says, competition, experiment and stimulation for the regular system.

Los Angeles has 13 Charter schools out of its 650 public schools. Superintendent Reuben Zacarias has said:

> We have to give credit to charter schools for taking the lid off and making administrators think about what is possible. I believe the system will begin to look more and more like charter schools as all of us move to focus on results. In that regard, the charter school movement is more important as a philosophy than as an organisational structure. (Centre for Educational Reform, 1999)

For discussion

School–business partnership: risks and rewards?

The future

> The vast majority of secondary schools take children on a non-selective basis. What parents want to see are schools which provide diversity within the campus and meet the needs of all children, whatever their talents, abilities or learning needs. ...We have already doubled the number of specialist schools and will double it again to at least 800 schools – nearly one in four of all secondary schools by 2003. These schools, all with strong support from business, have improved their performance at twice the rate of the average comprehensive. They are providing not only higher standards but increasing diversity. (Blunkett, 1999)

It seems from the above quotation from the Secretary of State's address to the CBI that Labour's idea for diversity is three-fold. First, voluntary schools provide education within a religious ethos, at present mainly Christian. Secondly, all maintained schools deliver the revised National Curriculum from September 2000, but with some local additions. Thirdly, specialist schools or colleges emphasise certain aspects of the National Curriculum. From the CBI speech, it seems that the Government sees the specialist schools as the chief instrument of diversity.

At present, most specialise in technology. The Government appears to acknowledge this as a trend that could escalate to the detriment of other sorts of specialism. Almost simultaneous with his CBI address, the Secretary of State for Education joined the Secretary of State for Culture, Media and Sport in signing *All Our Futures* (NACCCE, 1999). This report affirms that the present educational programme lays down the basics and establishes traditional structures of knowledge, and asks, what next? Its answer is a call for creative and cultural development through formal and informal education. In the language such reports are usually written in, it pleads for education that will develop flexibility of mind The strategy should, the report says, be based on three objectives: (i) all schools should explicitly identify their cultural and creative aims, (ii) staff should explicitly identify with those aims, and (iii) schools should reach out to business and grasp opportunities.

Admittedly, there is something of the converse of a crescendo about this declaration. The first two clauses are very welcome. They are refreshing antidotes to the business-oriented rhetoric of the Department for Education and Employment. Then, just as one thought that some such phrase as 'Government will back this initiative to the hilt' would appear, the rather anti-climactic 'schools should reach out to business' brought us back to earth. Nevertheless, a need for diversity and creativity is identified. As for choice, it seems now to belong within school partnerships rather than between schools. Though 'rooted' (the Secretary of State's word) 'in their own schools', able children could be sent to study in other, better schools, called 'beacons' or 'specialist' where they would be 'stretched'.

Where is the difference in substance, then, between Conservative and Labour on selection? Matthew Parris, writing in *The Times* (23 March 1999, p.2), has a flight of fancy as a Government spin-doctor:

> After a trial run, announce that clever inner-city kids should not be confined to 'beacon' schools within their area. After all, why should top teachers and facilities in state schools in leafy suburbs be out of bounds? Come to that, why should independent schools deny education to our top 10% in inner cities? Force them to open their doors to some of the best (reimbursing them, of course). Perhaps all that stands between Conservative and Labour is the fortified LEA.

Further reading

Glatter, R., Woods, P.A. and Bagley, C. (1996) *Choice and Diversity in Schooling: Perspectives and Prospects*. London: Routledge.

References

Bichard, M. (1998) 'Policy Priorities', *Education Journal*, September, 7.

Blunkett, D. (1999) Presidential Address to the CBI (19 July). London: DfEE.

Centre for Education Reform (1999) *Charter Schools Progress Report: Part III* at http://edreform.com./pubs.

Chadwick, P. (1998) *Shifting Alliances: Church and State in English Education*. London: Cassell.

Department for Education and Employment (1998) *Home–School Agreements: Guidance for Schools*. London: DfEE.

Department for Education and Employment (1999) *Excellence in Cities*. London: DfEE.

Gilborn, D. (1998) 'Racism, selection, poverty and parents: New Labour, old problems?', *Journal of Education Policy*, 13(6), 726.

Hargreaves, D. (1994) *The Mosaic of Learning*. London: Macmillan.

O'Hear, A. (1999) 'Bungling bureaucracy and this betrayal of bright children', *Daily Mail*, 25 September, 4.

Taylor, A. (1998) 'Courting business: the rhetoric and practices of school–business partnerships', *Journal of Education Policy*, 13(3), 395–422.

The National Advisory Committee on Creative and Cultural Education (1999) *All Our Futures*. London: DfEE.

Tooley, J. (1995) *Disestablishing the School*. Aldershot: Avebury Press.

Tooley, J. (1996) *Education without the State*. London: Institute of Economic Affairs.

Vincent, C and Tomlinson, S (1997) 'Home–school relationships: the swarming of disciplinary mechanisms', *British Educational Research Journal*, 23(3), 366.

West, A. and Pennell, H. (1998) 'School admissions: increasing equity, accountability and transparency', *British Journal of Educational Studies*, 46(2), 188–200.

Chapter 12

Disengagement, Truancy and Exclusion

Jane Lovey

Introduction

The three issues in the chapter heading, which are inextricably linked in a conundrum of cause and effect, have attracted more and more media interest during the last 15 years of overwhelming educational changes. With this there has been a growing awareness that some of this country's most vulnerable children are outside the educational system. Many have been excluded from school, while others, for a variety of reasons, have excluded themselves by not turning up at school, registering and then walking away, or truanting from selected lessons. Added to these pupils are those who attend nearly every day but totally fail to engage in the curriculum. These children have always existed but not in such numbers as in recent years.

The numbers of pupils permanently excluded from school in England stood at around 3,000 in 1990/91, rising by almost a third to nearly 4,000 during the next two years (Social Exclusion Unit, 1998). By 1996/97 it had escalated to 12,700 (13% from primary schools, 83% from secondary and 5% from special schools), but then fell back by 3 per cent to 12,300 in 1997/98 (more than four in five boys); to this figure has to be added around 100,000 fixed term exclusions (DfEE Statistical First Release, 11/99). The figures for truancy are also depressing, representing 1 per cent of school time in secondary schools and 0.5 per cent in primary schools, the only mitigating factor being that they are relatively stable. But about a million children (about 15% of all pupils) absent themselves for at least a half day without official permission (*ibid.*).

Why have numbers generally been rising, and more so than in other western European countries? The Social Exclusion Unit (1998) notes that much of truancy appears to be condoned by parents for shopping, looking after brothers or sisters or helping out in the home, while the influence of friends is even more important. But there are also educational factors: poor attendance seems to be associated, for example, with poor reading attainment, anxiety about deadlines for GCSE coursework, fear of bullying, dislike of particular lessons or teachers, and perceptions of school or the National Curriculum as irrelevant. Many of these factors apply also to excluded pupils, among whom there is a high incidence of family stress or disruption, poverty or unemployment, a low level of basic skills, and poor relations with pupils, parents or teachers. Other factors relate to the educational climate, particularly pressures on schools to meet performance targets.

But the concern goes wider than overall numbers. Research by Carl Parsons and his team (Castle and Parsons, 1997) suggested an ethnic bias in the figures, with African Caribbean boys six times more likely to be excluded than their white counterparts. Recent official figures show there are still marked variations among ethnic groups, with the exclusion rate for Black Caribbean pupils standing at 0.76 per cent compared with 0.17 per cent among white pupils and 0.18 per cent among all pupils (DfEE Statistical First Release, 11/99). Other groups that are disproportionately likely to be excluded are children with special needs and children in care (Social Exclusion Unit, 1998).

According to Carol Hayden (1997), the problem begins at primary level, which accounts for about one in ten of all excluded children. In many cases, children excluded from primary school have special needs, are 'looked after children' or live in homes that are chaotic or deprived. Moreover, some of the very children who should be receiving extra support in school are often not even on the roll of a school because they have been excluded. Both Parsons and Hayden link the increase in exclusions to the advent of pupil-led funding arrangements and the importance attached to league tables.

Previous policy

Management of behaviour

In response to the increasing problems that some teachers were experiencing in schools and a number of high-profile violent incidents reported in the media, the Conservative Government set up a committee, chaired by Lord Elton, to examine the issues involved. The Elton Report (DES, 1989) was accepted by the Government as a positive contribution to the problem, with its focus on classroom management skills, staff providing mutual support, and involving parents, governors, and pupils in managing the school community. As a result, practical training in managing pupil behaviour was made a compulsory part of teacher-training programmes, grants were given to local authorities to tackle problems of truancy and unacceptable behaviour, and all schools were advised to develop behaviour policies.

Exclusion from school

In response to a series of well-publicised cases, legislation in the mid-1980s addressed one aspect of the exclusions problem by trying to inject some common justice into the procedures for suspending or expelling. In one intractable dispute, Manchester LEA had tried to reinstate a child against the wishes of the school; in other situations, parents had not been properly informed about their child's exclusion or had found the appeal arrangements seriously wanting. The Education (No. 2) Act 1986 marked a watershed in being the first piece of legislation to regulate exclusions, laying down procedures to clarify the responsibilities and rights of headteachers, governors, parents and local authorities in the arrangements for excluding pupils and ordering their reinstatement. (The policy has since been somewhat amended by the School Standards and Framework Act 1998, as explained in the next section.)

In response to the continuing escalating figures, the School Teachers' Review Body suggested in June 1992 that teachers in schools with low excluding rates might be given extra remuneration for their efforts in containing the situation and that, conversely, schools with high rates should be penalised through the pay structures. In the event, the Government dismissed this approach and instead suggested other ways in which schools might be encouraged to contain pupils whose behaviour was unacceptable (DfE, 1992a). One of these included the publication of exclusion figures in annual performance tables.

However, the Government recognised two dangers in such a move: one was that it might serve to discourage teachers from recommending exclusion in cases where such action would be an appropriate response to the problem; the other was that it could tempt schools to pressurise parents into withdrawing their children 'voluntarily' and so save having to record a formal exclusion. Other suggestions were financial: either to give schools financial support for 'difficult and disruptive pupils' or, more contentiously, to fine schools for excluding pupils. As the Government acknowledged, however, the first idea would raise problems of definition and the second would mean that schools lost not only funding for the excluded pupil but multiples of that amount.

The 1993, 1996 and 1997 Education Acts tightened up exclusions procedures still further. 'Indefinite exclusion' was no longer an option for heads, who now had to ensure that any exclusions were 'fixed term' or 'permanent'. To ensure that schools receiving pupils excluded from elsewhere were not financially disadvantaged, arrangements were made for funding to follow the pupil. To address the dangers of pupils being without any kind of educational provision, every LEA had to ensure that children unable to attend school because of illness, exclusion or 'otherwise' received full- or part-time provision in a Pupil Referral Unit.

Under the 1997 Education Act, schools were obliged to publish a discipline policy but were also given more power to deal with unacceptable behaviour. They were allowed to keep children in after school without their parents' permission, to exclude pupils for longer periods (up to 45 school days in any school year instead of the previous 15 days per term), and to make the offer of a place conditional on the signing of a home–school agreement. Also, parents whose children had been excluded from two or more schools were deprived of their right to choose a new school.

Truancy

From 1992, all maintained schools were required to ensure that their prospectuses and annual reports contained rates of unauthorised pupil absence, and from 1993 this information was added to national performance tables. In a White Paper of the same year, the problem of truancy was strongly linked with crime, an aspect highlighted by the murder of a toddler by two primary school children who were found to be persistent truants:

> Boys and girls who stay away from school, or who having been entered on the register then absent themselves for substantial parts of the school day, are more likely to grow up unhappy and unfulfilled, leave school much less qualified than they might be and worst of all sometimes get drawn into a life of crime. (DfE, 1992b, section 1.25)

The Audit Commission's report *Misspent Youth* (1996) also strongly linked crime with exclusion from school and truancy. We should note, however, that not all truants or excluded pupils get drawn into crime. On the other hand, there is a grave danger of social exclusion, with many living a lonely life within the four walls of their homes.

Disengagement

The Conservative policy which promised choice and diversity for all proved to be one under which more and more pupils became disaffected, and at an earlier and earlier age. The nature and demands of the National Curriculum and its associated testing arrangements appeared to be associated with increased problems of pupil disengagement. The matter was compounded as competition between schools widened the gap between those who were empowered by the choices they were offered and those for whom there was little or no choice. It also created sink schools as well as prosperous ones. In these situations, it was difficult for children to see education as the key to all doors.

The vouchers for nursery education also put many vulnerable children at a disadvantage: their parents often found the system difficult to understand, and in any case they could not afford to top up the voucher for provision of their choice. This was another example of a well-meant policy that had potential to produce winners and losers, this time at pre-school age. Before long there were reports in the media of nursery children being excluded from an environment where they should have been nurtured and allowed to develop social skills.

Support for schools

Another problem during the Conservative years concerned the support that schools were given for addressing behaviour problems. Since the mid 1970s there had been a rag-bag of off-site provision for pupils who had either been excluded from school or had been persistent non-attenders. Although there were a number of very skilled and experienced teachers working in these units (unfortunately referred to in some of the media as 'sin bins'), there were others who had no qualifications in the support of children with behaviour problems, and the units were seen by many outsiders as simple containment facilities. After the publication of the Warnock Report (DES, 1978) on special needs and the 1981 Education Act, there was a will to close special off-site units and cater for those children in mainstream schools with the support of teachers experienced in special needs.

In many instances authorities replaced off-site units with outreach teams of teachers who would go into schools to work with the children who were displaying disruptive, disturbing and challenging behaviour. While some of these schemes were successful, many schools were dissatisfied with the service they received because a large number of outreach teachers were from the previous units and in some cases had had no recent experience of mainstream teaching. In another move, the DfEE published a series of six circulars called *Pupils with Problems* (1994) which gave guidance to schools on a range of concerns – pupils' behaviour and discipline, the education of pupils with emotional and behavioural difficulties, exclusions from school, the education by LEAs of children otherwise than at school, the education of sick children, and the education of children being looked after by local authorities.

In tandem with these changes was the advent of the purchaser–provider culture in education, which had an enormous effect on support for special educational needs and behaviour difficulties. Because of the number of schools that were leaving LEAs to become grant-maintained, LEAs were trying to appease those who stayed within their control by delegating to them an increasing proportion of the school budget, but out of this schools had to buy in special needs support. Agencies, however, could not afford to retain those support teachers whose services the schools did not wish to purchase. Why should a school purchase expensive behavioural support for pupils who were already in their final months of schooling? It became more cost-effective to exclude them (Lovey *et al.*, 1993). In this way, the excellent intentions behind school behaviour policies were overtaken by other policies to make schools more competitive.

Present policy

There is now general recognition that the issues of disaffection, truancy and exclusion often affect the same tranche of the population and are linked as being a powerful barrier to inclusion in present day society. In forming the high-profile Social Exclusion Unit, the present Government has taken a holistic approach to the consequence of disengagement and its relationship with truancy and exclusion. When Peter Mandelson, as Minister without Portfolio, announced the Government's intentions at a Fabian Society Lecture in the summer of 1997, he made it clear that the unit was not only inter-departmental and based in the Cabinet Office but focused on preventive rather than reactive strategies:

> One challenge above all stands out before we can deserve another historic victory: tackling the scourge and waste of social exclusion. The Prime Minister has decided to establish a special unit in the Cabinet Office to take decisive action at the heart of the government machine. This will promote co-operation between departments, drawing together a panoply of new initiatives, shifting the focus of government programmes towards preventing social exclusion and effectively to attack social exclusion. All policy decisions will be made by the appropriate Cabinet Committee. . . . It is so important that the Prime Minister himself will steer the unit with whatever support is necessary at ministerial level. (Quoted in BBC *News Online*, 10 August 1997)

In seeking to reduce the number of exclusions, while also making available suitable educational provision for all who are excluded, New Labour is continuing most of the policies initiated by the previous government. However, the consultation paper *Excellence for All* (DfEE, 1997) is emphatic that exclusion is a last resort, and the Government is committed to reducing exclusion and unauthorised absence by one-third by 2002. The policy is for LEAs to work more closely with social services and youth justice teams to maximise the opportunities offered by education to those whose lives are already placing them on the outside of the mainstream. Among ways that it is hoped to achieve this are:

- LEA support for schools in improving the management of pupil behaviour, with a view, among other things, to preventing unauthorised absence and exclusion;
- improvement in the type and nature of provision available outside mainstream schools for pupils with behavioural problems;
- arrangements for supporting the education of excluded pupils;
- arrangements for effective co-ordination between relevant local agencies, and for involving the youth service and the voluntary sector. (DfEE, 1997, p.57)

Local authorities must include targets for reducing truancy and exclusion in their Education Development Plans. From 2002, they must also provide full-time education for pupils within 15 days of their exclusion from school, though the Audit Commission (1999) suggests that some authorities are currently taking up to 11 weeks to do this. LEAs must also have in place Behaviour Support Plans, monitored for their effectiveness, covering four areas outlined in DfEE Circular 1/98:

- strategic planning for pupils with behavioural difficulties, including arrange-ments for effective co-ordination between relevant agencies;
- support for schools in improving the management of pupil behaviour with a view, among other things, to minimising unauthorised absences and exclusions;

- support for individual pupils with behavioural difficulties in mainstream schools;
- the type and nature of provision available outside mainstream schools for pupils with behavioural difficulties, including support for re-integrating them into the mainstream, where appropriate.

The Government has further introduced a new power that enables the Secretary of State to require a maintained school with significant attendance problems to set targets for reducing absence. Action to address problems of truancy and exclusion are also central to Education Action Zones.

The White Paper of 1997 acknowledged the part that self-esteem plays in promoting achievement in school. It is a pity that this is juxtaposed with the section on the importance of homework, which is probably one of the most demoralising issues for children from homes where the conditions for completing academic work are not present. However money has been made available for homework clubs, although in many places these depend on the goodwill of teachers. There is recognition of the fact that at an increasingly early age many boys are ceasing to engage with the curriculum, and in some areas links are being made with Premier Football League Clubs to sponsor study support centres (DfEE Circular 13/97).

DfEE News 26/99, headed '£65 Million to Tackle Truancy and Disaffection', heralded an important step to improving pupil behaviour. For the first time Government money was specifically ringfenced to provide full-time education for pupils permanently excluded from schools. A further amount was allocated for 14- to 19-year-olds beginning to disengage themselves from the curriculum to have a fresh start at further education colleges and to pay for alternative courses and examinations.

The early years Sure Start and Nurture Group initiatives are important developments in the strategies to combat social exclusion. The Sure Start programme, targeted on areas where there are high levels of deprivation and social exclusion, could be effective in cutting the incidence of disengagement with education later on. The programme recognises a clear link between the quality of a child's experience in its earliest years and future achievement at school. It is to be hoped that the Sure Start initiative will be successful in its aims to increase the language capacity and physical and emotional health of children starting school, and in the longer term cause a decline in disengagement, truancy, youth crime and teenage pregnancies.

The Nurture Groups initiative that is now being encouraged by the Government was successfully pioneered by the former Inner London Education Authority in the 1970s, but it gradually faded away at the break up of the ILEA. However, nurture groups continued to operate in the Borough of Enfield, and a research paper confirms their effectiveness in reducing the need for more expensive provision for excluded and vulnerable children in later years (Iszatt and Wasilewaska, 1997). They are based on John Bowlby's attachment theory, which holds that healthy emotional development is dependent upon the formation of attachment bonds with a caring adult. The groups are therefore fairly small, catering for around 10 five- to six-year-olds, with a teacher and specially trained support assistant. They are usually placed in a mainstream school so that the children remain on the role of a regular class, with which they are gradually re-integrated (Cooper and Lovey, 1999).

One of the values of the nurture groups is that life in the classroom, unlike in many of the children's homes, is predictable with a regular pattern to the day. The adults pay careful attention to what children need to learn next as they go through a day of eating together, formal work, story-time and play. Nothing is taken for granted: children absorb or are quite explicitly taught the behaviour needed to manage in a group. The nurture group could make a difference to those children excluded from school before the age of eight. Despite these initiatives, however, many early educationists regard it as a cause for concern that the early learning goals now being introduced in nursery schools could see greater numbers of children experiencing failure and becoming disengaged at an earlier and earlier age.

The School Standards and Framework Act 1998 made it compulsory for schools to draw up home–school agreements, elements of which are related to social behaviour. Parents must be invited to sign these, but the offering of a place in the school is not conditional on their assent. The same Act redefined the law on exclusion from school, abolishing certain special provisions that previous grant-maintained schools had enjoyed. Basically, the arrangements that now operate for all maintained schools are as follows:

- As before, headteachers may exclude pupils on a fixed-term basis for up to 45 days in a school year.
- They do not need to inform school governors of fixed-term exclusions of five days or less unless any previous exclusions mean than the five day limit for the term is being exceeded or the pupil will miss an examination. Longer fixed-term exclusions must be considered by the governors.
- All permanent exclusions must be considered by the governing body, which must hear any representations from the parents and can instruct the head to reinstate the pupil if it believes the exclusion to be unfair.
- All exclusions that must be referred to the governing body must also be reported to the LEA, together with the governors' decision. The LEA can no longer overrule the school's decision, but it can make representations.
- If the LEA agrees that a pupil should be excluded, the governors must inform the parents of their right to appeal. An appeal panel consists of three or five members, and its decision is binding on all parties.

The DfEE provides guidance on exclusion procedures in Circular 10/99. Here it advises that exclusions should not be used for minor incidents such as failure to complete homework, poor academic performance, lateness or truancy, pregnancy, breaching school uniform policy (including hairstyle or wearing jewellery) or because of lack of co-operation by the pupil's parents (e.g. in not attending a meeting about the problem). Circular 11/99 outlines responsibilities for managing and enforcing attendance, for pupils at risk of exclusion, or arranging education outside school and for re-integrating excluded pupils. It also summarises arrangements for Pupil Referral Units.

While legislating for the most disadvantaged section of the population, the Government has to be aware of the priorities of the rest. It is therefore understandable that it has retained elements of the previous government's policies such as performance league tables, which unfortunately can create a society of winners and losers. However, there does seem to be a will to invest in creating an inclusive society in which more can feel there is hope of advancement.

Issues for debate

1. Mentoring

For the last decade or more, small mentoring initiatives have been implemented in a number of authorities. In May 1999, Estelle Morris, the Schools Standards Minister, announced a £340,000 fund to 'help us to continue evaluating last year's mentoring projects, initiate new schemes and expand our knowledge of this crucial area by seeing what works best in any given situation' (DfEE News 211/99). She went on to say: 'Mentoring can make a world of difference to young people by building their confidence and self-esteem. ...We have seen this unique contribution to education working – and we are keen to develop it further.' Two areas of need that had already been identified were (a) support the commitment to business and community mentoring under the Excellence in Cities initiative and (b) to address the particular needs of ethnic minority groups.

A number of mentoring schemes have been in place for some time. Research by the Cambridge Institute of Education (Cooper *et al.*, in press) came across the following examples:

- A small secondary school where all the staff had agreed to mentor three or four students during their GCSE year. The students knew that if they had a problem with course work, something at home that was distracting them, or they just wanted reassurance, they could talk to this teacher sometime during the day or after school.
- In a very large secondary school, volunteer sixth formers had been trained to listen to the problems of students further down the school. Two sixth formers were attached to each tutor group. One sixth former commented that there were certain children who needed calming down after unhappy weekends and felt that this was a useful role she could play.

- In a medium-sized school, volunteer teachers were available at break times and after school for some of the most vulnerable students to come and talk to.

All these schemes were reliant on the goodwill of teachers or sixth formers to 'go the extra mile' that would encourage a young person with problems to feel cared for and included in the mainstream school setting.

The Government hopes that it will be possible to recruit people in the community to act as mentors to students who need a reliable adult to be available to speak to. Unfortunately this is the kind of informal work with vulnerable young people that can attract some adults who prey on just this type of young person. Whatever schemes are set up will have to be well organised and run by experienced people who can be accountable for the safety of the young people.

For discussion
Might pro-active mentoring of children during their transfer to secondary school and during Key Stage 3 be effective in reducing levels of disengagement, truancy and exclusions at Key Stage 4?

2. Curriculum needs

Unacceptable behaviour, both in and out of school, and disengaged behaviour (staying at home or sitting in the classroom but not joining in the lesson) are inextricably linked to self-esteem, which some aspects of the educational system seem geared to depress. Performance targets and league tables, for instance, encourage schools and the public to value only those young people who achieve the 'national standard' or the top three of seven grades at GCSE. In a small school just one persistent non-attender can materially affect the examination and the absence tables. The national testing system tempts schools to teach to the key stage tests, while parents are encouraged by the Qualifications and Curriculum Authority to buy their official booklets containing test papers and bearing the slogan 'Help your child get the best result'.

The system of transfer to high school, whereby some pupils find they have no school place until those who have been offered more than one place decide which to accept, is bound to erode the self-esteem of whole families. To counter these possible effects, however, the Government has taken a number of steps to enable more children to succeed with the school curriculum. Apart from the national literacy and numeracy strategies, we now have homework clubs, study support centres, mentoring schemes, Education Action Zones, Sure Start and the various Excellence in Cities initiatives. The National Curriculum has been slimmed down, with more flexibility for options and opportunities for 'vocational pathways' and opportunities to attend FE colleges at Key Stage 4, and there is a greater focus on personal education.

Any government that has the aims of achieving full school attendance and reducing the level of exclusions must find ways of making the curriculum fulfilling and empowering. Exclusion is not an appropriate sanction for those who find attendance difficult. Many educational welfare officers describe cases where they have worked to return disaffected, depressed children to school, only to find they are excluded before the week is out for such incidents as failing to hand in homework or attend detention, or for being in conflict with teachers for work missed during absence. Schools that succeed with these pupils are those that invest resources into putting in place a caring induction for them to settle back into the system, arranging for a named adult to be on hand to mediate in difficult situations.

One study at the beginning of the 1990s (Lovey *et al.*, 1993) focused on the types of activities that were successful with students who had either been excluded from school or had become persistent non-attenders. The most popular of the options were work experience and attendance at colleges of further education. More recently, a study by the Cambridge Institute of Education, in which the present writer has been involved, makes clear that these are still popular options. In explaining why so few Year 10s in a large school were becoming disaffected, a deputy head explained how 'sending to college' was a proactive rather than a reactive measure: 'We spend money on giving them a taste of college. It costs, but it is worth every penny for the ten week course. They come back knowing exactly what they want to do at college, and knowing exactly what GCSE passes they will need. It motivates them for the rest of their time here.'

Work experience used as part of a complete package, including skills training can also be a motivating factor for students in this age group – especially if, when they come back from a couple of weeks in the work place, they are treated as young adults by their teachers. Once students have been on work experience, or if they have a weekend job, they often develop and become different people. It is now possible for 14- to 16-year-olds to secure extended work experience by dropping two of science, design and technology or a modern language.

However, some practices seem counter-productive in this respect. There are schools, for example, that seem to connive at their less able students becoming cheap labour in firms which will replace them with another 'work-experience' boy or girl as soon as they can leave school. The condoning of pupils of school age working in unskilled jobs is at best misjudged and at worst patronising and prejudiced. In this way the children of unskilled parents are often being denied choices when they leave school since they have nothing to show for their education. If the most disaffected students are to be allowed to have life choices they must be offered programmes that can be accredited and that give them transferable skills. It is not good enough just to contain these young citizens. There must be a pathway, such as GNVQ, where all can achieve some success and upon which those tired of education can build later, when they have recovered the self-esteem that has been robbed from them because of failure in an overly academic curriculum.

Although there is now more general *recognition* of the complexity of factors that lead pupils to be excluded, most of the *responses* are in terms of the pupil's deficits and the need for alternative educational provision, rather than on changes that are needed in the educational arrangements to meet the needs of all pupils (Rustique-Forrester, 1999). Yet whatever legislation is made by successive governments, it will only be won if senior teachers are allowed to exercise their professional judgements over the content and aims of the curriculum for individual students. They must be satisfied that what they are learning is relevant to their aspirations, ability and future working life. Perhaps it is only when vocational pathways are afforded as much respect as academic pathways that the issues of disengagement and truancy will be solved.

For discussion

To what extent can schools become more empowering for the growing minority in danger of disengagement from schoolwork? Does the answer lie in individual school initiatives, or are further changes needed in national policy?

3. Pastoral support programmes

The DfEE (Circular 11/99) suggests that pupils who do not respond to the school's efforts to combat disaffection, and who are therefore at serious risk of permanent exclusion, may need a Pastoral Support Programme (PSP), devised with external services, to prevent them dropping out of school altogether. The PSP 'should identify precise and realistic behavioural outcomes for the child to work towards' in a series of fortnightly tasks over a short period (perhaps 16 weeks) with rewards for success and sanctions for the occurrence of certain behaviours. It should be overseen by a nominated teacher, and reviewed at least half way through the period.

To set up a PSP, the DfEE advises the school to invite the parents and a representative from the LEA to discuss the situation and determine a course of action. Other agencies – social services, housing departments, the youth service, careers services, ethnic minority community groups – should also be involved, as appropriate. Although the Department insists that 'a PSP should not be used to replace the special educational needs assessment process', it also suggests that 'in drawing up a PSP schools should...review any learning difficulties, particularly literacy skills, that may affect behaviour...and consider, or reconsider, disapplying the National Curriculum to allow for specific learning activities' (paras 5.3 and 5.6). Placement in a learning support unit is also given as a possibility. The school is also advised to consider whether special support is needed for social problems such as bereavement or alcohol or drugs dependency. Also in the checklist is the possibility of joint registration with a Pupil Referral Unit (which could assist re-integration) or even a 'managed move' to another school to provide a fresh start. Illustrative models are given in the Circular.

For discussion
Examine the advice on PSPs given in DfEE Circular 11/99. What do you see as their potential strengths? What conditions would need to apply for them to work successfully?

Conclusion

The title of this book contains the phrase 'Raising the Standard?', echoing part of the title of the 1998 Education Act. It is to be hoped this does not refer to the narrow academic pursuits, in which those who have different styles of learning and ways of making sense of the world have little chance of success. 'The drive to raise standards may be taking its toll on pupils as one in five suffers from anxiety or worse' is the subheading of a piece in the *TES* (25 June 1999, p.12), referring to a report by the Mental Health Foundation. The study notes that the number of children suffering depression, anxiety and psychosis is rising. Formerly these problems were often laid at the door of the home or the section of society from which the children came. Now it is not surprising to learn that 'the potentially negative impact of a narrowly-focused academic definition of raising standards can be seen in recent research showing increased pupil distress in primary school and of new pressures in secondary school'.

Understanding exclusion and disengagement demands going beyond the student's behaviour and includes the nature of the matrix of contexts in which the students operates (Lovey and Cooper, 1997; Parsons, 1999). The standard that needs raising is the one that recognises the diverse needs of every child and values achievements outside a narrow academic remit. Academic targets from the nursery upwards will only lead to the earlier disengagement of those young people without the academic learning style of those who make the policies. Any lip-service to inclusion is a sham if only those young people who aspire to academic education are celebrated.

There is a cycle of disengagement and truancy that often leads to either exclusion from school, or later exclusion from society. New Labour is trying to work proactively to change the inevitability of the disengaged in society becoming the disinherited – those who have little to look forward to. At the beginning of July 1999, Schools Minister Charles Clarke spoke of the Government's concern to raise the standards for these vulnerable children. The recommendation of a link teacher in each school for children 'looked after' by the local authority, for instance, might lessen the scandal of the neglect of this part of the child population. In the past, the various off-site units for excluded pupils have been a reactive response to problems caused by the rigid assessment of performance in a narrow academic curriculum. Money now spent to engender pro-social skills in all under-fives, the mentoring of pupils with home/school problems at high-school transfer, and the option of an alternative curriculum at 14+ might well reduce the number of young people who have difficulty in becoming stakeholders in the society in which they live.

Further reading

Blythe, E. and Milner, M. (1996) *Exclusion from School: Multi-Professional Approaches to Policy and Practice.* London: Routledge.

Carlen, P. *et al.* (1992) *Truancy: The Politics of Compulsory Schooling.* Buckingham: Open University Press.

Collins, D. (1998) *Managing Truancy in Schools.* London: Cassell.

Cooper, P. *et al.* (in press) *Exclusion is not a Solution.* London: Routledge. This book is about alternatives to exclusions.

DfEE (1999) *Social Inclusion: Pupil Support* (Circulars 10/99 and 11/99) (obtainable from DfEE Publications Centre, 0845 6022260).

The following publications published by the National Foundation for Educational Research, Slough:

Kinder, K. (1998) *Raising Behaviour!*

Kinder, K. and Wilkin, A. (1998) *With All Respect: Reviewing Disaffection Strategies.*

Kinder, K. *et al.* (1995) *Three to Remember: Strategies for Disaffected Pupils.*

Kinder, K. *et al.* (1997) *Pupils' Views on Disaffection.*

Kinder, K. *et al.* (1997) *Exclusion: Who needs it?*

References

Audit Commission (1996) *Misspent Youth: Young People and Crime.* London: Stationery Office.

Audit Commission (1999) *Missing Out.* London: Stationery Office.

Castle, F. and Parsons, C. (1997) 'Disruptive behaviour and exclusions from school: redefining and responding to the problem', *Emotional and Behavioural Difficulties,* 2(3), pp.4–11.

Cooper, P. and Lovey, J. (1999) 'Early intervention in emotional and behavioural difficulties: the role of nurture groups', *European Journal of Special Needs Education,* 14(2), pp.122–131.

Cooper, P., Drummond, M.-J., Hart, S., Lovey, J. and McLaughlin, C. (in press) *Exclusion is not a Solution.* London: Routledge. This book is about alternatives to exclusions.

Department for Education (1992a) *Exclusions: A Discussion Document.* London: HMSO.

Department for Education (1992b) *Pupils with Problems* (Circulars 8 to 13). London: DfE.

Department for Education and Employment (1997) *Excellence for All.* London: Stationery Office.

Department of Education and Science (1978) *Special Educational Needs.* Report of the Committee of Enquiry into the Education of Handicapped Children and Young People. London: HMSO.

Department of Education and Science (1989) *Discipline in Schools: Report of the Committee of Enquiry Chaired by Lord Elton.* London: HMSO.

Hayden, C. (1997) *Children Excluded from Primary School: Debates, Evidence, Responses.* Buckingham: Open University Press.

Iszatt, J. and Wasilewaska, T. (1997) 'Nurture groups: an early intervention model enabling vulnerable children with emotional and behavioural difficulties to integrate successfully into school', *Educational and Child Psychology,* 14(2), pp.121–39.

Lovey, J. and Cooper, P. (1997) 'Possible alternatives to school exclusion', *Emotional and Behavioural Difficulties,* 2(3), pp.12–22.

Lovey, J. *et al.* (1993) *Exclusion from School: Provision for Disaffection at Key Stage 4.* London: David Fulton Publishers.

Parsons, C. (1999) *Education, Exclusion and Citizenship.* London: Routledge.

Rustique-Forrester, E. (1999) 'The dynamics and dilemmas of growing school exclusion in the UK: a review of the research and policy literature'. Paper presented to the Annual Meeting of the British Research in Education Association, University of Sussex, September 1999.

Social Exclusion Unit (1998) *Truancy and School Exclusion.* London: SEU.

Index